Practitioner Series

Springer

London
Berlin
Heidelberg
New York
Barcelona
Hong Kong
Milan
Paris
Santa Clara
Singapore
Tokyo

Other titles in this series:

Ian Warren

The Renaissance of Legacy Systems

Method Support for Software-System Evolution

With contributions from
Markus Breuer, John Favaro, Jane Ransom,
Eirik Tryggeseth and Claude Villermain

 Springer

Ian Warren
Computing Department, Bradford University, West Yorkshire, BD7 1DP

ISBN-13: 978-1-85233-060-6

British Library Cataloguing in Publication Data
Warren, Ian
    The renaissance of legacy systems : method support for
    software-system evolution. - (Practitioner series)
    1.Systems software 2.Software engineering 3.Software
    maintenance
    I.Title
    005.1'6
    ISBN-13: 978-1-85233-060-6

Library of Congress Cataloging-in-Publication Data
Warren, Ian, 1970-
    The renaissance of legacy systems : method support for software
    -system evolution / Ian Warren.
        p.   cm. -- (Practitioner series)
    Includes bibliographical references and index.
    ISBN-13: 978-1-85233-060-6   e-ISBN-13: 978-1-4471-0817-7
    DOI: 10.1007/978-1-4471-0817-7
    1. Computer software--Evaluation. I. Series.
    QA76.76.E93W38   1999
    005.1'4--dc21   98-37227

Typesetting: Ian Kingston Editorial Services, Nottingham, UK

34/3830-543210 Printed on acid-free paper

Dedication

We would like to thank Ian Sommerville for his guidance and support throughout the development of this book.

Contents

Preface

Today, software professionals recognize that change in software systems is inevitable. There are many systems currently in operation, however, which were developed before the need for change was understood. Such systems are commonly referred to as "legacy systems", and were developed with relatively short lifetimes in mind.

Software engineering is a relatively young discipline which is continually improving to provide better support for the development of software systems. What were once state-of-the-art techniques, tools, and processes are now dated, and have resulted in systems which are not responsive to change. For historical reasons, dated development practice traded maintainability for other system attributes, such as cost and performance.

A significant number of legacy systems remain in operation because they are critical to the business processes which they support. The combination of extended lifetimes and poor maintainability means that legacy systems are expensive to change, and in many cases they cannot accommodate emerging requirements. This is clearly an undesirable situation, which, until recently, has been tackled by replacing the system or attempting to maintain it.

Replacing a legacy system is dangerous, since you face the risk of losing vital business knowledge which is embedded in many old systems. In many cases, system replacement is not cost-effective. Conversely, if you attempt to maintain a legacy system, there is often little return on the investment in maintenance effort and the system remains difficult and expensive to change.

"Reengineering" is a relatively new approach to software evolution which falls between the two extremes of system replacement and continued maintenance. Reengineering improves a system in some way and results in a system which is more responsive to change.

The costs of reengineering a system are typically lower than replacing it. Reengineering can also mitigate significant risks associated with replacement and continued maintenance. The starting point for reengineering is an existing system. This means that you do not discard a legacy system, so you reduce the risk of losing any critical business knowledge embedded in it. Unlike maintenance, however, the result of reengineering is a system which you can evolve to meet new requirements cost effectively.

What is this Book About?

This book introduces a method, Renaissance, which helps you to recover control over the process of legacy system evolution. We have written this book to help you understand the problems of reengineering and to provide you with a body of practical advice for reengineering systems.

Today's technology enables you to build new systems which are evolvable. Techniques and tools have also emerged to support system reengineering. However, the software industry lacks a method which supports system evolution. This book addresses this real need by disseminating our experience and results gained from the RENAISSANCE project, whose goal was to develop a method for transforming legacy systems into an evolvable form.

Renaissance supports software evolution from project conception through to deploying the reengineered system. We have designed Renaissance for information systems, but much of it is applicable to other classes of system. In short, Renaissance helps you answer two critical questions:

- *What is the best way to evolve a legacy system?* There are three general evolution strategies: continued maintenance, reengineering and replacement. Renaissance provides practical advice and techniques for choosing the right strategy based on technical, organizational and business factors.

- *How do I implement an evolution strategy?* Once you have selected a strategy, Renaissance offers guidance on managing activities which are specific to evolution projects.

Why Has this Book Been Written?

The developed world is now very much dependent on the information systems in which it has invested. These systems must change in order to remain useful to the organizations which operate them. Factors which trigger change include changing user requirements, new technology, changes in business goals, and the need to exploit new opportunities. These factors sustain the demand for change, but with constrained IT budgets and the accumulation of legacy systems, system evolution must become a more controlled and cost-effective process.

Who Should Read this Book?

We have written this book for industrial practitioners who are involved in making changes to software systems.

IT managers, consultants, and software managers will benefit from the method's practical advice concerning planning and controlling evolution projects. We help you to determine the best way of evolving a legacy system and, where some action is necessary, how to plan the evolution activities. We also discuss the issues involved in delivering and deploying a reengineered system.

The book will also be of value to software engineers who are responsible for technical activities. Part of the book is devoted to building system models, which are designed to improve your understanding of legacy systems. In addition, we describe how to perform evolution planning tasks and introduce techniques for migrating legacy systems to distributed architectures.

How do we Communicate the Material?

Table 1 shows the structure of the book.

Table 1 Book structure

Chapter 1	Background
Chapter 2	Renaissance: a Method for System Evolution
Chapter 3	Evolution Planning
Chapter 4	Modelling for Evolution
Chapter 5	Migration to Distributed Architectures
Chapter 6	Case Study 1: Evolution of a Legacy System
Chapter 7	Case Study 2: Evolution of a Modern System

We begin with an introductory chapter. Chapter 1 provides an overview of software evolution. We explain why change is an inherent property of software systems. We present the legacy problem, with its causes and consequences, and explain why software maintenance has, in general, been ineffective for managing change. We discuss techniques and tools for developing evolvable systems and introduce the topic of reengineering.

In Chapter 2, we present an overview of the Renaissance method. Renaissance defines a process for managing evolution. It also describes a document repository, which identifies and structures information which you may gather over the course of an evolution project. To perform the process, Renaissance defines a set of responsibilities which you can assign to individuals involved in an evolution project. We describe how you can customize Renaissance according to particular project and organizational factors. Finally, we describe Renaissance's origins.

Chapters 3, 4 and 5 provide practical advice and techniques which support the process described in Chapter 2.

Chapter 3, "Evolution Planning", describes how you can assess a legacy system, from technical, business and organizational viewpoints, to determine whether the system is a candidate for evolution. Based on this assessment, we explain how you can develop a suitable system evolution strategy. We describe a set of general evolution strategies, which span continued maintenance, reengineering and replacement, and point out their relative costs, benefits and risks. In this chapter, we also describe approaches to cost estimation and risk management for evolution projects, and evolution project planning.

The activities presented in Chapter 3 demand a sufficient understanding of the subject legacy system. In Chapter 4, "Modelling for Evolution", we describe how you can build system models to gain the necessary understanding. Chapter 4 explains how to build models, at a range of levels of abstraction, of both legacy and "to-be" systems. Context models are high-level models which capture a system from several viewpoints. Technical models are more detailed and focus on a system's implementation. We demonstrate how you can use the UML to construct both types of model.

Chapter 5, "Migration to Distributed Architectures", is a technically oriented chapter which introduces a number of distributed architectural models. We describe how these models have developed and point out their strengths and drawbacks. We also describe several architectural models for structuring a system in terms of software layers and explain how you can integrate parts of a legacy system with a distributed architecture.

Chapters 6 and 7 provide case studies to illustrate the material contained in the preceding chapters. Chapter 6 is based on a combination of legacy systems which we have been exposed to. This chapter describes how you can apply Renaissance to two contrasting scenarios. Both scenarios share the same legacy system (a 1970s mainframe system which typifies many of today's legacy systems), and extend it with different technical, business and organizational characteristics.

Chapter 7 supports Chapter 6 with a particular case study which we have managed using Renaissance. The second case study is based on a modern client/server system which was developed as a pilot project for a new technology. We have included this case study to show that the use of modern technology does not guarantee an evolvable system. In this case, the development team lacked experience with a 4GL which resulted in a modern system that exhibits some legacy characteristics.

What is RENAISSANCE?

RENAISSANCE is a collaborative project, funded by the European Esprit commission. The RENAISSANCE consortium (Table 2) is a collection of industrial organizations and universities which have worked together to develop the Renaissance method. We have used several of the application

Table 2 RENAISSANCE consortium

Application provider	Technology developer
CAP Sesa Hoskyns, France	CAP Gemini Innovation, France
debis Systemhaus, Germany	Intecs Sistemi, Italy
Engineering, Italy	Lancaster University, UK
Telesoft, Italy	Sintef/NTNU, Norway

providers' legacy systems to understand the problems of evolving them, and to develop, evaluate and refine the Renaissance method.

RENAISSANCEWeb is a WWW site which provides information about the project and software reengineering in general. Its URL is:

```
http://www.comp.lancs.ac.uk/projects/renaissance/
```

Additional Material

This book is supported by additional RENAISSANCE documents, which you can download from RENAISSANCEWeb without charge. In particular, the following documents are available:

● The "Method Handbook", which is a complete and detailed definition of the Renaissance method.

● Three consultancy reports which supplement Chapters 3–5. These reports give a more detailed account of the advice and techniques which we present in this book:

– Evolution Planning

– Architectural Modelling

– Client/Server Migration

The appendices contain details of WWW sites for reengineering, CASE tool vendors and implementation technology vendors. We do not endorse any of the vendors or their products and do not claim that the appendices are complete. We have, however, included this information as a starting point for you to make your own enquiries.

1. *Background*

Objectives

- To introduce legacy systems. In particular, we describe factors which have led to their existence and identify the problems they present to organizations.
- To explain why change is fundamental to software systems.
- To expose the shortfalls of software maintenance.
- To present a paradigm which provides for controlled system evolution.
- To introduce software reengineering.

Contents

It is not uncommon to find that many of today's data processing systems have been in operation for as many as 30 years. Although the original developers may not have expected their products to be providing useful service in the 1990s, we now know that long lifetimes are an inherent property of many software systems. It is inevitable that any non-trivial system must change over the course of its lifetime. Over a long lifetime, a system will accommodate a large number of changes.

"System change" is a fundamental phase of the software life cycle. Some systems remain in service considerably longer than originally intended, while others have been built with long anticipated lifetimes. In both cases, change is the longest and most expensive phase in the development cycle which consumes considerable effort. As software engineers, we should look at how we can reduce these costs.

System change has been managed by a process termed "maintenance", which, historically, has been an add-on to the software life cycle. This separation means that, in many cases, software developers have different skills from maintainers. Systems are often developed by one organization and maintained by another. In many cases, temporary contractors are employed to maintain systems. The discontinuity between development and maintenance results in systems which are perplexing to understand, difficult to change and ultimately expensive to evolve.

The traditional develop-and-maintain model is unsuitable for long-lived systems. A model which is based on continuously changing systems is more appropriate. This ideal is an underlying principle of the method described in this book and results in "evolutionary systems". We use the term "evolution" to reflect a controlled approach to system change.

Despite significant advances in software development, evolution has not enjoyed the same interest. The consequence of this is that there are many legacy systems which are difficult to change. The continued service of many legacy systems is, however, critical to the organizations which use them. The method in this book addresses how to manage the transformation from legacy to evolutionary systems.

1.1   Legacy Systems

The term "legacy system" describes an old system which remains in operation within an organization. Legacy systems have, typically, been developed according to dated development practice and technology. They have also had long lives and have incurred extensive change.

Many legacy systems are business critical and have high maintenance costs. It is this subset of legacy systems that is of particular interest to us in this book. These systems must remain operational and able to accommodate subsequent change if they are to continue to serve their organizations well. The legacy dilemma is:

> A legacy system, which is business critical, must remain operational, in some form, within its organization. However, continued maintenance of the system is expensive and the scope for effectively implementing further change is heavily constrained. Moreover, the costs of replacing the system from scratch are prohibitively high.

Organizations therefore face a difficult decision as to the future of such legacy systems. The penalty for making the wrong decision can be very expensive for the organization concerned. Attempting further change using maintenance techniques may turn out to be hideously expensive and fail to satisfy new requirements because the system cannot accommodate additional change. In this scenario, the effort and costs invested in the system are wasted. Conversely, replacing the system may be too expensive. In addition, where business knowledge is embedded in the system there is a significant risk of losing this knowledge and developing a system that does not satisfy its requirements.

Many legacy systems were developed before the introduction of structured programming. Process models and basic principles such as modularity, coupling, cohesion and good programming practice emerged too late for them. These systems were developed according to *ad hoc* processes, and often used programming techniques that do not scale up to large systems development.

There are three reasons why many legacy systems were not designed to accommodate change:

1 *Short life expectancies.* At the time of their commission, it was not anticipated that today's legacy systems would be in service decades later.

2 *Failings in process models and software engineering culture to treat evolution as a first class activity.* You can extract evolution requirements from business goals, but according to traditional practice, these requirements are largely ignored during the specification phase of development. Furthermore, since maintenance has been divorced from development, change has not been effectively managed.

3 *Satisfying constraints that existed at the time of development.* Hardware, in particular, has become considerably more powerful and significantly cheaper since the development of today's legacy systems. Memory and processing power were once scarce resources which constrained software design decisions. Techniques were employed to make economic use of these resources, but at the expense of maintainability. For long-lived business systems, maintainability is the fundamental measure of system quality.

Figure 1.1 shows the situation for many of today's business legacy systems. In this case, systems are composed of several different programs which share common data. These systems have been implemented using flat or structured files, rather than a database management system (DBMS). Data is often duplicated because the same information may be represented in different ways in different files.

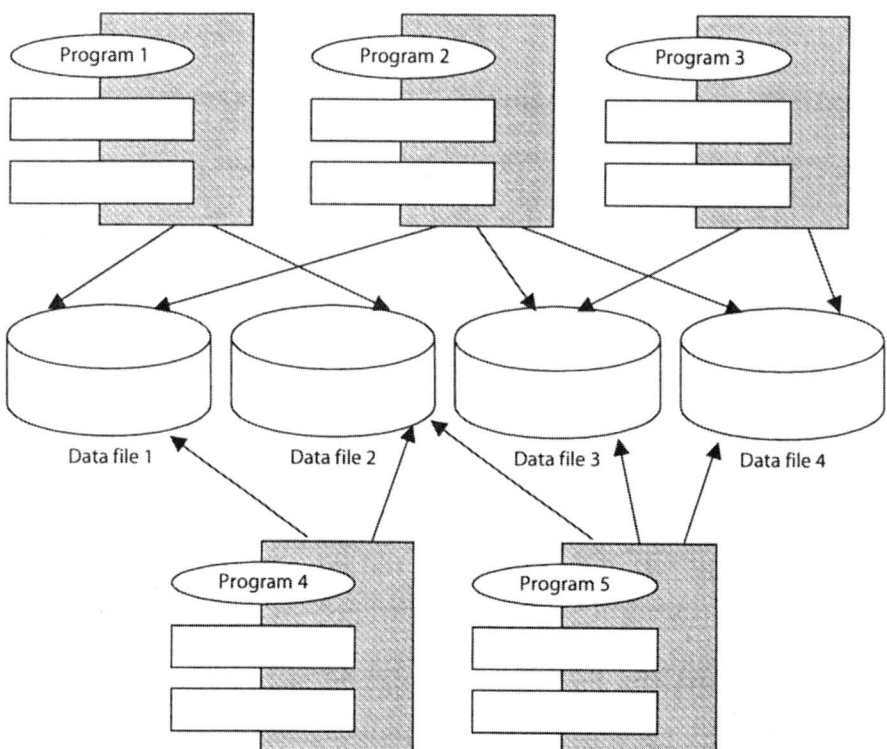

Fig. 1.1 Common legacy application structure.

Unlike DBMSs, file-based data storage systems offer no insulation against changes to data structures, since programs which use the files are tightly integrated with the data structures. Where programs share data files, you should consider changes to the data structures carefully, as they can literally ripple across the system. The situation is more extreme for large information systems, where several systems share common data using files, or where each system duplicates data.

The combination of employing dated processes, techniques and technology, coupled with the long lifetimes over which legacy systems have been changed, results in systems which may suffer from the characteristics shown in Table 1.1.

Table 1.1 Legacy system characteristics

High maintenance costs
Complex software
Obsolete support software
Obsolete hardware
Lacking technical expertise
Business critical
Backlog of change requests
Poor documentation
Embedded business knowledge
Poorly understood by maintainers

Legacy systems are generally associated with high maintenance costs. The root cause of this expense is the degraded structure that results from prolonged maintenance. Systems with contrived structures are invariably complex, and understanding them requires considerable effort. System understanding is a prerequisite for implementing changes. It enables you to assess the feasibility of making changes and to determine the impact of them on the rest of the system.

Some systems operate with obsolete system software or hardware. For business-critical applications this is clearly undesirable, because you may be unable to correct component failures. You should try to avoid this situation by assessing vendors of hardware and system software for survivability. Where support for system products is withdrawn, you should replace them with products which are not only supported today, but which are likely to remain supported for the system's anticipated lifetime.

Over the long lifetimes of legacy systems, several individuals have probably maintained them. Experienced maintenance staff are valued assets when it comes to technical application knowledge. Without them, individuals with less experience are assigned to maintenance. This often results in increased maintenance costs, since inexperienced staff need time to understand the system and may introduce new errors.

In many cases, business knowledge, rules and procedures are embedded in legacy systems. Information of this sort may not be documented elsewhere. Where a system has high maintenance costs you may consider replacing it, but if it embeds critical business rules you face the risk of losing this knowledge. You can reduce this risk by reengineering the system. We provide an overview of reengineering in Section 1.3.1

Many legacy systems are poorly documented. Over several years, documentation typically becomes out of step with the system it documents. It is often the case that quick bug fixes are not documented. Unreliable documentation is, in part, why managers do not want to lose experienced maintenance staff. Inconsistent documentation is misleading and adds confusion to system-understanding exercises. Where documentation is non-existent, maintainers resort to the system's source code. In extreme scenarios, source code is missing too, and maintainers must understand the system by studying its behaviour.

Factors such as inexperienced maintenance staff, poor documentation, and complex systems mean that legacy systems often have a backlog of change requests. Under these conditions, the times required to integrate changes with legacy systems rise dramatically. The paradox is, often, that as systems age, they may be expected to incorporate increasing frequencies of change.

Figure 1.2 shows the constituent parts of a legacy system. Each of these parts contributes to a system's evolveability:

1 *Business.* An organization's business goals are its long-term objectives. They generate future system requirements. The more radical the business goals, the harder, in general, it is for systems to accommodate the changes. Unless systems are designed explicitly for change, radical changes can only be accommodated after extensive rework.

2 *Organizational.* The "development" organization is responsible for maintaining the system. Where a legacy system is poorly documented and several key

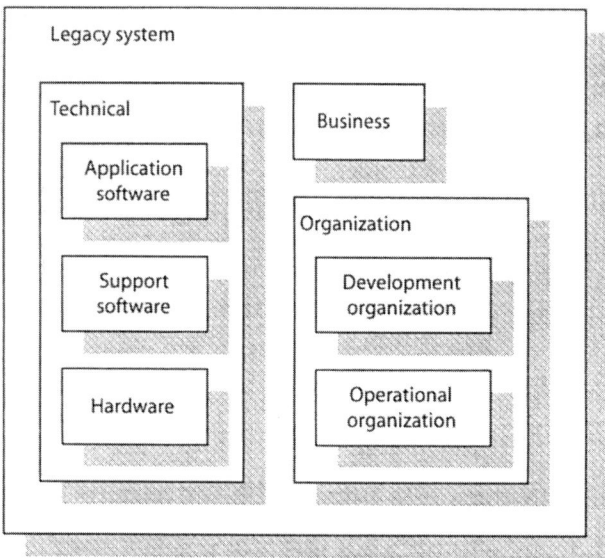

Fig. 1.2 Legacy system composition.

individuals who have maintained the system retire, the organization is typically less able to evolve the system further. A legacy system provides services to its "operational" organization. An organization's attitude to change affects system evolvability. Some organizations are reluctant to accept change, for example. If change is imposed on a workforce by senior management, the workforce may reject the software system which implements those changes.

3 *Technical.* From a technical point of view, you can decompose a legacy application into application software, system software and hardware. The condition and quality of application software, including its documentation, are significant factors in determining how well a legacy system can evolve. A contrived software architecture, or inconsistent documentation, for example, means that the system is not readily evolvable. Where a system's hardware is no longer supported, it would be unwise to continue to invest in the system without replacing its hardware.

You should assess a system's technical, business and organizational parts to determine its future. We return to this topic in Chapter 3.

1.2   System Change

Change is an inherent and necessary stage of a system's life. The importance of change is reflected in the distribution of software costs. Estimates show that 65–75% of total software costs are subsumed in maintenance activities [1].

Software systems change for two basic reasons:

1 *The environment in which a system operates is dynamic.* This is a natural phenomenon, and unless software systems change to accommodate their changing worlds, they will progressively become less useful. Lehman and Belady (in [1]) have conducted a series of studies on system change. The results of their studies are five observations, which have become known as Lehman's laws (Table 1.2). Their first observation emphasizes the inevitability of change.

Table 1.2 Lehman's laws

1	Continuing change	A program that is used in a real-world environment necessarily must change or become progressively less useful in that environment.
2	Increasing complexity	As a program changes, its structure tends to become more complex. Extra resources must be devoted to preserving and simplifying its structure.
3	Large program evolution	Program evolution is a self-regulating process. System attributes such as size, time between releases, and the number of reported errors are approximately invariant for each system release.
4	Organizational stability	Over a program's lifetime, its rate of development is approximately invariant for each system release.
5	Conservation of familiarity	Over the lifetime of a system, the incremental change in each release is approximately constant.

2 *Software development invariably introduces errors.* Errors ranging from misunderstood requirements through to more trivial programming errors may be introduced during change activities. In his fifth law, Lehman suggests that the rate at which new functionality can be integrated with an existing system is limited. If too much functionality is introduced in any one release, a new release will be required fairly quickly to correct the errors introduced in the previous release.

Earlier, we described how a legacy system is decomposed and how its parts constrain system evolvability. Collectively, these units form the system's environment. Each part represents an evolution driver – a trigger for change. Figure 1.3 shows the inter-dependencies between each of the system's constituent parts. For example, a system's technical components are dependent on its business process. A change in the business process may require a change to the system's technical components.

Advances in hardware technology provide for new capabilities and performance gains. Modern data storage media allow today's systems to provide rapid online access to vast quantities of data. Changing hardware, for whatever reason, is often very disruptive, as the changes may propagate to both support software and application software. Replacing a computer, for example, may require a new operating system, which, in turn, may lead to application software changes.

System software products are subject to change, and periodically vendors release new versions. New releases may correct errors in earlier releases or they may provide

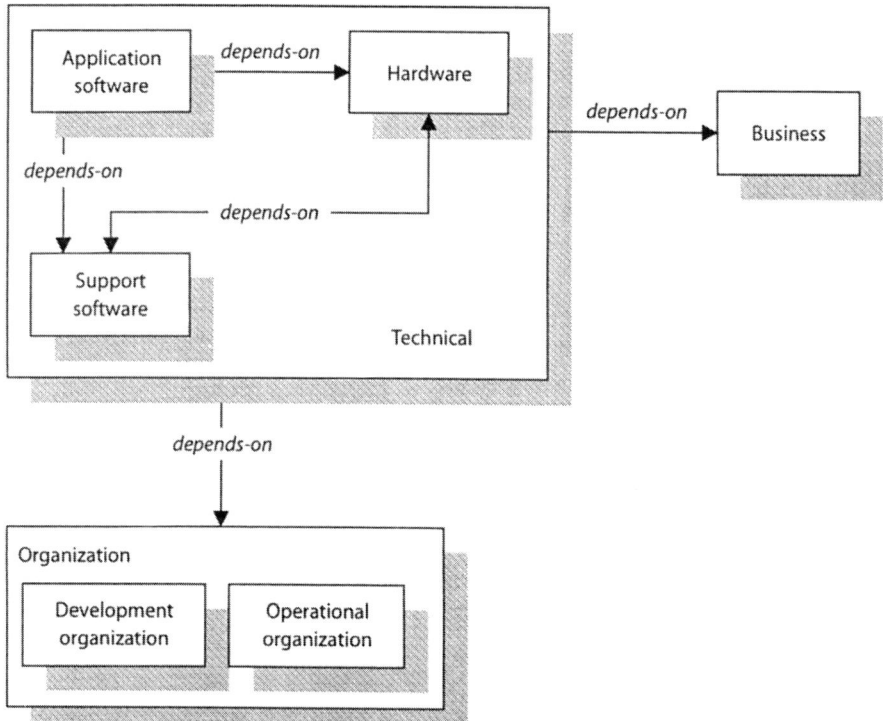

Fig. 1.3 Evolution drivers and their dependencies.

functional or non-functional enhancements. Support software vendors often encourage customers to install new releases of products by discontinuing support for previous releases. Later releases may propagate changes to application software where the system software API (Application Programming Interface) has changed. In other cases, changes to system software may demand additional memory or processing capabilities which force hardware upgrades.

The users in a legacy system's operational organization have needs which change over time. Changes in user needs produce change requests which generate functional or non-functional requirements. Many business systems accumulate vast quantities of data over time. There may come a point where the system takes an intolerable period of time to process that data. Users may generate a performance enhancement requirement which results in a hardware upgrade or software modification.

To survive, organizations should respond to their changing market-places. Business process changes are likely to generate new requirements that must be satisfied by supporting software systems. Business process reengineering often results in radical changes to the working practices of organizations, which in turn generate extensive system changes. In cases of radical business process reengineering, it is often inappropriate to attempt to change the existing system, because the changes are so great. In other cases which involve less business process reengineering, the system's technical components may be able to accommodate the changes.

1.2.1   Software Maintenance

Maintenance in many engineering disciplines means preserving the good condition of some artefact. A car is composed, in part, of a number of mechanical artefacts: its engine is an obvious example. Maintaining a motor car includes replacing engine oil and making adjustments to the fuel and ignition systems. The aim of maintenance is to keep the engine in good working order.

In software engineering, however, maintenance is the accommodation of change after the system has been delivered and deployed. There are three different types of software maintenance, with blurred distinctions between them. "Corrective maintenance" is concerned with fixing reported errors in the software. "Adaptive maintenance" means changing the software to some new environment, such as a new version of an operating system. The software functionality does not radically change. "Perfective maintenance" involves implementing new functional or non-functional requirements.

The idea of preventative maintenance is analogous to taking remedial action to preserve and simplify the structure of software. Preventative software maintenance requires an investment of resources in the system. The return on that investment is often difficult for customers to appreciate, but as Lehman's second law states, the more a system is subjected to maintenance, the more its structure will erode. The result of structural degradation is a system which is more difficult to understand and ultimately more expensive to change. Where practised, preventative maintenance improves a system's evolvability.

The costs of making changes to software after it has been put into operation are usually much greater than incorporating the changes during original development, for the following reasons:

- Maintenance is often assigned to junior staff because of its poor image, shared by more experienced engineers.

- As we pointed out earlier, many legacy systems have been developed to be efficient rather than maintainable. The techniques used to improve efficiency do not necessarily improve maintainability.

- Assessing the impact of proposed changes is difficult when the system has suffered from structural degradation.

- Documentation is often inconsistent and cannot be relied on as an accurate representation of the system. Documentation often suffers as a consequence of budget and resource constraints.

Some of these problems can be addressed by more effective software maintenance. For example, remedial action could be taken periodically to reduce structural degradation. However, what is really needed is an approach to software development which recognizes change as an integral part of it.

1.3   System Evolution

An "evolutionary system" is capable of accommodating changes over an extended operational lifetime. Evolutionary systems are designed explicitly for change; an evolutionary system is built with an initial capability and, over time, evolves to become more capable. There is no end to evolutionary system development. This is a significant departure from the traditional develop-and-maintain model and advocates continuous improvement of software systems.

To overcome the drawbacks of the develop-and-maintain model, the evolutionary paradigm is a controlled process which is based on sound engineering principles. Many legacy systems have been developed according to *ad hoc* techniques rather than engineering practice. *Ad hoc* development is a craft, where software quality is totally dependent on the skill and experience of the individuals involved in the process. Software engineering requires adherence to a body of well-defined good practice which includes standards, techniques, measurements and notations. In short, engineering means technical maturity.

A process to manage evolutionary system development should:

- *Use established management techniques.* A mature evolutionary process should manage activities such as risk analysis, configuration management, quality assurance, process improvement, and metrics collection. You should continue to use tools and techniques which have proven effective in your experience to support these activities.

- *Recognize pre-planned product improvement.* Pre-planned product improvement accepts that systems do change. We noted earlier that business goals can be used to predict how a system will change. Business goals generate evolution requirements, which you should consider during requirements and design activities.

- *Capture requirements effectively.* Requirements change during the development of many systems. Traditional development processes freeze requirements early on. This factor contributes to the development of systems which do not meet their users' real needs. Modern requirements-capture techniques are based on iteration, user involvement, viewpoints and prototyping.

- *Support rapid accommodation of change.* The dynamic environments of many of today's data processing systems demand that you should implement new requirements quickly. In addition to an effective requirements engineering process, there is a need for technology which is responsive to change. Solutions include software reuse and user-configurable systems.

- *Make effective use of existing assets.* In many cases, software projects are managed independently of each other. Other than source code, there has been little reuse across them. For families of related systems, requirements, designs and software components can be better exploited. Software architecture, in particular, promotes reuse of software design documents and coarse-grained components.

- *Develop information-rich systems.* A system's change record should be part of its documentation. Information such as why a system has been changed and how was it changed allows you to better understand the system. Without a system evolution record, you have only a snapshot of the system, which means that you are less able to make informed decisions as to how you can implement new change requests. To be practical, you should use tools to browse and update the system evolution record.

Table 1.3 describes technology which enables an evolutionary system process. Table 1.4 maps those technologies onto particular evolutionary process properties.

1.3.1   Reengineering

Evolutionary systems are only part of the solution to the legacy problem. A method for transforming today's legacy systems into evolutionary systems is required. System replacement is overkill in many cases, and typically incurs great expense and risk. Reengineering is often considerably cheaper than replacement and it reduces the risk of losing any critical information embedded in the existing system.

Reengineering is one of three broad strategies for managing change:

1 *Continued maintenance.* This approach involves maintaining the system according to the traditional develop-and-maintain process model described earlier. However, you can employ some evolutionary system concepts, such as starting to manage a system evolution record.

Table 1.3 Enabling technology

Technology	Description
Software architecture	A system's architecture makes explicit its decomposition into subsystems and the framework for control and communication. It provides engineers with a top-level view of the system.
Reusable components	Componentware and distributed object technology are recent technologies which aim, in part, to improve software reuse. Using these technologies, you can compose an application of many components, each implemented in a different programming language and running on a different platform. Components map, naturally, onto objects and encapsulate application and system services.
System families	Applications which serve a common domain can be built from similar configurations of components. This encourages a development approach based on customizing a generic application, rather than building new systems from scratch.
User-configurable systems	User-configurable systems provide users with an intuitive interface which allows them to make changes to their applications. These systems can accommodate simple changes rapidly by not requiring engineers to respond to change requests.
Prototyping	Prototyping technology enables rapid application development and requirements validation. Today's 4GLs provide for both rapid application development and rapid accommodation of change.

Table 1.4 Process property enabling technology

Property	Software architecture	Reusable components	System families	User-configurable system	Prototyping
Established management practice					
Pre-planned product improvement					
Effective requirements capture	✓				✓
Rapid accommodation of change		✓	✓	✓	✓
Effective use of existing assets	✓	✓	✓		
Information-rich systems					

2 *Reengineering.* Tilley [3] provides a generally accepted definition of software reengineering:

> Reengineering is the systematic transformation of an existing system into a new form to realize quality improvements in operation, system capability, functionality, performance or evolvability at a lower cost, schedule, or risk to the customer.

Table 1.5 Benefits of reengineering

Benefit	Description
Lower costs	Evidence from a number of US projects suggests that reengineering an existing system costs significantly less than redeveloping it. Ulrich [2], for example, reports on a reengineering project that cost $12 million, compared to estimated redevelopment costs of $50 million.
Reduced risk	Reengineering is based on incremental improvement of systems, rather than radical system replacement. The risk of losing critical business knowledge which is embedded in a legacy system, or of producing a system that does not meet its users' real needs is drastically reduced.
Better use of existing staff	Existing staff expertise can be retained and extended to accommodate new skills during reengineering. The incremental nature of reengineering means that existing staff skills can evolve as the system evolves. The approach carries less risk and expense which is associated with hiring new staff.
Revelation of business rules	As a system is reengineered, business rules that are embedded in the system are rediscovered. This is particularly true where the rules govern exceptional situations.
Incremental development	Reengineering can be carried out in stages as budget and resources are available. The operational organization always has a working system. End users are able to adapt gradually to the reengineered system.

This definition emphasizes the greater return on investment than could be obtained through a new development. Reengineering is a bad idea if estimates show redevelopment to carry less risk or to be less expensive. Table 1.5 shows the benefits which reengineering offers when it is an appropriate evolution strategy.

3 *Replacement.* You may replace the existing system with a new system, developed from scratch. Replacement may be necessary where reengineering is not technically viable, or for other reasons such as organizational policy or radical change of the business process.

A combination of evolution strategies may be the most appropriate way to change a legacy system. You can apply different strategies to different parts of the system. For example, a legacy system may be in good order except that its data schemas have become overly complex. In this case, an evolution strategy might include data reengineering and continued maintenance of the application logic.

Reengineering is an umbrella term which covers many forms of system improvement, many of which are tool supported. We give details of such tools in Appendix B. Despite little consistency among terminology in the reengineering community, Arnold [4] classifies several forms of reengineering:

● *Source code translation.* The simplest form of reengineering is program translation from one source language to another. The target language may be an updated version of the original language, such as COBOL-74 to COBOL-85.

Source code translation may be necessary when you replace a system's hardware and operating system. In this case, compilers for the original application programming language may not be available for the new platform. In other cases, source code translation may be required to combat skills shortages. This is particularly true where a system is written in an obsolete or proprietary language, since the system becomes more evolvable if you code it in a language that is readily understood and supported.

You can often perform source code translation using automation tools. This is especially so when the target language is an updated version of the source language. In other cases, you may need to intervene with manual techniques where there is no corresponding construct in the target language for the source language. For all but very small systems, source code translation is only practical if you have appropriate tool support.

- *Program restructuring.* Programs with a "spaghetti" structure are particularly difficult to evolve. Automatic program restructuring tools are now relatively common for popular languages such as COBOL and FORTRAN. These tools transform poorly structured programs to functionally equivalent programs coded using modern programming constructs. The resulting programs are more evolvable because they are easier to understand and change.

- *System restructuring.* Program restructuring does not improve the system's architecture because programs are improved in isolation from the rest of the system. System level restructuring takes a global view of the system's software architecture and aims to make the structure explicit. At this level, you should analyze the relationships between modules. Improving a system's architecture is typically a manual exercise, because you need an understanding of the responsibility or function of each module.

  Where a legacy system comprises several programs which manipulate global data structures, restructuring often propagates data reengineering. This is because of the tight coupling between programs and data.

- *Data reengineering.* Data reengineering involves analyzing and reorganizing a system's data structures and, in some cases, its data values. In many cases, data reengineering means migrating from file-based data management to a relational or object-oriented DBMS. Using modern DBMS technology, you can recover the situation shown in Fig. 1.1. The result of data reengineering is a logical model which describes the data and a DBMS which encapsulates the data's implementation details (Fig. 1.4).

- *Reverse engineering.* Reverse engineering is the process of analyzing software with the objective of recovering its design and specification. In most cases, source code is available to generate documentation using automation tools. Reverse engineering is typically a prelude to other reengineering activities. This is because you should understand a system before you attempt to reengineer it. You can use the results of reengineering to provide engineers with a better understanding of a legacy system and to determine whether any reengineering is necessary.

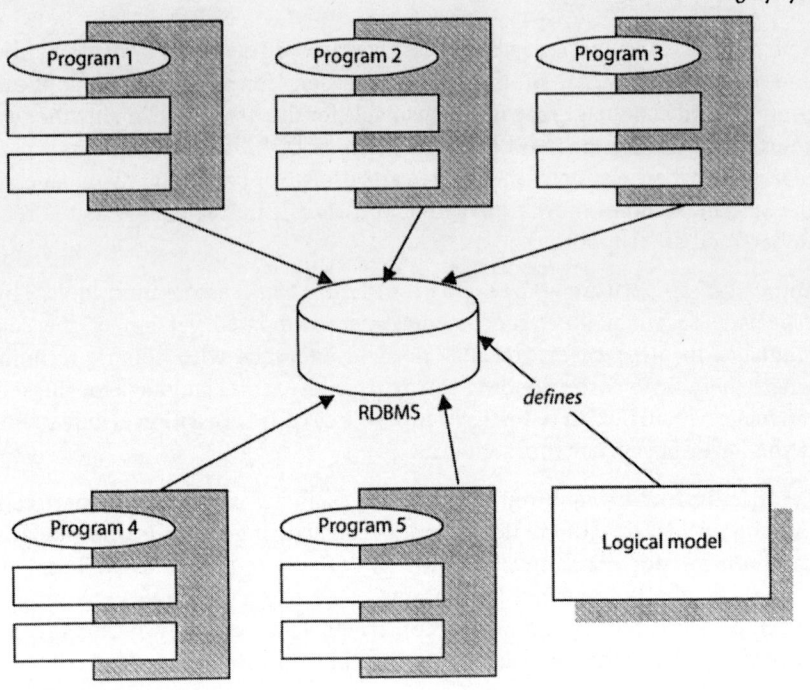

Fig. 1.4 Data centralization.

● *Retargeting.* Retargeting involves migrating an existing system to a new hardware platform. The motivation for retargeting includes obsolete hardware and organizational policy.

Software reengineering is often associated with business process reengineering (BPR). You should not, however, confuse these terms. Software reengineering is the improvement of software systems. The objective of BPR is to increase the efficiency of an organization's business processes. BPR often, however, goes hand-in-hand with software reengineering.

It is important to view legacy systems from the wider perspective, which includes the business processes supported by these systems. Software reengineering is of little value if you improve a system in a way that is not suited to the business process it should support.

References and Further Reading

[1] Sommerville I. (1995) *Software Engineering*, 5th edn. Addison-Wesley, Reading.
[2] Ulrich W.M. (1990) The Evolutionary Growth of Software Reengineering and the Decade Ahead. *American Programmer*, 3(10), 14–20.
[3] Tilley S. (1995) *Perspectives on Legacy Systems Reengineering*. Reengineering Centre, Software Engineering Institute (SEI), Carnegie Mellon University, USA.

[4] Arnold R.S. (1994) *A Road Map Guide to Software Reengineering*. IEEE Computer Society Press.

Bennet K. (editor) (1995) Special edition on legacy systems. *IEEE Software*, 12(1).

Key Points

- Legacy systems are operational systems which have been developed according to dated practice and technology. Over their long lifetimes, they have probably been subjected to extensive change.

- Legacy systems are often difficult to change because they were not designed for maintainability.

- Change is an inherent property of software systems. System change is necessary to respond to a system's dynamic environment and to correct software errors. An application's environment is made up of business, technical and organizational parts.

- Software maintenance is part of the traditional develop-and-maintain model. The separation of maintenance from development contributes to the difficulties of accommodating change in legacy systems.

- Evolutionary systems are designed explicitly for change. They require a controlled approach to development, based on engineering principles and appropriate enabling technology.

- Reengineering is a means for transforming a legacy system to its evolutionary complement. Where appropriate, reengineering offers several benefits not shared by maintenance or system replacement.

2. *Renaissance: a Method for System Evolution*

Objectives

- To summarize the rationale for a method which supports software evolution.
- To introduce the method's process model.
- To describe how information is produced and managed by the method.
- To show how human resources are managed in an evolution project.
- To illustrate how the method can be customized according to project and organizational factors.

Contents

Engineers have developed several techniques, based on software engineering, for practising software evolution. However, software evolution has yet to reach its full potential because, to a large extent, these techniques are not integrated. While technologies such as "reengineering", the "evolutionary" paradigm, and "reverse engineering" make significant contributions to the field, they are difficult to use together in an effective way.

Currently, the building blocks for supporting software evolution are in place. What is needed, however, is a management approach to bring the above technologies, techniques and tools into a coherent whole. In this chapter, we present a method, "Renaissance", which has been developed to meet this real need. Renaissance provides end-to-end guidance, from project conception through to system deployment, for managing evolution projects. The ultimate product of following Renaissance is an evolutionary system which can continue in service.

Renaissance comprises:

- *A well-defined process.* The method's process model guides practitioners through the activities in evolution projects. The process is generic and it is intended that practitioners customize it according to their own project's profile.

- *Advice for performing its activities.* The process model is complemented with practical advice and techniques for performing its activities. This includes guidance on how to use the UML for modelling legacy and evolutionary systems, risk management for evolution projects, and techniques for assessing the evolvability of legacy systems.

- *An information repository.* Renaissance identifies a set of documents which can record information that is gathered and refined during the course of the method. Sample documents capture business goals, context models of the legacy system, evolution strategy information and deployment plans.

- *Personnel responsibilities.* We define the responsibilities of individuals involved in evolution projects.

This book is supported by a number of documents, one of which is a reference for the method. You can download them from the Renaissance WWW site:

```
http://www.comp.lancs.ac.uk/projects/renaissance/
```

2.1   The Process Model

Renaissance consists of four top-level "phases", which are decomposed into more specific "activities". Figure 2.1 shows the four-phase structure. The entry point for Renaissance is phase Plan Evolution, which addresses the question, "what" is the system's future? During this phase, you make a broad decision whether to decommission the system, continue to maintain it, improve it in some form through reengineering, or to replace it. This is a non-trivial process, which may consume considerable effort. Consequently, a complete phase is devoted to it.

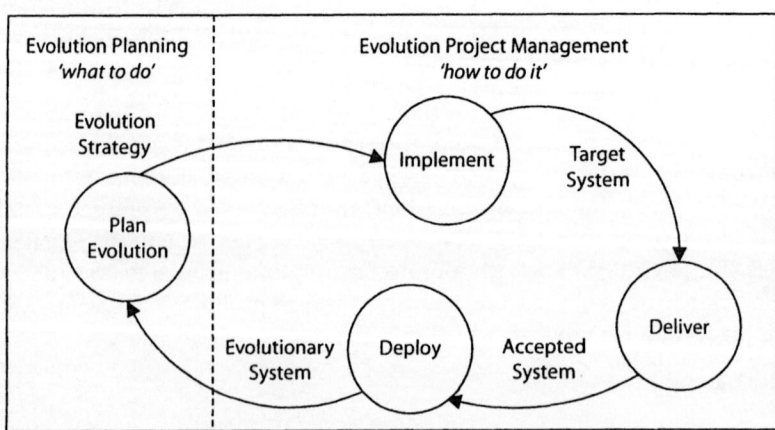

Fig. 2.1 Top level view of the method's process model.

The decision you reach in Plan Evolution determines whether you proceed with the remaining three phases. Where the system has no useful future, there is obviously no need to carry on. If you decide to reengineer or replace the system, phases Implement, Deliver and Deploy and Use help you to plan and implement the evolution project. These phases deal with "how" you tackle the project.

In Chapter 1, we explained how continuous improvement is fundamental to evolutionary systems. Renaissance supports development of these systems by allowing a legacy system to be evolved incrementally. Incremental evolution is advantageous because it carries less risk than "Big Bang" radical reengineering or system replacement. In addition, it can accommodate evolution as organizational, technological and budgetary constraints dictate.

To illustrate an incremental approach to evolution, an organization may decide initially to upgrade a system's user interface from a text-based system to a windows solution. Subsequently, after users gain experience with the system and when sufficient budget is available, the system may then migrate to a client/server infrastructure.

Before we elaborate on each of the four phases, we introduce a graphical notation for describing their decomposition into activities. Figure 2.2 summarizes the notation. In particular, control and data flow among activities are represented by arrows from source to target activities. A vertical line in the phase icon separates major concurrent activities; you can perform those on the left side of the line in parallel with those on the right. Activities may be further decomposed into units which we refer to as "tasks".

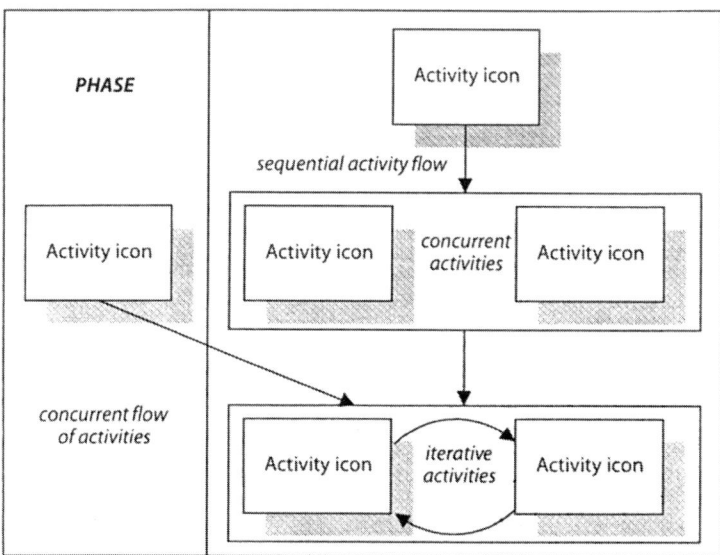

Fig. 2.2 Graphical notation.

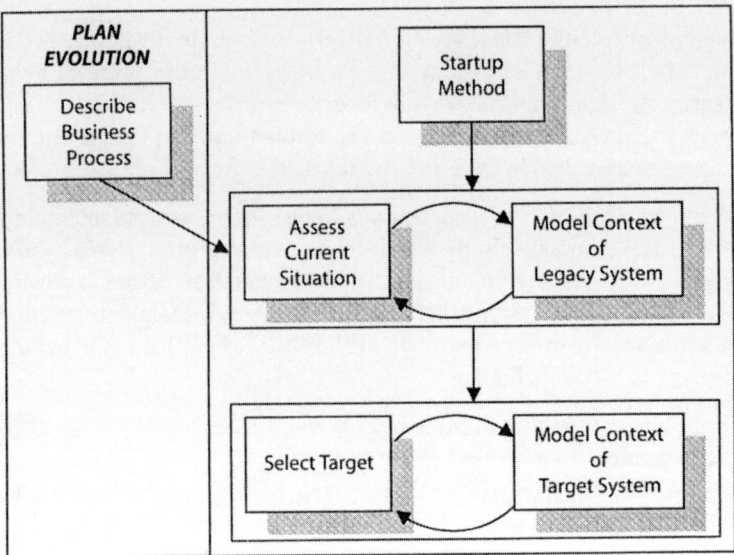

Fig. 2.3 Plan Evolution

2.1.1 Evolution Planning

The key to successful evolution planning is a thorough assessment of the legacy system and its operational context. You tackle this activity by using techniques to measure the system's "technical quality" and "business value". Obtaining accurate measures for these attributes is critical to choosing the right System Evolution Strategy. This is the principal result of Plan Evolution (Fig. 2.3) which drives the evolution project.

Plan Evolution represents a major cost factor for evolution projects. Assess Current Situation can easily consume considerable effort where legacy systems are poorly documented and lack experienced engineers. There is a real risk that budget and time are exceeded in these circumstances. To manage this risk, you should select a "cost/risk trade-off" which is appropriate to your project. Plan Evolution has been designed to offer this trade-off by iterative execution. For example, you can assess the current situation relatively quickly with little effort to gain an estimate of the system's technical quality and business value. With subsequent iterations, you can refine the initial approximation and obtain a more accurate result.

Before progressing to phase Implement, you should always put sufficient effort into Plan Evolution. Choosing the wrong evolution strategy may be very expensive for the organization which relies on the system. However, a quick and approximate estimate is appropriate in many cases to eliminate systems which are not evolution candidates. For example, where it is clear that a system has a high technical quality and a low business value, there is no point in proceeding with a thorough assessment of it. Effort is better spent on other applications.

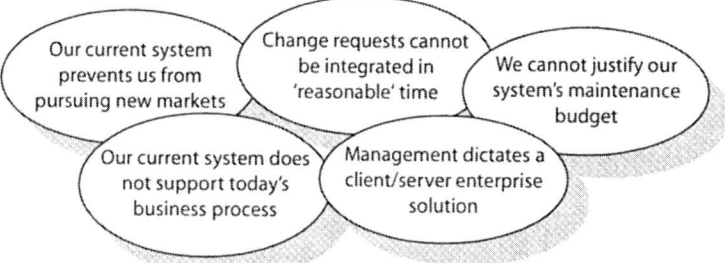

Fig. 2.4 Evolution scenarios.

Once you decide on the right cost/risk trade-off for your project, you begin Plan Evolution with activity Startup Method. What you do here is dependent on your own project scenario. Figure 2.4 shows a number of scenarios which might motivate evolution.

Startup Method requires you to perform the following tasks:

● *Customize the method.* Every organization is different, so Renaissance has been designed for you to customize it according to your needs. For example, you may not require all its activities, or may want to change their ordering. In addition to process model changes, you decide how to perform the activities you select. We suggest particular techniques for doing so, but you may prefer to use techniques and tool support that you have experience with. Customization also includes deciding what individuals take on project responsibilities and defining the information repository.

● *Record the operational organization's business goals.* You should identify business goals because they generate evolution requirements. Tomorrow's system requirements enable you to make a decision as to what extent the system needs to change in order to accommodate them. In some cases, the requirements may be so radical that the only cost-effective evolution strategy is to replace the legacy system.

● *Document the problem statement.* You must understand the need for evolution. Are users dissatisfied with the legacy system? Can the system no longer accommodate change? Has new functionality been requested? In addition to the need for change, you should document any constraints on the solution, such as budget or time.

● *Gather information about the legacy system.* Legacy information sources include source code, documentation, maintenance staff, users and managers. The availability of these varies from project to project. You should collect information about the system and arrange interviews with individuals who are available.

As a concurrent activity to Startup Method, you should understand the business process supported by the legacy system. The justification for Describe Business Process is to combat the risk, associated with evolution projects, that business rules (embedded in a software system) may be lost during evolution. This is a critical success factor for many evolution projects.

System users, managers and senior personnel from the system's operational organization are good sources of information for capturing the business process. In other cases, the only record of business rules may be embedded in the system itself. Here, you can build context models to extract the business process from the system.

After Describe Business Process, you should determine how good a fit the system is to the business process. In many cases, business process changes have not been incorporated by the system. Users find themselves fitting their work processes to the behaviour of the system, rather than using the system as a tool to assist them. Where this is the case, you should use the Business Process Description to generate target system requirements.

You are now in a position to proceed with Assess Current Situation. The product of this activity is an understanding of both the application and its role in the enterprise. Together, these provide the foundation for choosing the right System Evolution Strategy. The first step is to identify the "assessment level" for the application. This depends on the cost/risk trade-off you have chosen and your project's characteristics.

Where an approximate assessment will suffice, you do not need to assess the application in great detail; rather, a high-level assessment is appropriate. In other cases, where you know the system is essential to the organization, you should decompose the application and assess its constituent parts. This enables you to identify which "components" are in good technical condition and those that need attention.

In some evolution projects, senior management mandates a new IT solution. In this case, there is no need to assess the system's technical quality because the decision to replace it has already been made. For other projects, it may be clear that some system components are irrelevant. For example, where evolution is driven by a need to reduce "software" maintenance costs, the hardware and system software need not be assessed. In this case, you should assess the application software to determine what action is necessary to make it more evolvable.

You should assess each of the selected components at the appropriate level of detail, using the techniques we introduce in Chapter 4. For each component, you derive a measure of its technical quality and business value. In general, components which have a low technical quality but a high business value are good candidates for evolution. Deciding whether a component is an evolution candidate often requires more than a superficial analysis. Consider the following scenarios.

- Components with relatively low business value might benefit from replacement with commercial off-the-shelf software (COTS). Technical quality is often of little concern in such cases.

- Components with high business value and high technical quality might be evolution candidates. An application software component, for example, might satisfy functional and non-functional requirements today, but may not be able to accommodate a critical business goal. This component, clearly, is an evolution candidate.

You may need to build system models of the legacy system during assessment. The degree of modelling required depends on the availability of technical and business personnel, the presence and quality of documentation, and the technical condition of the application. You should build context models where you do not have a sufficient understanding of the system. Modelling is time-consuming, but is invaluable in cases where suitable personnel and system documents do not exist. In Chapter 5, we explain how to build models which capture the system from the technical and business viewpoints.

After assessment, you should select appropriate evolution strategies for each component. This forms part of the Select Target activity. There are a several ways in which a particular system component can evolve. To help manage this potential strategy explosion, we define six typical evolution strategies, which span continued maintenance, reengineering and system replacement. Chapter 4 introduces them and describes each strategy's costs, risks and benefits.

Where you identify several evolution strategies for a particular component, you should record the relative costs, risks and benefits of each strategy in the Cost Benefit Risk Analysis document. Questions you should raise during this process include:

- *Does this strategy pose a risk which is difficult to mitigate or avoid?* An evolution strategy which involves migrating to new technology requires suitably qualified engineers. If your organization lacks them, you may consider outsourcing, hiring appropriate personnel or training your existing workforce. Each of these responses are themselves associated with risk. Depending on project factors, it might be better to choose an alternative evolution strategy.

- *What is the cost of this strategy?* A strategy may incur costs which exceed the project's budget. In this case, you might choose an alternative strategy, or, where possible, select an incremental strategy. For example, where a system's structure has degraded, restructuring its application code is often the first stage in an overall incremental strategy which aims to migrate the system to a new platform.

- *Does this strategy support incremental evolution?* As we said earlier, incremental evolution is often preferable to radical evolution because it reduces risk and allows costs to be distributed over a greater period of time.

As you converge on a particular evolution strategy for each component, you should develop a model of the target system. Where context models of the legacy system have been produced, you should use them as the starting point for target system models. Similarly to legacy system modelling, you only need to model the context of the target system. You should show how it supports any revisions made to the business process and model its technical composition at a high level.

The ultimate product of Plan Evolution is a System Evolution Strategy. You may have a single strategy for the whole system, or a hybrid strategy with a separate sub-strategy for each component. Table 2.1 shows a hybrid evolution strategy. The former is common where assessment has been performed at a high level or where you intend to migrate the system to a new technological infrastructure. For example, transforming a 3GL mainframe-based application to a 4GL client/server solution usually offers little scope for reusing individual legacy system components.

Table 2.1 Hybrid evolution strategy

Evolution strategy	Component(s)	Description
Restructure	Application modules	Restructure modules (3GL programs) to improve their evolvability.
Revamp	Application modules	Introduce GUI middleware to interface between new GUI components and application modules.
Rearchitecture	Database Application modules Operating system Processors	Encapsulate application modules, legacy data, and system services using distributed object technology and middleware interfaces. Introduce new hardware.

At the end of Plan Evolution, you should have gained an understanding of the system's role within its operational organization. You know whether the application features in the organization's future. If it does, you know how, and what changes are expected of it. The target system is defined in terms of its architecture. You may chose to perform another iteration of this phase to reduce the risk of selecting an inappropriate strategy. When you are satisfied that you have the right System Evolution Strategy, and where that strategy involves evolution, you should then start developing a project plan for the evolution project.

2.1.2   Project Implementation

Figure 2.5 shows the configuration of activities for Implement, which is concerned with making the transition between the legacy and target systems. The first activity, Plan Evolution Project, is similar to project planning for new development projects. You should identify project tasks and their dependencies, estimate cost and effort,

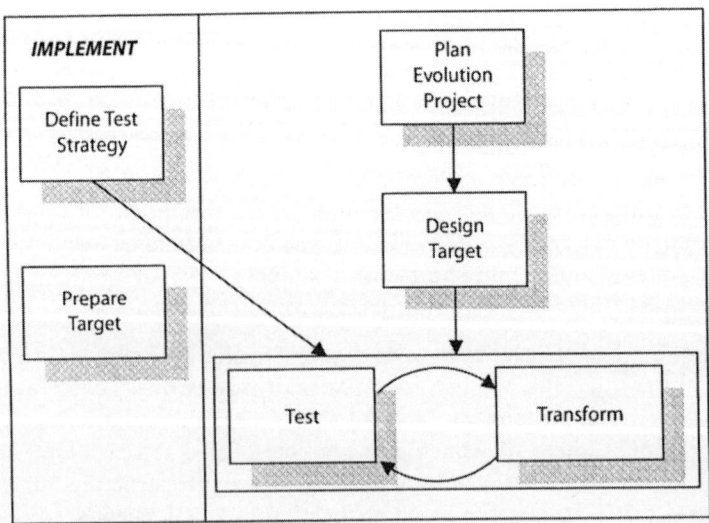

Fig. 2.5 Implement.

Table 2.2 Evolution project issues

Issue	Description
Data migration	Many evolution projects require you to migrate data from the legacy system to the target system. Data migration tasks include identifying data which must survive evolution, converting data to new formats, and integrating legacy data with the target solution.
Incremental evolution	For incremental evolution strategies, you should perform many of the method's activities in iterative cycles.
Target system deployment	In most cases, the legacy system should remain operational until the target system is deployed. You will often need to minimize the changeover period during deployment.
Legacy system integration	Many evolution strategies involve integrating legacy components into a new system architecture. In these cases, you may need to identify reusable components, manage them according to a configuration management programme, and evolve them so that they are compatible with the new architecture.

allocate effort to project tasks, manage risk and so on. The costs and risk identified in the Cost Benefit Risk Analysis document are an important input to project planning.

Table 2.2 identifies a number of issues which arise because of the fundamental differences between development and evolution projects; the latter's starting point is an existing system. The extent to which these issues affect your project depends on your System Evolution Strategy. In general, the more radical your strategy, the greater the impact of these issues. You should address them in Plan Evolution Project and use the resulting Project Plan to manage the remaining project phases.

Several tasks depend on the availability of migrated data, so you should ensure that sufficient data is migrated for use by other tasks. For example, you can exploit the availability of "real" data during testing if you migrate the data beforehand. This contributes to a realistic test environment, and is an issue you should consider during Define Test Strategy.

In other cases, a project constraint may state that the target system must be deployed with a minimal changeover period between the legacy and target system. Here, you should migrate as much data as possible preceding deployment.

An incremental System Evolution Strategy results in an iterative Project Plan. Consider, for example, the strategy presented in Table 2.1. You can manage this strategy in three increments: restructure, revamp, and then rearchitecture. In this case, your plan should ensure that users are trained before you deploy the second and third increments. You should plan a testing activity for each increment. In other cases, you may also have to manage additional tasks iteratively, such as data migration.

During Design Target, you should build on the target system's Context Model and develop a Technical Model. In Chapter 4, we discuss how to refine context models into technical models. The Technical Model captures the target system's system design. Where your strategy involves migrating to a new architecture, Chapter 5 provides guidance on designing it.

Your System Evolution Strategy may dictate that the target system is to be built from a combination of existing and new components. In this case, you should decide on the legacy system's components to be reused. Before they can be reused, you may need to evolve them in some way. For example, if your strategy involves migrating to a distributed architecture, you may need to write an interface to encapsulate the reusable components. In other cases involving data reuse, there are a number of possible solutions. Chapter 5 describes how to integrate legacy data components with a distributed architecture.

You should perform activities Test and Transform according to the Project Plan. Prepare Target is an activity which you can run in parallel with other Implement activities. It requires little effort except when your System Evolution Strategy involves new hardware. When migrating from a mainframe system to a PC-based distributed client/server architecture, you need to physically install and configure the new network and hardware. You should complete Prepare Target before acceptance testing.

2.1.3   System Delivery and Deployment

Having implemented and tested the system, you should proceed with Deliver (Fig. 2.6) and Deploy and Use (Fig. 2.7). Activities which are of particular interest to evolution projects are Plan Deployment, Migrate Data, Document Revised Business Process and Do In-Use Evaluation.

During Plan Deployment, you describe your deployment approach in the Deployment Plan. There are three broad approaches to deploying the target system. The suitability of each approach is governed by your System Evolution Strategy.

1 *Incremental deployment.* This approach is well suited to incremental evolution

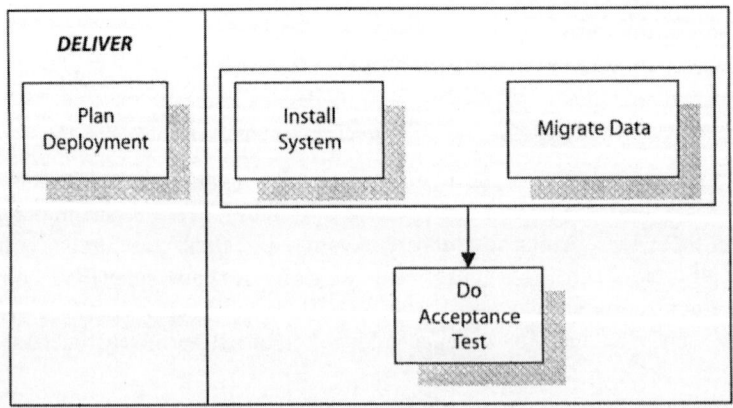

Fig. 2.6 Deliver.

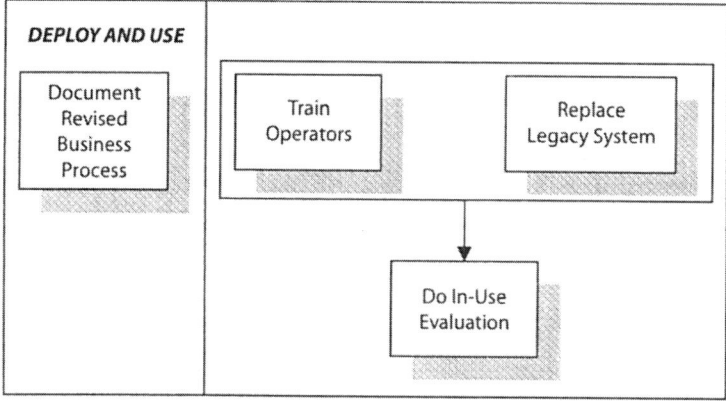

Fig. 2.7 Deploy.

strategies which do not involve radical reengineering or system replacement. As you reengineer a particular component, you build a new system version which integrates that component. The legacy system evolves to become the target system. In many cases, this can be achieved without affecting system users.

2 *Coexistence of the legacy and target systems.* Where your evolution strategy involves migrating to a new implementation technology, such as from a 3GL to a COTS package solution, it is not usually feasible to use the first deployment approach. In such cases, there are two coexistence solutions:

(i) *Incremental replacement of legacy system components with target system components.* In this approach, you develop and deploy the target system incrementally. Unlike incremental deployment, however, two incomplete systems operate concurrently. As you deploy target system services, they replace the corresponding services of the legacy system. Deployment ends when you have migrated all legacy system services to the target system.

(ii) *Parallel running of the legacy and target systems.* This solution differs from approach 2(i) in that when you deploy target system components, they do not replace the corresponding legacy system components, but run in parallel with them. Both approaches may incur the overhead of maintaining data consistency between the legacy and target systems.

3 *"Big Bang" deployment.* Big Bang deployment means that you decommission the legacy system prior to deploying the target solution. This is often the only solution for deploying systems which are implemented using fundamentally different technology or which support non-trivial business process changes. The drawback of this approach is that there is, inevitably, some disruption of computer support during deployment.

In cases where evolution strategies are constrained by a need for continuous system service, approach 1 is most appropriate. An evolution strategy which involves restructuring application logic is a good candidate. In this case, components are application modules, which may simply be extracted, restructured and reintegrated with a new system version. When the system is not in use, you can deploy the new system version. You should repeat this process for every module you restructure. This approach is, however, only feasible for a subset of evolution strategies.

Incremental deployment is inappropriate when you change the system's architecture. This may involve moving from a centralized CICS system to a client/server solution where much of the computation work is distributed at clients. Migrating from a centralized to a distributed architecture means extensive reengineering.

Where the gap between the legacy and target systems is too great for incremental deployment, system coexistence may be appropriate. It is particularly suited to service-oriented systems or systems which can be decomposed into independent concerns. Coexistence can support changes to both software and hardware architectures.

An enterprise system, for example, which includes payroll and inventory functions can be divided into payroll and inventory concerns. You can migrate each subsystem independently of the other. Operators who use the payroll system could move over to the target technology, while inventory system users continue to use the legacy system.

System coexistence is a bad idea when subsystems are interdependent. This is particularly true when they share data. If you deploy the subsystems in separate increments, you must ensure that each subsystem maintains consistent copies of common data. In principle, this is possible, but in practice it is complex and error-prone. System coexistence may also be inappropriate simply because of physical constraints on duplicate hardware.

Thorough planning can reduce the period of system unavailability associated with Big Bang deployment. Where you rearchitect or replace a system which cannot be managed by coexistence, you should ensure that as many activities as possible are performed before you deploy the system. These include preparing the target environment, acceptance testing, training operators and data migration. For data-intensive systems, data migration can be particularly time-consuming. During deployment, you want only those activities which could not be performed earlier to remain.

To reduce the volume of data to migrate during deployment, you should classify the legacy system's data to be migrated as either "static" or "dynamic". As a general rule, static data equates to master data and dynamic data to transaction data. Static data does not change often and you should migrate it before deployment. This involves keeping a copy of the data in the target system's data format. Between migrating static data and decommissioning the legacy system, you should ensure that any changes made to the legacy system's master data are recorded in your copy. You should delay migrating dynamic data until you decommission the legacy system.

Once deployed, you have an evolutionary system. The repository documents serve to document it from technical and business perspectives. You should be proactive in ensuring that it retains its evolutionary status. This means documenting changes to the ways in which the operational organization works (Document Revised Business

Process) and evaluating the system. You should track business goals and record evolution requirements. Without this information, it is difficult to evolve the system so that it continues to provide effective support to its organization.

During Do In-Use Evaluation, you assess users' satisfaction of the system. This includes functional and non-functional requirements and should involve a representative body of users. You should feed the results of evaluation into the system's cycle of continuous evolution.

2.2   Information Management

In the preceding text, we referred to several "documents" which you develop as a consequence of following the method's process, such as System Evolution Strategy and Deployment Plan. To manage these documents, Renaissance suggests that you should establish an information repository. Figure 2.8 shows that the repository is a structured collection of "folders". Each folder groups logically related documents. Tables 2.3–2.8 describe each of the documents according to the folder they belong to.

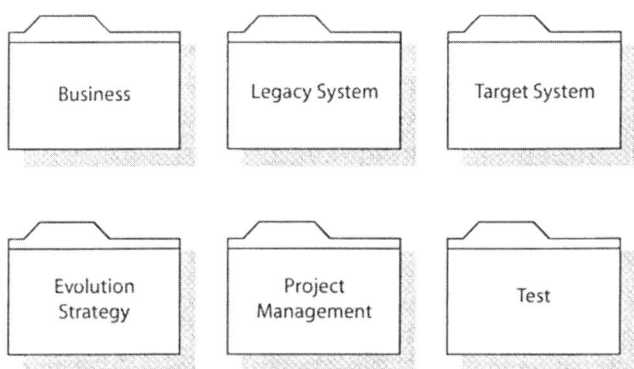

Fig. 2.8 Repository structure.

Table 2.3 Business documents

Document	Description
Business Goals	A description of the operational organization's business goals. Business goals form part of the organization's strategic plan; you should use them to generate evolution requirements.
Business Process Description	A description of the business processes which are supported by the legacy system. You should use this description to determine how well the current system supports them.
Problem Statement	A description of motivating factors for evolution. In addition, you should record any constraints on the solution space.

Table 2.4 Legacy system documents

Document	Description
Assessment Report	A document which records the system's business value and technical quality. You use these measures to decide the most appropriate evolution strategy.
System Documentation	Documents which may accompany the system. These include user guides, design documents, test plans, and change histories.
Context Model	A conceptual model of the system which may comprise technical and business viewpoints. You should build context models when you require a better understanding of the system.
Technical Model	A refinement of the context model. This model captures the system's software structure. Technical models help you during implementation to make the transition between the legacy and target systems.

Table 2.5 Target system documents

Document	Description
Context Model	An architectural model. You should build context models as you consider alternate evolution strategies. They help you to understand the product of each strategy.
Technical Model	A model which captures the system's design.

Table 2.6 Evolution strategy document

Document	Description
Possible Evolution Strategies	A set of possible evolution strategies for each component which has been assessed. Each evolution strategy represents a possible form of evolution for the associated component.
Cost Benefit Risk Analysis	For each possible evolution strategy, you should document its costs, benefits, and risks. You use this document to help develop the evolution strategy.
System Evolution Strategy	The set of evolution strategies for legacy system components. There may be several strategies or one strategy for the complete system.

Table 2.7 Project management documents

Document	Description
Project Plan	A description of the tasks which must be performed to transform the legacy system to the target system according the evolution strategy. You use this plan to manage the evolution project.
Deployment Plan	A description of the approach you intend to take to deploy the system. You should use this plan to prepare and manage delivery and deployment tasks.

Table 2.8 Test documents

Document	Description
Test Strategy Plan	A description of the approach you will use to test the system.
Test Data	The data which are to be used for testing. In many evolution projects, you can use real data for testing purposes.
Test Report	A report which details the results of the testing exercise.

The repository helps you to manage evolution project information in two ways:

1 *Statically.* The repository captures documents which are common to typical evolution projects. These documents identify the kind of information which you should generate as you follow the method's process. You should select only those documents which are relevant to your project. You may find that additional documents, not defined by Renaissance, are needed in your case.

2 *Dynamically.* As you apply the method, you use the repository to manage documents. Effective document management contributes to the success of any engineering project.

The repository may be realized as a database management system or as a collection of files in a directory structure. In other cases, it could be entirely paper-based. It is most likely however, that the repository will be realized as a combination of paper and electronic documents.

Table 2.9 shows the mapping of folders to process model phases. In general, when you produce a document in one phase it is used by subsequent phases. In some cases, you add or refine existing documents in subsequent phases. For example, in phase Implement, you refine the target system's context model into a technical model.

The form and content that each document takes are dependent on the characteristics of your project. In many cases, availability of resources dictates the documents' form. A Test Plan may be a paper document or a script from an automated testing tool. In

Table 2.9 Production and consumption of repository documents

Repository folder	Process model phase			
	Plan Evolution	Implement	Deliver	Deploy
Business	produced used	used	used	used
Legacy system	produced used	used		
Target system	produced	produced used	produced used	used
Evolution Strategy	produced used	used		
Project Management		produced used	produced used	used
Test		produced used	used	

other cases, the cost/risk trade-off associated with Plan Evolution influences what information you should record. A context model of the legacy system may be a textual summary of a discussion with a senior maintainer or a multiple viewpoint model expressed in UML.

2.3 Responsibilities

Renaissance identifies a generic set of the responsibilities of individuals involved in a typical evolution project. Similarly to activities and documents, you should select those responsibilities which can or need to be met in your project. In the case that there are no experienced maintenance staff you will not be able to meet the responsibility of Legacy Implementation Expert. In other cases, you may need to identify additional responsibilities.

Table 2.10 introduces project responsibilities which you can meet by assigning them to operational personnel. In Table 2.11, we describe responsibilities which can be met by engineers. As part of project planning, you should assign responsibilities to individuals. The same person may have several different responsibilities. For example, a particular software engineer from the development organization may have the responsibilities of Software Project Manager and Data Modeller. Conversely, several system operators may meet the responsibilities of User.

2.4 Method Customization

Some methods suffer from being too prescriptive in terms of what activities you should perform and how they should be performed. This causes many of them to be uneconomic because the costs incurred by following them exceed their benefits.

Table 2.10 Operational organization responsibilities

Responsibility	Description
Application Business Expert	An individual who has a sound knowledge of the business sector supported by the system. He or she assists the operational organization to define appropriate business goals and target system requirements. An external consultant may meet this responsibility.
Client Representative	The contact person for the operational organization. This responsibility involves making available business and organizational information and general decision-making on behalf of the operational organization.
Legacy System Functional Expert	A responsibility which involves individuals who understand the behaviour of the current system. In particular, people who know the rationale for system functionality and who understand how the system supports the business process are required. They are often middle to senior employees of the operational organization.
User	A range of system users, including those who physically operate the system and those who benefit only indirectly from its services. Each class of user represents a stakeholder with different, and potentially conflicting, interests in the system.

Table 2.11 Development-oriented responsibilities

Responsibility	Description
Legacy System Developer	This responsibility requires engineers who have developed a good working knowledge of the current system from a technical perspective. It is a desirable responsibility, but can only be met by engineers who are experienced in maintaining the system.
Modeller	A specialist in legacy and modern implementation technology. This responsibility involves modelling legacy and target systems to help promote an understanding of them on which to base decision-making.
Quality Engineer	An independent team of engineers is responsible for verifying and validating the transformation between the current and target systems.
Software Architect	Where evolution involves migrating to a new architecture, to a client/server solution from a mainframe system for example, a software architect should ensure that the target system is designed according to engineering principles. This is particularly important to ensure evolvability of the target system.
Software Engineer	Many technical developers are likely to be involved in implementing the target system. They should be trained in the target system's implementation technology to ensure that it is used appropriately. Inappropriate use of technology often results in a system which is not evolvable.
Software Project Manager	An individual who is responsible for planning, coordinating, and overseeing the evolution project.

Furthermore, organizations, quite wisely, are reluctant to abandon their tried-and-tested processes, techniques and tools in favour of those mandated by a new method.

Earlier, we mentioned how the method's process model, information repository and responsibilities can be adapted to the needs of a particular evolution project. In this section, we elaborate on how you can customize Renaissance according to project and organizational factors.

You should ask the following questions when you consider project issues:

● *At what level should I perform phase Plan Evolution?* You should carry out this phase with an appropriate cost/risk trade-off. For feasibility studies, it is generally more cost-effective to develop a System Evolution Strategy based on an approximate assessment of the legacy system. The effort required to develop an approximation is considerably less than for a detailed assessment. Where appropriate, you should perform a subsequent iteration of Plan Evolution to reduce the risk of selecting the wrong strategy.

● *Are there any project specific constraints? If so, what are they?* Renaissance provides for managing open-ended evolution projects. In practice, however, a project is inevitably constrained. For example, senior management may mandate an enterprise IT solution, or demand that when the target system is deployed there should be no break in system service. In other cases, the project budget may preclude evolution of particular system components. It is more often the rule, rather than the exception, that constraints dictate how you should use the method.

● *Do I need all method phases?* Not all evolution projects are complete life cycle projects. For example, a feasibility study could be supported by phase Plan Evolution, without ever continuing to implementation. Conversely, where an organization intends to deploy a mandated solution, you may only need phases Deliver and Deploy and Use.

To calibrate Renaissance with the local development organization, you should ask:

● *What are my organization's tried-and-tested techniques?* A technically mature development organization will have adopted its own techniques for performing activities, such as managing risk, estimating effort and cost, and designing software. We suggest techniques to support Renaissance, but you should replace these with techniques which you have found effective.

● *What processes are encouraged or compulsory in my organization?* Organizations which are technically mature typically conform to well-defined process standards. These may be specified internally, or require adherence to an external standard, such as ISO 9000. When in place, standards will affect how you customize Renaissance.

● *What tools do I use?* Similarly to techniques and processes, Renaissance does not prescribe particular tools. You should use those tools with which you are familiar, and which are appropriate to support your project's activities.

In keeping with the concept of evolutionary systems, you should subject Renaissance to a cycle of continuous evolution. As you gain experience in using the method, you should continue to customize it so that it better meets your needs. Further changes to Renaissance will also be necessary to exploit advances in the field of software evolution.

2.5   The Method Framework

In this section, we describe the underlying framework for Renaissance. You do not need to read this section to understand and use the method, but we include it to present the origins and motivation for Renaissance.

The framework serves as a blueprint for the method and comprises:

● A model which captures the environment of a legacy system.

● An abstract process model for system evolution.

● A number of abstract roles which are relevant to system operation and evolution.

● Knowledge capture and preservation.

We have borrowed ideas from two "business" process change models, but have applied them to software systems. The first is business process reengineering (BPR), which advocates radical rethinking of a business process. You can use BPR to significantly improve the efficiency of an organization's ways of working. However, if you misunderstand the organization's requirements, you may develop a process which is inefficient. For large organizations BPR is complex, and developing the wrong business process can be very expensive.

In contrast to BPR, "Kaizen" is a slow process which involves continually improving a process by accommodating small changes. It avoids the main risk associated with BPR, of creating an inadequate business process, but is constrained to relatively minor changes.

There are parallels between business process change and software evolution. BPR is analogous to replacing a software system, since you face the risk of developing a system which fails to meet its users' real needs. In many cases involving legacy systems, the probability of this risk occurring increases because they often embed business rules in their source code. If you decommission a legacy system, it is easy to discard the business knowledge it contains.

Kaizen and the evolutionary paradigm both share the principle of continuous improvement. However, for a software system to improve continuously, it must be able to accommodate change. Software reengineering falls between the two extremes of system replacement and continuous improvement. You can reengineer a legacy system to transform it to an evolutionary system, which is responsive to change.

Our approach to software evolution is, thus, a two-step process. First, and where feasible, you should recover a stable basis through software reengineering. You should then adopt the evolutionary paradigm to continuously improve the system and ensure that it reflects any changes in its environment.

Figure 2.9 shows three views of a legacy system. Collectively, these views enable you to develop a complete understanding of the system, upon which you can base your decision-making. Each view acts as a filtering mechanism and focuses on a related set of factors.

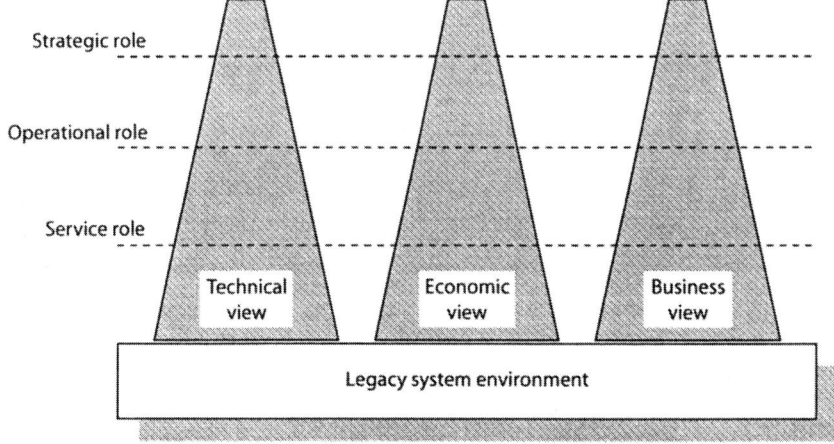

Fig. 2.9 Framework structure.

The "technical" view captures the technical quality of the system, any documentation, the system's implementation technology, and the development and maintenance processes used. The "economic" perspective addresses the business value of the system. Both the technical and economic views support the "managerial" view by providing sufficient knowledge to support critical decision-making.

To support these views, the framework identifies three abstract roles. The "strategic" role is concerned with long-term decision-making. It involves defining market strategies, improving quality and identifying future needs of information systems subject to constraints, such as reducing costs. The "operational" role performs managerial functions to provide effective control over an evolution project. The "service" role meets the objectives of the strategic and operational roles. Service roles include system operators and technical personnel who evolve the system.

Figure 2.10 shows the abstract process model, which complements the framework's static structure. The process model is logically divided into two concerns: "what-to-do" and "how-to-do" activities. The former addresses the decision-making process which is necessary to support the choice of evolution strategy. The latter implements that strategy.

The first activity, "trade-off analysis", concerns long-term planning and involves a thorough investigation of open technical issues, market trends and business goals. It

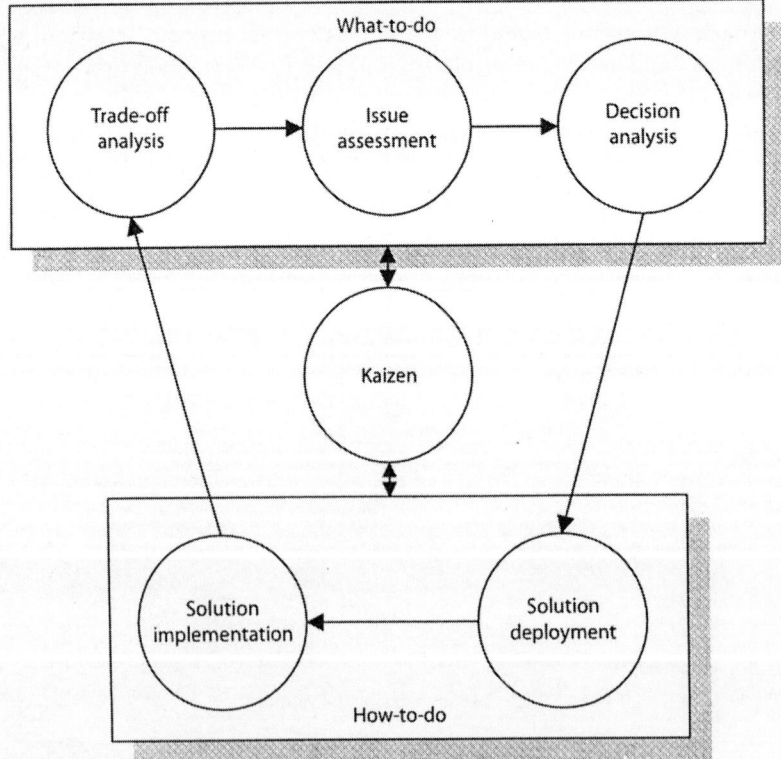

Fig. 2.10 Abstract process model.

is supported, primarily, by the strategic role. "Issue assessment" uses the technology and business information from trade-off analysis to define the scope and direction of the evolution project. Part of this activity is assessing the legacy system.

"Decision analysis" involves a cost/benefit/risk exercise to develop a suitable evolution strategy based on the earlier project, technology and business considerations. "Solution implementation" follows decision analysis with project planning and target system development tasks. After the solution has been validated, it can be deployed during "Solution deployment".

Similarly to providing for continuous improvement of software systems, the framework applies "Kaizen" to the method. With experience, you can improve the preceding activities so that they better support your organization and subsequent projects.

Table 2.12 shows the mapping of framework concepts onto the method. The framework builds on many of the ideas of the evolutionary paradigm, introduced in Chapter 1. In particular, it promotes:

- *Use of established management practice.* The process model is a high-level description which is independent of particular techniques and tools. We have carried this through to the method to encourage you to use those procedures, techniques and tools with which you have gained experience.

- *Pre-planned product improvement.* A significant part of the framework's process model involves long-term planning. You should consider whether a legacy system plays a role in your organization's future, and if so, how. By examining business goals, you can anticipate changes in system requirements.

- *Effective use of existing assets.* The framework is reengineering oriented. System replacement is a drastic and risk-prone form of evolution which we only

Table 2.12 Framework to method mapping

Framework	Method
Kaizen	Customizable method
Abstract process model	Process model
"What-to-do" activities	Phase Plan Evolution
"How-to-do" activities	Phases Implement, Deliver, Deploy and Use
Abstract roles	Responsibilities
Strategic	Application Business Expert Client Representative
Operational	Client Representative Software Project Manager Quality Engineer
Service	Legacy System Functional Expert User Legacy System Developer Data Modeller Software Architect Software Engineer
Knowledge capture	Document repository

recommend when reengineering is not technically feasible or is likely to be more expensive than replacement. We develop a core set of reengineering strategies that enable you to integrate parts of a legacy system with a target solution.

● *Information-rich systems.* Understanding a system is an essential and often expensive process which precedes system evolution. Knowledge grows with each iteration of the process model and should be preserved to reduce subsequent evolution costs.

References and Further Reading

RENAISSANCE Consortium (1998) *Renaissance Method Handbook.* http://www. comp.lancs.ac.uk/projects/renaissance/.
RENAISSANCE Consortium (1998) *Renaissance Method Framework.* http://www. comp.lancs.ac.uk/renaissance/.

Key Points

■ Renaissance provides a method which offers end-to-end guidance for managing evolution projects.

■ A process model, an information repository and a set of responsibilities define the method. Each of these elements is generic and you should customize them according to project and organizational factors.

■ The process model is made up of four phases. The first, Plan Evolution, assists you to develop the right evolution strategy for your system. The remaining phases guide you in implementing that strategy.

■ The method is not prescriptive in terms of particular techniques and tools. You should use the techniques and tools which you find effective.

■ Renaissance is iterative. You can apply it several times to a particular application and build on the information you gather in each iteration.

■ Renaissance is evolutionary. As you gain experience in practising it, you should evolve it to further meet your needs.

■ You can download further Renaissance documentation from http://www. comp.lancs.ac.uk/projects/renaissance.

3. *Evolution Planning*

Objectives

- To introduce evolution planning for evolutionary systems.
- To provide guidelines for assessing whether a legacy system is suitable for evolution.
- To introduce a set of "evolution strategies". Each strategy classifies a particular form of evolution.
- To describe how to develop an appropriate evolution strategy for a legacy system.
- To discuss project planning issues for evolution projects.

Contents

Evolution planning involves both "long-term" and "project" planning. Long-term planning addresses how a system should evolve over an extended operational lifetime. Long-term planning is necessary to manage evolutionary system development. Project planning is similar to planning for development projects, but is concerned with implementing an evolution strategy.

Figure 3.1 shows the distinction between long-term and project planning; the former is "product" oriented and the latter "project" driven. Traditionally, development projects have been managed with a short-term project view. In such cases, project planning is concerned with tasks like allocating resources, estimating costs and managing risks that are associated with system development. In this context, project planning does not address system evolution.

In Chapter 1, we described how continuous improvement is fundamental to evolutionary systems. Throughout the lifetime of an evolutionary system, you should manage its continuous improvement by a series of evolution projects, where each evolution project implements a particular form of improvement. Evolution project planning tasks are similar to those for development projects, but you should perform them in conjunction with the foresight of long-term planning.

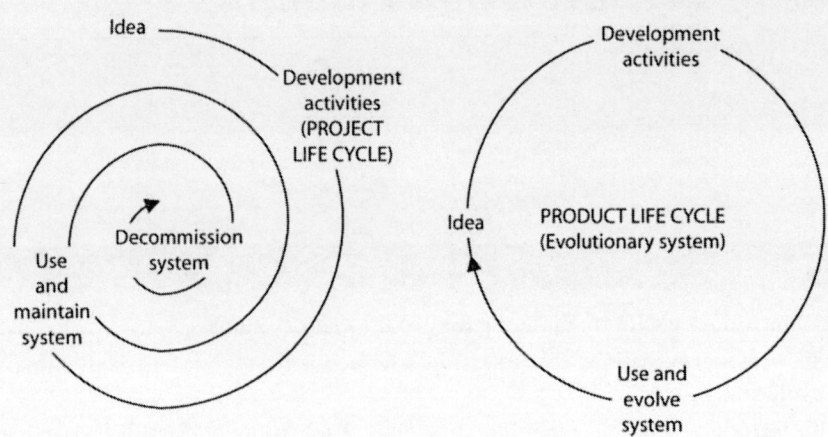

Fig. 3.1 Project and product life cycles.

Long-term planning is concerned with establishing a legacy system's future. From a business perspective, you should investigate whether the operational organization needs the system. If the answer to this is yes, you should determine for how long. It may be that the system is business-critical today, but that the operational organization's long-term strategy involves the introduction of an enterprise IT solution. In this case, you should not invest heavily in a reengineering programme because the system will shortly be replaced.

In addition to a business case analysis, you may assess the technical quality of the system. Measurements for business value and technical quality enable you to decide whether the application is an evolution candidate. If it is, you should develop an evolution strategy which identifies how the system can be improved. In many cases there are several alternatives, and you should make your decision based on their relative costs, benefits and risks. Some strategies, for example, may be too expensive or require resources which are unavailable.

Where you develop a system evolution strategy that can be justified on business and economic grounds, you should proceed by planning the project which implements the improvement. For large organizations, you may have several systems which are evolution candidates, but insufficient resources to evolve them concurrently. Here, you should prioritize them and start project planning for high-priority cases.

Evolution planning is a time-consuming process which can be very expensive. To avoid unnecessary planning, you should distinguish between critical and non-critical activities. You can do this by thinking of system evolution as a journey (Table 3.1). For a journey, you can develop a "plan" which identifies a "route" from a "starting point" to a "destination". Before planning, you need to know the starting point, the destination and the "reasons" for the journey. You should use this information to identify possible routes and assess them according to your reasons for making the journey. Only then can you make an informed decision as to the best route.

Table 3.1 Journey analogy

Step	Journey planning	Evolution planning
1	Determine reason for journey	Defines evolution project constraints
2	Unfold map	Define business goals and processes
3	Locate starting point	Understand legacy system
4	Locate destination	Formulate possible target systems
5	Identify possible routes	Develop possible evolution strategies
6	Assess possible routes	Assess evolution strategies
7	Choose route	Choose appropriate evolution strategy
8	Plan journey	Plan evolution project

For evolution planning, you should first identify the problem statement (reasons for the journey). The operational organization's business goals and business process description provide you with a map. The next step requires you to understand the legacy system (starting point). You should then identify one or more target systems (destinations) and evolution strategies (routes) for reaching them. You should select the evolution strategy which best satisfies the problem statement's aims and constraints.

Whether you should carry out all the steps in Table 3.1 depends on your project. There will almost certainly be constraints which affect the extent to which you need to carry them out. Various factors have to be considered:

1   You should specify any constraints, including time and budget, before proceeding with evolution planning. This helps prevent unnecessary and costly work. For example, where target hardware has been mandated, there is no point in considering target systems which do not use that hardware.

2   You should document business goals and the current business process description. There is nothing to be gained from examining the internal composition of a system where it no longer supports the business process.

3   To understand the legacy system, you should assess it from technical and business viewpoints. You may need to collect information and build models to support each of these views. The degree of modelling required depends on your system and the availability of knowledgeable personnel.

4   You should consider target systems which address your problem statement, subject to the constraints identified in step one. A budget constraint may preclude target systems which require a new hardware infrastructure for example.

5   Similarly to step four, there is no point in considering evolution strategies which fail to meet your evolution requirements, or which cannot be implemented because of constraints.

6   To decide whether it is worth implementing a particular evolution strategy, you should estimate the effort, time and resources required.

7   Where you have developed multiple evolution strategies, you should select the most appropriate one by assessing the relative costs, benefits and risks of each strategy.

8 If you decide that evolution is necessary, you should develop a project plan to support implementation of the selected strategy.

In Chapter 2, we described how you can customize Renaissance to offer a cost/risk trade-off. You should capture sufficient information about the system and its future requirements, but do so with the minimum effort necessary. Renaissance supports you by providing a number of assessment levels and helps you narrow your focus on components which actually need to be reengineered or replaced.

Figure 3.2 shows how the documents introduced in Chapter 2 develop during evolution planning. In general, documents which you create in one step are used in subsequent steps. It is particularly important that you use all the information you have gathered when developing the Project Plan. Preceding documents contain vital information such as cost and risk assessments for the System Evolution Strategy.

The output of evolution planning is a project plan. Implementation of a strategy may involve substantial investment, and choosing the wrong strategy can be very expensive. You should gain accurate results from long-term planning activities, such as Assess Current Situation and Select Target, to develop a workable and realistic project plan. Figure 3.3 shows the dependencies involved in a successful evolution project.

You should include delivery and deployment procedures in the project plan. They impact what can and cannot be deployed. In cases where a solution cannot be

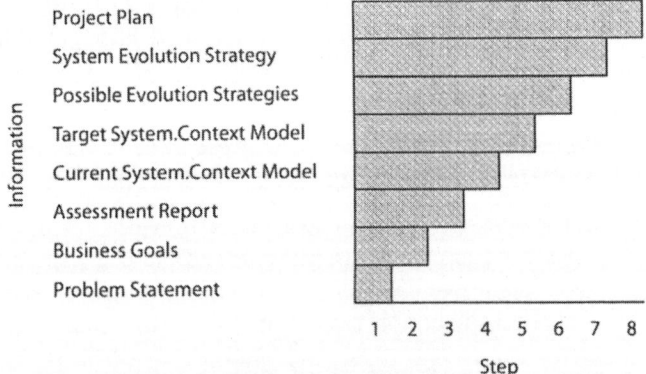

Fig. 3.2 Growth of information.

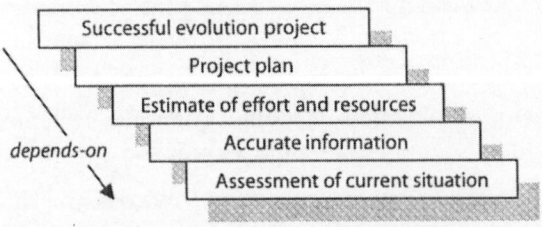

Fig. 3.3 Evolution planning dependencies.

deployed without involving intolerable disturbance to the operational organization, or where the organization cannot physically accommodate it, you should consider alternative strategies.

3.1   Legacy System Assessment

For the general case, you should assess a legacy system to determine its business value and technical quality. In addition, you should consider organizational factors which may affect your choice of evolution strategy. Large operational organizations may resist change, so a radical evolution project may prove unsuccessful.

Figure 3.4 shows possible information sources which you can use to gather information on which to base your assessment. Some of them may be unavailable in your case. For example, experienced maintenance staff are highly valued experts who can save you considerable time when developing a measurement of the system's technical quality. Without them, you need to study system artefacts and, where necessary, build system models.

System artefacts include source code, change history documents, development documents and user manuals. Where they exist, you should browse them to develop an understanding of the system. Often, however, documentation does not reflect the current state of the system. You should treat these documents cautiously, because relying on them too heavily can be misleading.

In other cases, documentation may be absent; you should use reverse engineering tools to help construct system models. In extreme cases, you will have nothing more than the operational system itself. Here, all you can do is study the system in use to see how it supports its business process. This can be of great value, however, because it may reveal business rules which are not documented elsewhere.

Experts are not constrained to technical maintainers, but include middle to senior individuals of both the development and operational organizations. In most cases, people from the operational organization who understand the rationale for the system are available. Managers typically understand the need for particular system functionality. You should interview these people because their contributions are invaluable when assessing the system's business value.

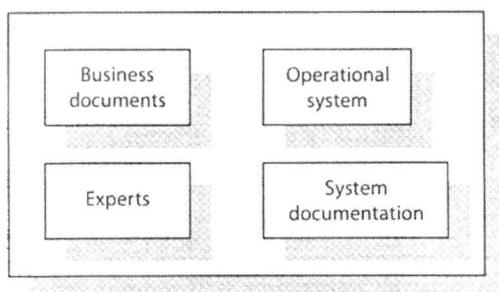

Fig. 3.4 Information sources.

Objective assessment requires that you base your assessment on measuring particular system "attributes". You should choose attributes which are appropriate to your project. For example, consider a simple analogy with a cube of ice. Possible attributes for measuring it include volume, weight and temperature. The choice of attributes depends on what you want to assess. If you intend to store a quantity of ice in a freezer, you should choose its volume. To carry it to the freezer, you would be more interested in its weight.

For legacy systems, you should select attributes whose values enable you to develop a suitable system evolution strategy, and on which to base estimates for cost, risk and resources during project planning. You should consider the availability of information sources and the Problem Statement when making your selection. Where assessment is focused on application software components, it does not make sense to choose attributes for measuring support software and hardware. In other cases, where you do not have the source code, it is meaningless to choose application software attributes such as complexity.

In Chapter 1, we introduced a model of legacy systems which captures their composition from technical, business and organizational components. Table 3.2 shows the attributes which you may choose to measure technical components. You should choose the level at which to assess the technical components according to your cost/risk trade-off. Figure 3.5 shows that there are three levels. At the "system" level, you view the system as a black box.

"Component" level assessment involves looking inside the system and identifying its processing components. These tend to be application programs and utilities; the latter include support software programs for tasks such as printing and sorting. In many cases, components are linked through a base of data. Where database or

Table 3.2 Technical quality attributes

Attribute	Hardware	Support software	Application software
Age	✓	✓	✓
Failure rate	✓	✓	✓
Ability to perform function	✓	✓	✓
Performance	✓	✓	✓
External dependencies	✓	✓	✓
Documentation	✓	✓	✓
Vendor/supplier	✓	✓	
Maintenance costs	✓		✓
License costs		✓	
Frequency of fixes/patches		✓	
Complexity			✓
Data			✓
Legality			✓
Maintenance record			✓
Size			✓
Security			✓
Test bed			✓

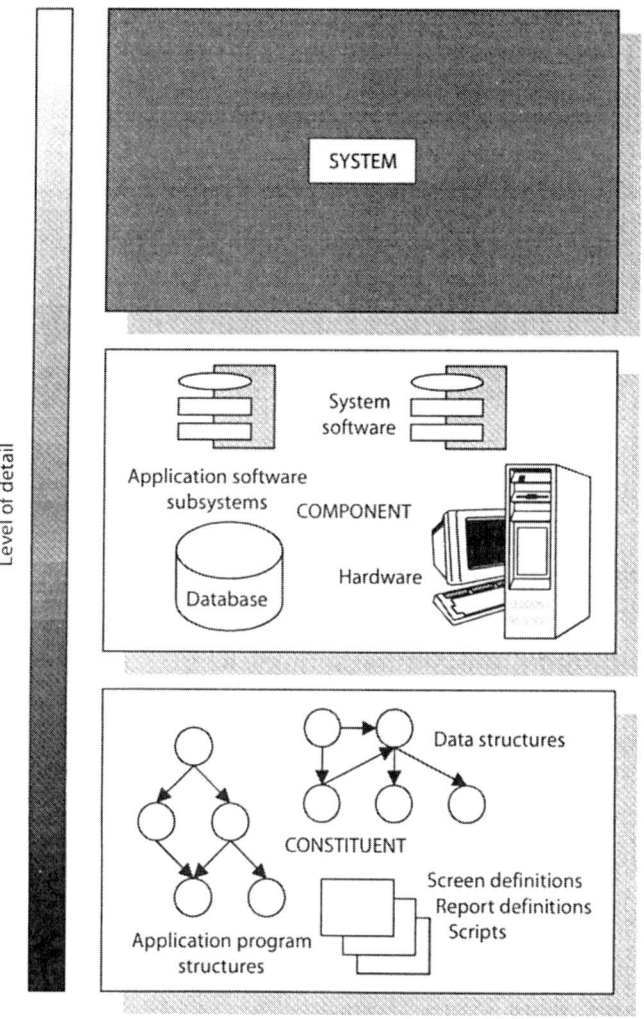

Fig. 3.5 Technical assessment levels.

transaction processing technology forms part of the system, you should assess them at this level. Often, you can identify inter-component relationships by studying job control modules, such as JCL and Unix shell scripts, and by following application software dependencies. You can use technical modelling and reverse engineering tools to help identify components.

For detailed assessment, you should decompose the system further into its "constituent" components. Constituent level assessment is only practical for application software components, as it involves examining their internal workings. Support software, such as 4GLs, compilers and operating systems, is generally supplied in binary form with a well-defined application programming interface (API).

At this level, you should assess the application software in terms of its programs and data schemas. Monolithic program structures do exist, but it is more common to find a main program which controls a hierarchy of subprograms. Constituent level components which you should assess include screen maps, report definitions, procedural code and data definitions. Each subprogram typically has a data definition section which describes its interaction with external data. This may be hard-coded or copied from a data dictionary at compile time. Similarly, procedural code may be hard-coded or included from a source library.

Once you have selected technical attributes, you should proceed by assigning each attribute a value. We use a four-point scale for each attribute, where 1 is a low score. You can develop an overall measure for technical quality by calculating a weighted average score.

To illustrate the approach, consider the "vendor/supplier" attribute for a hardware or support software component. A system fails to be an evolutionary system when it is composed of components which are no longer supported. For example, you should not operate a system which runs on obsolete hardware because it is unlikely that system software will be supported for it. The vendor/supplier attribute captures the degree of support available for a particular component. It is rated:

1 The worst case, where the component is not supported by any vendor or third-party organization.

2 A tolerable situation where the original vendor no longer supports the component, but there is support from a third-party organization.

3 The original vendor currently supports the component.

4 The original vendor not only supports the component today, but the vendor's future looks assured. This is the best scenario, because the vendor should continue to support the component.

You can assign values to attributes using either expert opinion or metrics. Expert opinion is well-suited to low-cost assessment, but obviously requires suitable experts. The use of metrics is particularly appropriate for detailed assessment where you can use tools. However, effective use of metrics requires historical records of process and product metrics which have been calibrated to your organization.

Unlike technical quality attributes, business value attributes are few, but common to all evolution projects. Table 3.3 describes two fundamental business attributes. They are less easy to quantify than technical attributes, but you should draw on the Business documents which you created during the method's Startup Method activity. In addition, you can study the system in use and interview operators, managers and senior personnel from the operational organization.

You should use the Business Process Description document to determine how well the system supports the operational organization's business process. Where the system supports key processes well, you should assign "business criticality" a high value. Additional factors you may want to consider include the system's market value and contribution to profit, and the significance of the system's data.

Table 3.3 Business value attributes

Attribute	Description
Business criticality	A system's business value is determined by the degree to which the business needs the system. If the system is essential to the continued operation of the business, it has a high business value.
Required lifetime	Business value is affected by the anticipated need for the system in the future. Business value is high where you find that the system is likely to remain business critical in the long-term.

To provide a measure for "required lifetime", you should consider the Problem Statement and Business Goals documents. The Problem Statement records whether the reason for evolution is a changing business process. If you expect the process to change radically, the required lifetime of the system may be short. Similarly, where business goals indicate radical change, the system may not be required for much longer. In these cases, we assume that the system cannot accommodate the anticipated changes. In other cases, you may be able to integrate business process change and emerging business goals with the system. In this case, the required lifetime of the system is extended.

Once you have generated measures for technical quality and business value, you should plot them on a graph (Fig. 3.6). This is a practical approach advocated by Nolan Norton and Co. (in [1]). Generally, you should invest reengineering effort in systems with high business value and low technical quality. Where you have many systems, you should plot them on a single graph. Those that fall in the lower right quadrant are priority cases.

The initial measurements you make are a "first cut". For effective and accurate assessment, you must adjust these measurements by further analysis. Where a system has both a high technical quality and a high business value, you should initially tag the system as a low priority reengineering candidate. A high rating for technical quality may hide an isolated low score for the hardware's failure rate. A

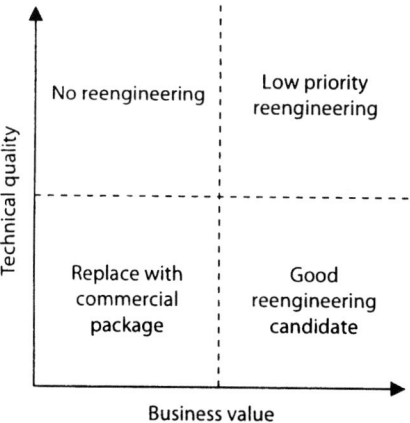

Fig. 3.6 Portfolio analysis.

system which is business-critical but which fails repeatedly is not a low-priority case. You should promote it to a good reengineering candidate.

In other cases, further analysis should take the form of a more detailed assessment. For example, a system-level assessment might reveal a performance deficiency, but it does not indicate which components are responsible for the problem. Here, you should carry out a component-level or constituent-level assessment to determine which components should be reengineered or replaced.

In addition to analyzing your results, you should consider the impact of organizational factors, such as those presented in Table 3.4. In cases where you choose an evolution strategy which involves a technology change, you should consider whether you have engineers who are competent to use the new technology. Where a system supports a revised business process, or has a different appearance, you should ensure that the operational organization is committed to operator training. Organizational factors are often critical success factors.

Table 3.4 Organizational factors

Factor	Description
Technical maturity	Technical maturity includes the use of modern software engineering methods and conformance to a defined and practised process. Mature organizations are committed to process improvement and formally record product and process metrics. To be successful, radical evolution projects require technically mature development organizations.
Training procedures	Personnel training is a critical success factor. Where the operational organization is not committed to staff training, the risk of an evolution project failing may be high.
Skill level	Engineers from the development organization should have skills in the legacy system's technology and any new technology which is to be used. Similarly to the operational organization, the development organization should train its staff.
Attitude to change	Many large organizations, especially those which are bureaucratic or employ dated structures, resist change. Radical reengineering may be unsuccessful in these cases.

3.2   Evolution Strategies

An "evolution strategy" describes a particular way of evolving a system. Renaissance defines a set of strategies, shown in Table 3.5. Reengineering is a general term which captures some form of system improvement. To help manage this generality, we define four popular classes of reengineering. Each strategy is associated with risks, which we summarize in Table 3.6.

Continued maintenance is often the most cost-effective evolution strategy. It requires a well-defined process, system documentation, experienced maintenance staff, historical change information and configuration management. For many legacy systems, however, continued maintenance is inappropriate. Motivating factors for reengineering or replacement include:

Table 3.5 Evolution strategies

Evolution strategy		Description
Continued maintenance		The accommodation of change in a system, without radical change to its structure, after it has been delivered and deployed.
Reengineering	Revamp	The transformation of a system by modifying or replacing its user interfaces. The internal workings of the system remain intact, but appear to have changed to the user.
	Restructure	The transformation of a system's internal structure without changing any external interfaces.
	Rearchitecture	The transformation of a system by migrating it to a different technological architecture.
	Redesign with reuse	The transformation of a system by redeveloping it utilizing some legacy components.
Replace		Total replacement of a system from scratch.

Table 3.6 Evolution strategy risks

Risk factor	Evolution strategy					
	Continued maintenance	Revamp	Restructure	Rearchitecture	Redesign with reuse	Replace
Lack of system knowledge	✓	✓	✓	✓	✓	✓
Experienced maintenance staff leave	✓	✓				
Inadequate or inconsistent documentation	✓	✓	✓	✓	✓	✓
Lack of skills for target technology				✓	✓	✓
Errors introduced during evolution			✓	✓	✓	✓
Unpredictable target system performance				✓	✓	✓
Operational organization not committed to staff training		✓		✓	✓	✓
Immature technology for target system				✓	✓	✓
Difficulties integrating legacy components with target system				✓	✓	✓
Lack of tool support			✓	✓	✓	✓
Loss of embedded business rules						✓
System will not meet evolution requirements	✓	✓				
Obsolete operational environment	✓	✓	✓			

- An anticipated reduction in maintenance costs following reengineering.

- Poor technical condition of the system, which makes continued maintenance difficult and expensive.

- Business process changes which cannot be adequately supported by the system.

- Obsolete system components.

● A need to integrate the system with other systems, but where continued maintenance precludes integration.

You should "revamp" a system when you want to improve its "look and feel".
Revamping gives the impression of a new application and is particularly suited to
migrating from a character-based user interface to a GUI. In this case, it requires
some investment in new hardware (terminals and pointing devices) and GUI
software. Revamping does not, however, resolve any difficulties in evolving the
system, because its application code and data are ignored.

During revamping, you may need to analyze the system's current user interface,
remove redundant forms, redesign the interface, and identify and replace interface
components. Revamping is only practical when the user interface and application
logic are loosely coupled (Fig. 3.7).

Where revamping is applicable, you can often use middleware between the legacy
system and new GUI components. Middleware describes software which provides
for interoperability between otherwise incompatible components. We discuss how
you can use middleware to integrate legacy and target system components in
Chapter 5. Figure 3.8 shows how middleware interprets the character stream of a
text-based user interface and generates GUI events. In many cases, you do not need to
change legacy source code.

Figure 3.9 shows how a system can operate with both a text-based interface and a
GUI at the same time. You can introduce GUIs for certain classes of user and
maintain existing text-based interfaces for other users. For example, a text-based
interface might be suitable for data entry clerks, but for managers GUIs may be more
appropriate. You can also incrementally revamp a system using the model shown in
Fig. 3.9.

In contrast to revamping, you can "restructure" a system to improve its internal
workings. You should consider restructuring systems when they are difficult and
expensive to change. Restructuring makes software easier to understand and evolve.

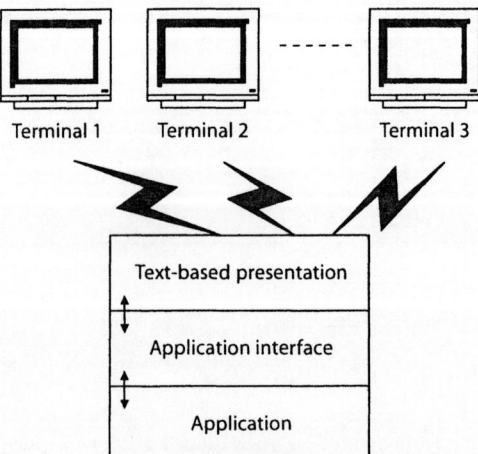

Fig. 3.7 Loosely coupled presentation and application.

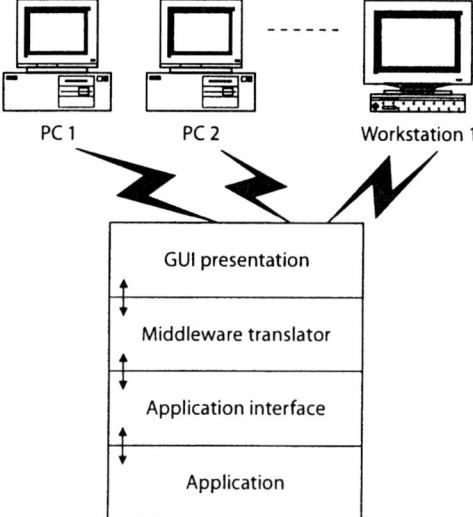

Fig. 3.8 Migrating to a GUI.

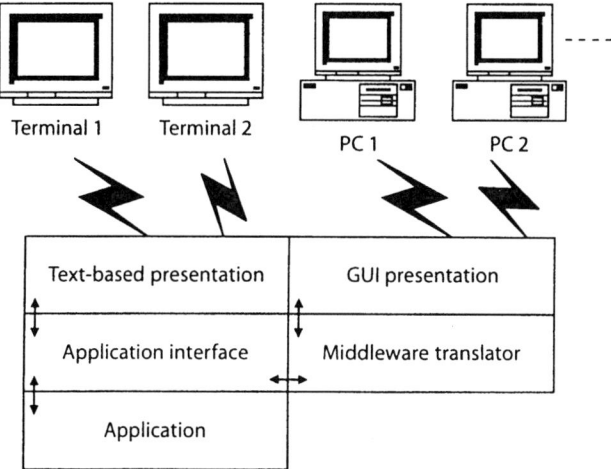

Fig. 3.9 Coexistence of text-based interfaces and GUIs.

During restructuring, you should identify software components which need reorganizing. They may be either procedural (subsystems and functions for example) or data-oriented, such as database schemas.

Restructuring aims to increase a system's understandability and maintainability without making semantic changes. It may involve transforming a system from a situation similar to that shown in Fig. 3.10 to that of Fig. 3.11. For procedural components, you should improve their control flow, remove redundant code, adopt coding standards and reduce dependencies among them. You can measure the improvement

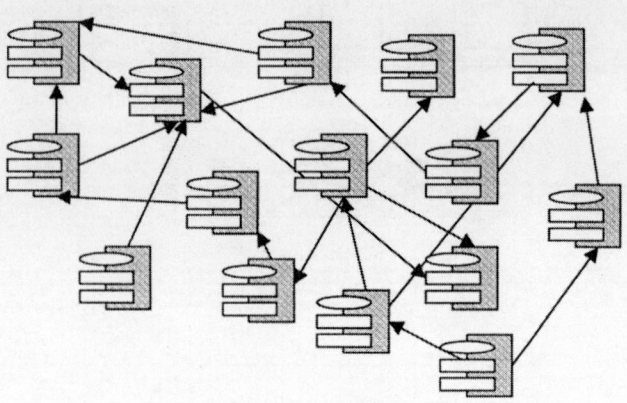

Fig. 3.10 Complex software structure.

External interfaces

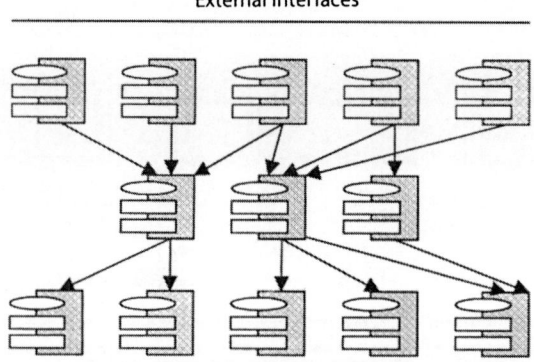

Fig. 3.11 Restructured system.

gained from restructuring by using complexity metrics on the pre- and post-restructured components.

For any non-trivial system, you should use tools which automate much of the restructuring in order to manage the volume of code. In any case, there is a risk that you will introduce errors in the restructured system because of the changes you make to it.

Unlike revamping, restructuring does not yield an immediate return on reengineering investment. It does, however, make a system easier to understand and reduces the chances of introducing new errors. The net result should be a drop in long-term maintenance costs and improvements in the system's reliability, testability and performance.

Legacy system architectures are often inflexible and resist change. Where they become obsolete, non-standard or too expensive to operate or change, you should consider system "rearchitecturing". Rearchitecturing involves transforming a centralized architecture (Fig. 3.12) to a distributed system (Fig. 3.13). Software rearchitecturing typically means adopting client/server and object-oriented technology. Hardware and software rearchitecturing are generally interdependent; a change in one generally requires a change in the other.

Chapter 5 provides guidance on choosing a distributed architecture and integrating legacy system components with it. To rearchitecture a system, you should analyze the legacy system's functionality and identify functions to be distributed to clients and servers. You may have to transform functional programs into object-oriented

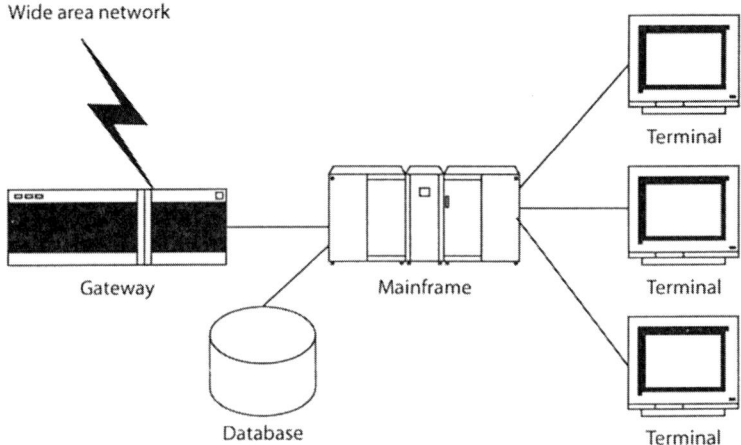

Fig. 3.12 Centralized architecture.

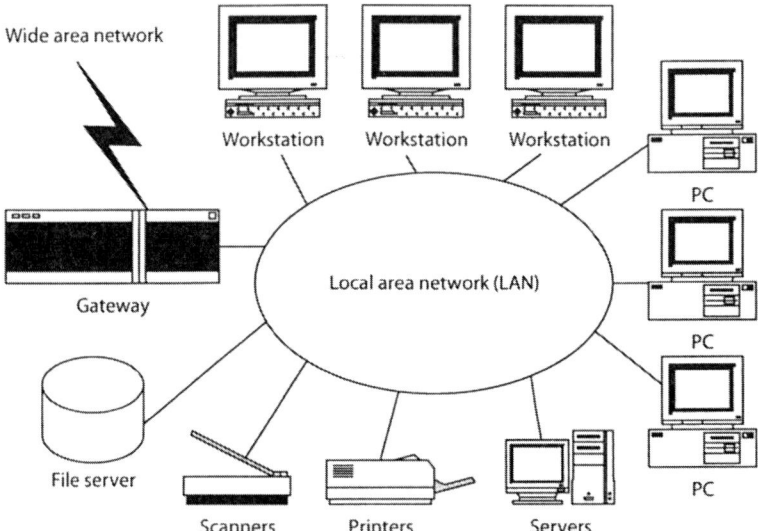

Fig. 3.13 Distributed architecture.

solutions. In many cases, you may choose to replace existing functionality with commercial off-the-shelf (COTS) components.

Rearchitecturing is generally more expensive and carries greater risk than revamping or restructuring, but its benefits are greater. A rearchitectured system is likely to be evolvable because it runs on modern well-supported hardware. Client/ server and object-oriented technology is generally more responsive to change and supports rapid accommodation of change. In addition, rearchitecturing realizes the benefits of distributed systems such as resource sharing, openness and scalability.

"Redesign with reuse" emphasizes legacy software reuse. It aims to preserve the knowledge and business rules which are embedded in legacy components by integrating them in a new software architecture. You can encapsulate both procedural and data components behind well-defined interfaces. For the former, you should use distributed object technology to package legacy components as distributable objects. You can use database middleware to encapsulate legacy data. We describe both of these approaches in Chapter 5.

You should not select the redesign-with-reuse strategy if your system has a monolithic structure. In this case, you will be unable to identify suitable reusable components. In less severe cases, you may be able to restructure the system to reveal reusable components before proceeding with redesign-with-reuse. Where you can find reusable components, you may need to change them so that they are compatible with any new software architecture technology.

Similarly to revamping, an encapsulated component retains any problems associated with its underlying legacy implementation. Redesign-with-reuse does, however, allow you to evolve an application incrementally. Initially, you can distribute legacy functions as objects and encapsulate legacy data using middleware. You can then select individual objects and reengineer their implementations.

System "replacement" is an expensive and risk-prone strategy. You should only consider it when continued maintenance or reengineering is not feasible. Replacement is subject to development project risks, such as building systems which do not satisfy users' real requirements.

In many cases, you will develop a hybrid evolution strategy. Different strategies are often appropriate for different system components. You might select revamping to provide senior users with GUIs and restructuring of the system's data schemas to improve its performance. In other cases, you should precede one evolution strategy with another. For example, before you can rearchitecture a system you may need to restructure it first so that you can identify components which can be cleanly distributed as servers.

3.3   Cost Estimation and Risk Assessment

Once you have assessed the legacy system and have developed, to some degree, a model of the target system, you will probably identify several candidate evolution strategies. At this stage, these strategies are based largely on technical and functional considerations. To select the right system evolution strategy, you should consider the relative costs, benefits and risks of each strategy. This cost estimation and risk assessment also forms the basis for subsequent project planning.

For each evolution strategy, you should use cost estimates to calculate its return on investment and time-to-market. You should quantify factors such as effort, duration, equipment costs and personnel costs. Precise cost estimation is based on accurate and detailed information. In cases where you need precise cost estimates, you should carry out a detailed assessment of your system. You will also need a sufficiently detailed context model of the target system, rather than a brief description.

Risk assessment is fundamental to cost estimation (Fig. 3.14). You may need to base cost estimates on uncertainty. For example, where a project's size and scope are not well defined, you have less confidence in any cost estimate than if these factors are known. In this case, you face the risk of developing an inaccurate cost estimate. You should deal with situations like this by stating any estimation assumptions and build contingency measures into your project plan.

A risk is an event which may adversely affect the operational organization. Risks include:

- The target system is never delivered.

- The target system is delivered late.

- The target system exceeds budget.

A risk may become a reality when a risk factor, such as one of those in Table 3.6, occurs. Risk management involves assessing and containing risk. For the former, you should monitor those risks that are associated with your strategy. For each risk, you should classify it as to whether it is avoidable or not, and to the degree of threat which it poses to the business. You should treat risks which can be avoided and which pose a significant threat to the business as high-priority cases for containment. To contain risk factors, you should bring them to the attention of interested parties and take remedial action to reduce their effects, or try to avoid them.

Where you have several candidate evolution strategies or a hybrid evolution strategy, you should follow the process shown in Fig. 3.14 for each strategy. This allows you to consider the relative costs and risks of each strategy and to establish an "economically driven" baseline for comparing them. You may need to assign more than one individual to cost estimation because it requires people who understand the legacy system, cost estimation and reengineering.

You should start by documenting any assumptions you will use to prepare your estimates. For example, you may have personnel with particular skills who are only available for a limited period of time. In other cases, you may assume that tools exist with particular capabilities. You should then identify cost items which have an impact on your evolution strategy. Table 3.7 shows a set of cost elements which are generally applicable to reengineering projects.

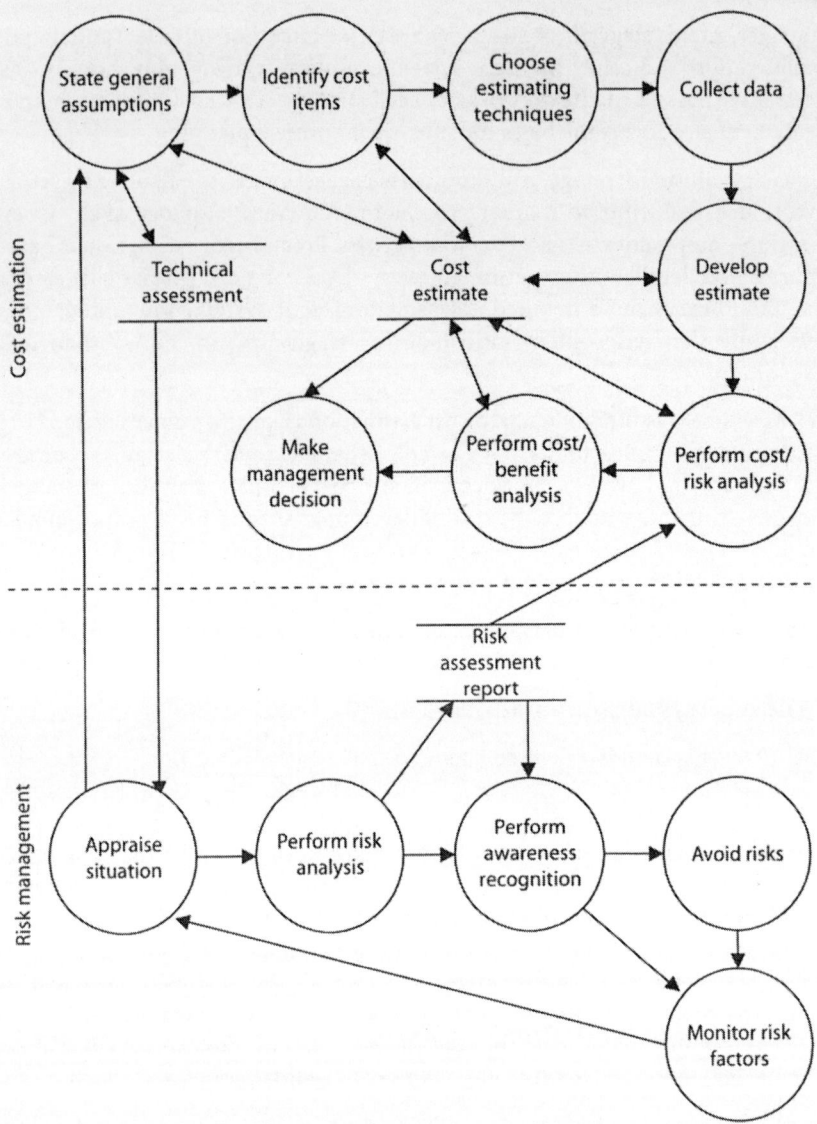

Fig. 3.14 Cost estimation and risk management.

You should select cost items which capture all costs incurred from the start of any reengineering effort to the end of the system's useful life. There are three cost groups you should consider:

1 *Reengineering investment costs (RIC).* This group represents those costs which are necessary to implement the evolution strategy. They include human resources for software development, modelling and training; and software and hardware procurement costs.

Table 3.7 Possible cost items

Code and unit test	Operational site activation
Integration test	Hardware
Requirements analysis	Training
Reverse engineering	Independent verification and validation
System design	Support environment
System integration	Data migration

2 *Operations and support costs for reengineered components (OSRC)*. Once deployed, those components of a system which have been reengineered need to be supported. Operational and support costs include licensing, hardware servicing and software evolution costs.

3 *Operations and support costs for legacy components (OSLC)*. You will typically need to support the legacy system throughout the evolution project. Only when the reengineered system is ready to deploy can you withdraw support for it. Where your evolution strategy involves retaining part of the legacy system, you should include the operations and support costs for these legacy components beyond reengineering too.

For each cost item, you should use an appropriate technique for estimating its cost. Table 3.8 describes a number of techniques. You should select the technique based on factors, such as availability of resources and time, the level of accuracy you require and the availability of the information necessary to make the estimate. In cases where a quick order-of-magnitude estimate for reengineering will suffice, you should generally use a top-down technique. Conversely, if you need a more precise estimate, you should use an alternative technique, bottom-up for example, with accurate inputs.

Table 3.8 Estimating techniques

Technique	Description
Expert judgement	This technique involves drawing on historical data and estimators' experience. Its use is dependent on your organization's technical maturity and availability of experienced personnel.
Analogy-based	Analogy-based estimation requires that you have estimated similar projects in the past. Often, the novelty of reengineering projects means that there is a lack of suitable projects to support this technique.
Top down	You derive the cost estimate from the global properties of the software product and split it amongst the product's components.
Bottom up	You develop the cost estimate starting with individual cost items and aggregate the results to produce an estimate for the whole project.
Parametric	Parametric models are typically based on some measure of system size, such as source lines of code (SLOC) or function points. Many models, COCOMO for example, use additional input variables which represent major cost drivers.

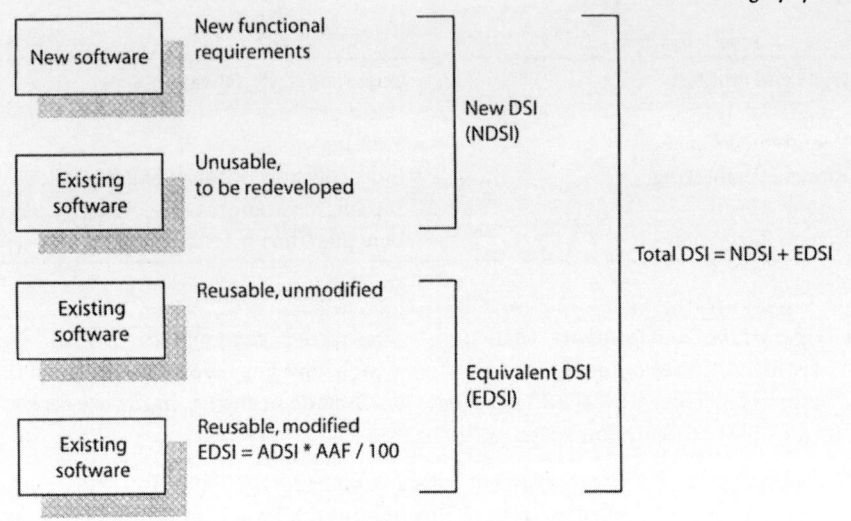

Fig. 3.15 Parametric model adaptation.

Cost estimation techniques have generally matured for development projects. You should adjust them before using them in reengineering projects. Many adjustments are based on the assumption that reengineering projects require less effort than development projects because of the potential for code reuse. You can calculate an adaptation factor (AAF) by considering the percentage of design, code and integration required for the reengineering project. You should then apply this factor to the adapted delivered source instructions (ADSI) to reduce the size of a reengineering project (Fig. 3.15). However, you should apply such techniques with caution and support them with experience.

As you develop the cost estimate, you should be aware of any time constraints which have been imposed on the project. Where they exist, you should develop a preliminary project plan before estimating the effort required. You can then allocate effort so that any time constraints are met.

3.4 Evolution Project Planning

Many projects fail because of a lack of coordination and communication, inaccurate estimating, poor quality assurance and bad contractual procedures. You can avoid project failure by effective evolution planning, which increases the degree of control which you have over the project. You should allow for contingency measures based on your planning assumptions and risk assessment. You should monitor progress according to the plan and respond to changes in project risk factors, which include those which you have identified for your evolution strategy.

The objective of evolution project planning is to develop a plan which describes "how", "by whom" and "with what" you will implement your system evolution

Table 3.9 Project plan

Item	Description
Assumptions	You should document any assumptions on which you plan the project.
Product descriptions	You may produce several deliverables, such as software components, documentation, and project reports. For each, you should describe its purpose, its dependencies on other deliverables, and the time which it is to be produced.
Quality assurance plan	You should plan for independent verification and validation of the evolution project's products.
Resource requirements	Project resources include personnel, skills, budget, time, hardware, and software tools.
Risk management plan	Based on evolution strategy specific risks and general project risks, you should develop a plan for monitoring and containing them.
Schedule	You should develop a schedule based on products and tasks. You should allow for contingency, based on assumptions and risk. The schedule should identify milestones and key deliverables.

strategy. Before you start project planning, you should ensure that you have accurate results from the preceding evolution planning activities. They provide critical inputs on which to build, and without them you will be planning to fail. Table 3.9 identifies the content of a typical project plan.

Figure 3.16 shows the process of project planning. In Chapter 2, we pointed out that evolution projects differ fundamentally from development projects in that they start with an operational system. This raises several issues which you should plan for. In particular, you should:

- *Plan human resources.* You may need to remove technical personnel from their normal duties throughout the course of an evolution project. They may be required to retrain in new technologies, to develop target system components and to help train operators. In addition to technicians, you may need to disrupt operational personnel to train them in the target system. In both cases, you need to address the effects of removing individuals from their normal work.

- *Procure, install, and configure new hardware and support software.* Where your evolution strategy involves new technology, you may need to introduce the technology incrementally or with some period of coexistence with the legacy and target systems.

- *Plan data migration.* In most cases, you will have to manage some data migration. In Chapter 2, we introduced "static" and "dynamic" data. You may need to plan for static data to be available for testing. In other cases, where you need to rapidly deploy the system, you should plan data migration tasks so that as much data as possible is migrated before the deployment period.

- *Consider system deployment.* In general, you should keep the legacy system operational until the target system is ready to deploy. You should make initial plans for deploying the target system because of the impact that deployment has on project

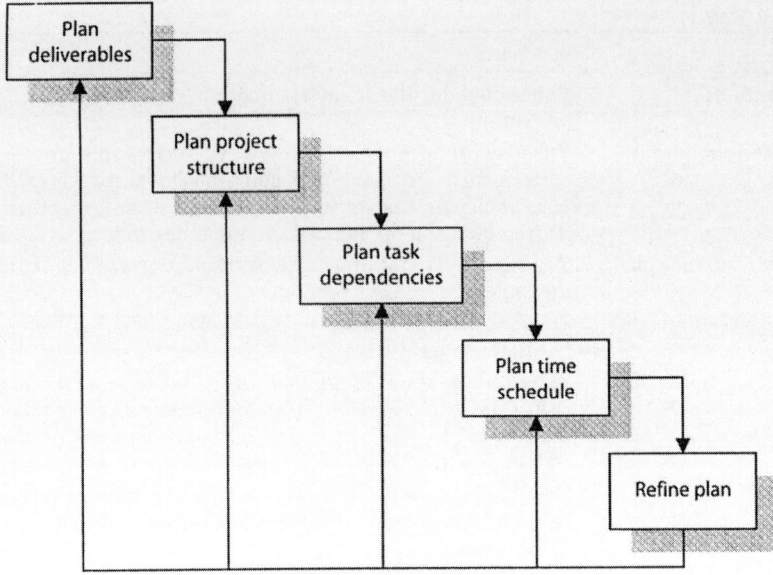

Fig. 3.16 Project planning.

planning. This is particularly true where a project constraint states that the deployment period should be minimal. In addition to data migration, you should plan to have the operational environment prepared, operators trained and the target system acceptance tested prior to deployment.

References and Further Reading

[1] Sneed H.M. (1995) Planning the reengineering of legacy systems. *IEEE Software*, **12**(1), 24–34.

Boehm B.W. (1991) Software risk management: principles and practices. *IEEE Software*, **8**(1), 32–42.
Ganti N. (1995) *The Transition of Legacy Systems to a Distributed Architecture*. John Wiley & Sons, Chichester.
RENAISSANCE Consortium (1998) *Evolution Planning*. Consultancy report, http://www.comp.lancs.ac.uk/projects/renaissance/.
Sneed H.M. (1991) Economics of software reengineering. *Journal of Software Maintenance: Research and Practice*, **3**, 163–82.
US DoD (1997) *Software Reengineering Handbook*. United States Department of Defense.

Key Points

■ Evolution involves both long-term planning and project planning.
■ Long-term planning addresses how a system should evolve over an extended operational lifetime.

- Project planning manages the transition between the legacy and target systems according to a particular evolution strategy.

- Evolution planning is an expensive process. To control costs, you should select tasks and the degree to which to perform them based on your project's characteristics.

- Accurate assessment is an essential contribution to developing the right evolution strategy. You should carry out a thorough assessment of business, technical and organizational factors.

- Where possible, you should avoid replacing a system. In cases where you need to take some remedial action, a reengineering-based evolution strategy is, in general, less expensive and carries less risk than replacement. It also, potentially, supports an incremental approach to evolution.

- Part of the process of selecting the right evolution strategy is to analyze the relative costs, benefits and risks of alternative strategies. You should use cost estimation and risk assessment techniques which have been tailored to evolution projects.

- You should use the information you gather during evolution planning as the basis for your project plan. The results of assessment and cost/risk analysis are critical inputs to effective project planning.

4. *Modelling for Evolution*

Objectives

- To explain why modelling is necessary for evolution projects.
- To introduce a set of modelling techniques which capture a system from several viewpoints and at a range of abstraction levels.
- To demonstrate how to use the UML and other popular techniques to build system models.
- To present general guidelines for evolution modelling.

Contents

Many legacy systems are difficult to understand. Several years of *ad hoc* maintenance leads to systems with contrived structures and documentation which is missing or outdated. These systems are prohibitively expensive to maintain, and they constrain the development of organizations which operate them. Evolution modelling addresses how to redocument these systems, with the aim of bringing them back under control. In addition, it enables you to document target systems and the transition between legacy and evolutionary systems.

In contrast with development projects, evolution projects are initiated to improve aspects of existing systems. Before you begin to improve a system, you must understand it. Software modelling assumes that abstract models convey information more effectively than source code. You should use abstract models to enhance your understanding of a system and to provide a common base for others to discuss it.

In this chapter we introduce system modelling from a reengineering perspective. We use the term "context model" for models which describe a system at a high level of abstraction. Context models describe "what" a system does. "Technical models" elaborate context models with more detail to describe "how" a system implements its behaviour. Figure 4.1 summarizes evolution modelling. It is based on the following rationale:

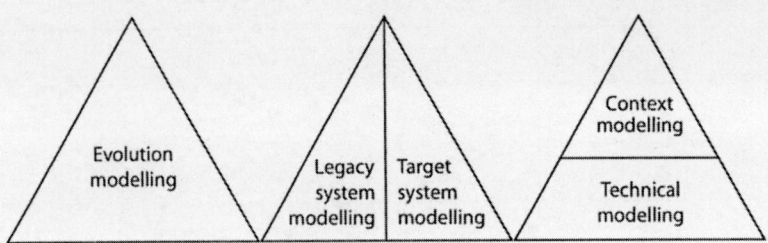

Fig. 4.1 Evolution modelling.

- You should understand a system in order to make an informed decision as to the best evolution strategy for it.

- It is difficult to understand a system from source code alone. You should develop context models to build a visual framework for discussing the legacy system and documenting the target system.

- You should build detailed models of selected legacy system components. Technical models support the transformation between the legacy and target systems and serve as target system documentation.

Figure 4.2 shows that evolution modelling is an incremental four-step process. You should follow this process to develop models which support system reengineering. In general, you should:

1 *Build a context model of the legacy system.* The input to this task is the source code and any documentation for the legacy system. You can use a number of modelling techniques, which we introduce shortly, to develop a context model. This is an iterative process where you should consult with operational individuals who have a good working knowledge of the system. Where technical personnel who understand the system are available, you should discuss the system with them to reduce the modelling effort needed.

2 *Build a context model of the target system.* Once you are satisfied that you have captured the interesting aspects of the legacy system (step one), you should augment that model with new business and technology constraints. The former includes new functionality; the latter documents new technology which is part of the target system, such as a GUI. The result is a context model for the target system.

3 *Build a technical model of the legacy system.* You should build technical models of legacy system components which you intend to integrate with the target system. You can use reverse engineering tools to help extract suitable abstractions. For all but the most trivial projects, reverse engineering tools are probably essential.

4 *Build a technical model of the target system.* In the same way that you can extend the legacy system's context model with target system constraints, you should augment the legacy system's technical model with implementation constraints. These constraints capture how legacy components will be integrated with target system components.

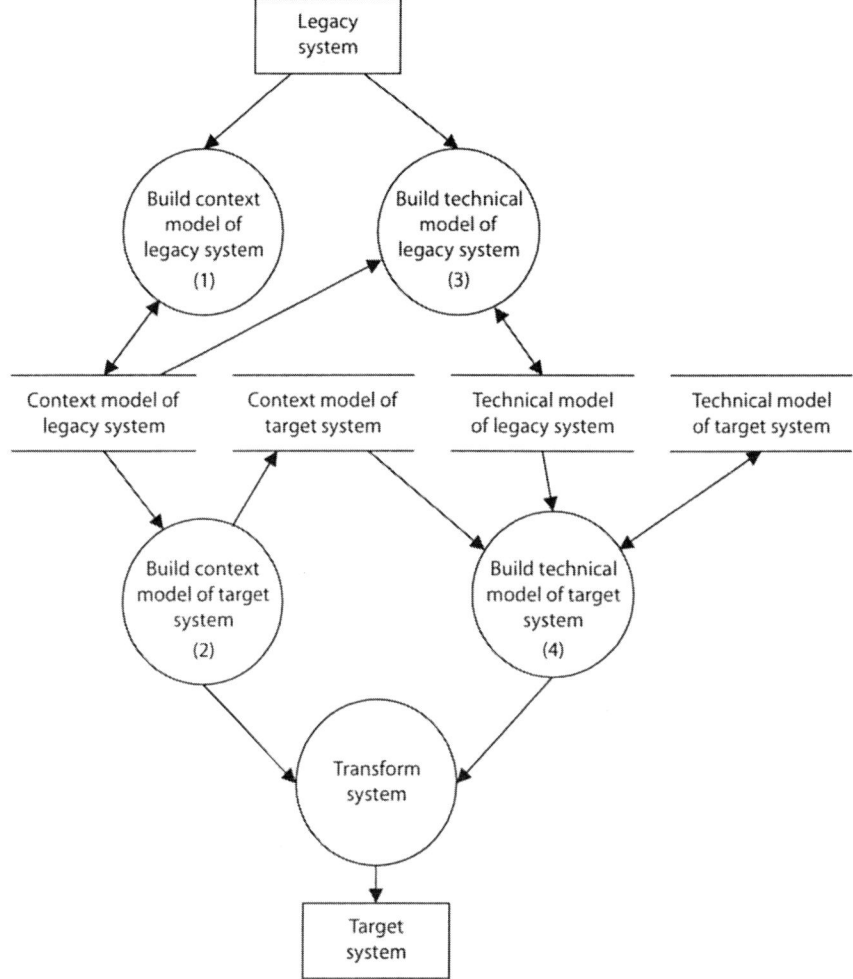

Fig. 4.2 Data flow diagram for evolution modelling.

4.1 Context Modelling

The aim of context modelling is to describe a system at an abstract level. You should capture a sufficient understanding of the system with which to make an informed decision as to an appropriate evolution strategy. The degree and content of context modelling which you need varies from project to project. Factors you should consider include availability of system experts, quality of existing documentation and any constraints on the solution space.

Context models should not contain too much detail. You need only capture the main system concepts, components and relationships. Requirements for modelling are stronger and more specific for the target system, however. This is because you not only need to understand the target system, but also to design and implement it too.

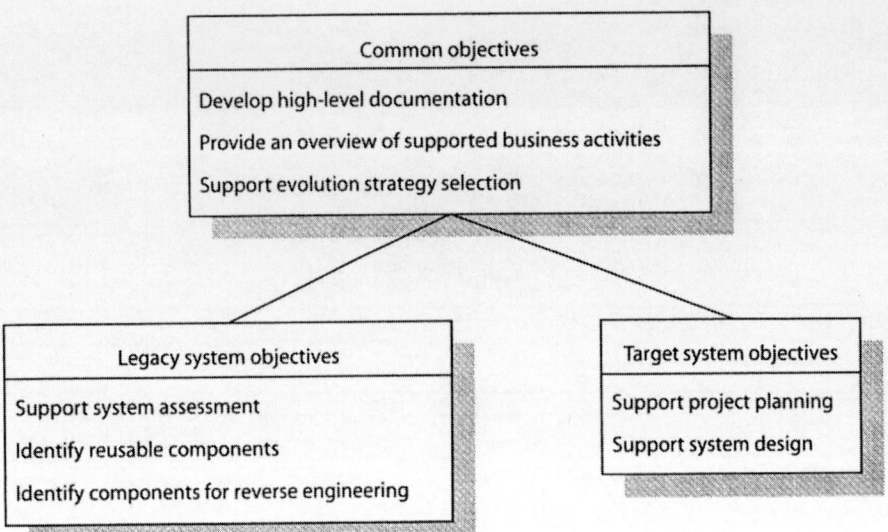

Fig. 4.3 Context modelling objectives.

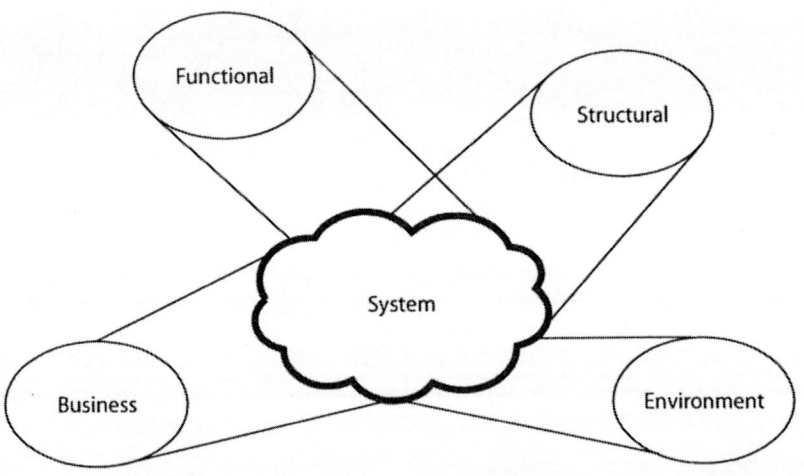

Fig. 4.4 Context modelling viewpoints.

Figure 4.3 summarizes the objectives of context modelling for both legacy and target systems. To meet these objectives, you should study systems from four viewpoints (Fig. 4.4):

1 *Business.* This viewpoint captures a system's support for business processes.

2 *Functional.* The functional view describes the system functionality which implements the business processes captured in the business view.

3 *Structural.* This view shows an overview of the system's software.

4   *Environment.* This is the physical system structure. It models the system's network
    organization and communication model.

You can structure the Context model documents for both legacy and target systems
in a common way. Table 4.1 shows the structure and identifies how each viewpoint
supports the document's constituent parts.

Table 4.1 Context model document

Model structure	Viewpoint			
	Business	Functional	Structural	Environment
System functionality	✓	✓		
Business process support	✓	✓		
Software architecture			✓	
Data structures			✓	
External interfaces			✓	✓
Software composition			✓	
System environment				✓

During context modelling, you should bear in mind that context models are abstract
and are intended to support non-technical participants in their decision-making.
You should keep diagrams both simple and focused, without too many concepts on
one diagram. Where you need to provide additional detail, you should use hierarchical decomposition to manage multiple diagrams.

To avoid unnecessary effort, you should focus on components that are of interest to your
project. Context models, particularly those which support the structural viewpoint, are
the starting point for technical modelling. You must develop context models for components that you need to understand or develop their internal workings.

Context modelling is an iterative process. At each iteration, you should refine your
model in terms of correctness and detail. You should stop when further iteration is
not cost-effective, or, in other words, when you have captured a sufficient understanding of the system. It is often difficult to know when to stop, but you may
consider the Pareto rule. This states that the last 20% of refinement, which is necessary to get a "perfect" model, will cost you 80% of effort.

To build a model which comprises all four viewpoints, you should use the techniques
identified in Table 4.2. Particular techniques include:

● *Use case diagrams.* Use case diagrams model how users interact with a system. You
  should use them to capture how a system supports its business process.

● *Data flow diagrams.* These diagrams, used in Structured Analysis, are useful for
  capturing processes and information flow at a range of abstraction levels.

● *Entity relationship diagrams (ERDs).* ERDs are well suited to data modelling. You
  can use these diagrams to support data reengineering.

● *Block diagrams.* You can use various flavours of block diagrams to capture
  relationships among software components.

Table 4.2 Context modelling techniques

Diagram		Viewpoint			
		Business	Functional	Structural	Environment
UML	Use-case	✓	✓		
	Sequence	✓	✓	✓	
	Collaboration	✓	✓	✓	
	Package			✓	
	Deployment				✓
Other	Data flow		✓		
	Entity relationship			✓	
	Block	✓	✓	✓	
	Hardware/network				

- *Hardware/network diagrams.* You should use these diagrams to document a system's hardware composition and the mapping of software components to it.

4.1.1   Business Viewpoint

From the business viewpoint, you should identify the business processes which the system supports. You should do this for both the legacy and target systems.

To model existing business processes, you should identify all classes of system users, from regular operators to occasional users. From each class, you should pick individuals and interview them to develop an understanding of how the legacy system is used. This may reveal that the system offers inadequate support for some processes. For example, old systems are often used differently from how they were originally intended. This may be because the original system is used to support a changed business process, or because data fields have been given new semantics.

Where user documentation exists, you should read it prior to interviewing users. This gives you a feel for how the system was intended to be used and helps you determine whether that functionality is still critical to the business today.

When you interview users, you should ask them how they use the system to support their main tasks. You should try to guide users in their answers so that most answers are at the same level of detail. If you get conflicting answers to questions from users of the same class, you should review the class structure. You should document each task you elicit as a "use case". Figure 4.5 shows a use case diagram for a simple library system.

Use case diagrams are an aid to defining who exists outside the system (actors) and what it performs (use cases). Components in a use case diagram are actors, use cases and the relationships between them. An actor is not a user, but represents a "role" that some user may play. Relationships model communication (participation) associations between actors and use cases.

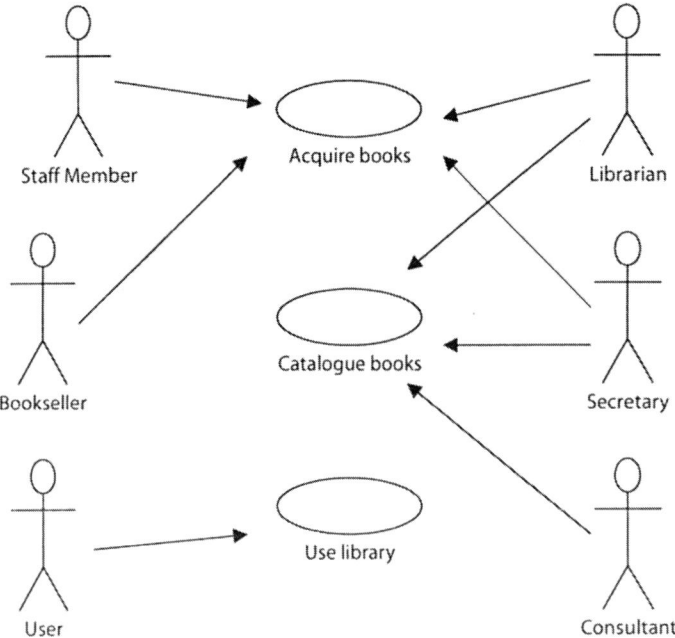

Fig. 4.5 Use case diagram.

An instance of an actor (a user) performs a number of different operations on the system. When a user operates the system, he or she performs a behaviourally related sequence of transactions with the system. This sequence is termed a use case. It represents a business process which the system supports. Use case diagrams differ from data flow diagrams in that they do not model data flow. Instead, they relate actors to business processes.

You can refine each use case diagram using a sequence or collaboration diagram. You should do this when you want to capture the ordering of events of a use case. Figures 4.6 and 4.7 extend the "Acquire books" case using sequence and collaboration diagrams respectively.

Both collaboration and sequence diagrams model the flow and ordering of messages between objects. They use different notations, but are semantically identical.

4.1.2   Functional Viewpoint

You should use the functional viewpoint to discover legacy system functionality and to document the functions of the target system.

System behaviour, which you record in the business view, requires functionality to support it. During functional modelling, you may find that the legacy system's functionality does not match the logical business structure. This is often the case for legacy systems and indicates that the system contains redundant functionality.

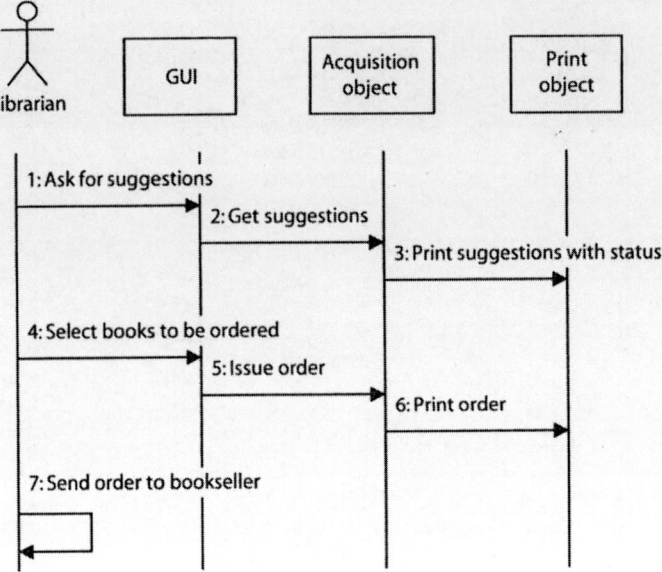

Fig. 4.6 Sequence diagram.

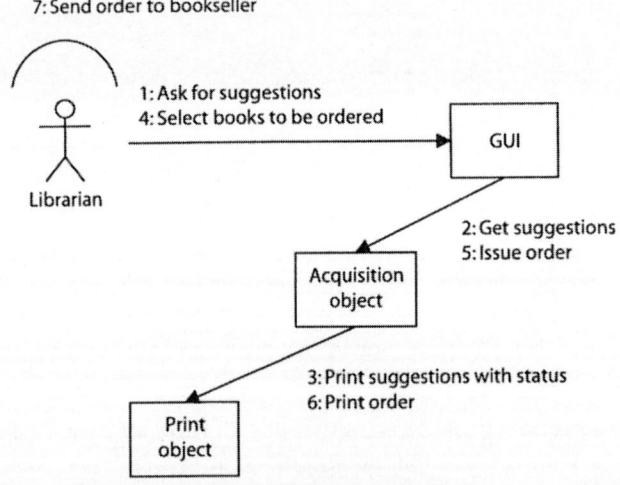

Fig. 4.7 Collaboration diagram.

In preparation for functional modelling, you should gather existing documentation and interview maintenance personnel. In any case, you need to make some analysis of the source code. You should use reverse engineering tools to support your analysis for all but trivial systems.

Data flow diagrams (DFDs) are particularly suited to functional modelling. They capture the main functionality of a system in terms of functions and data flows between them. Figure 4.8 shows an example DFD.

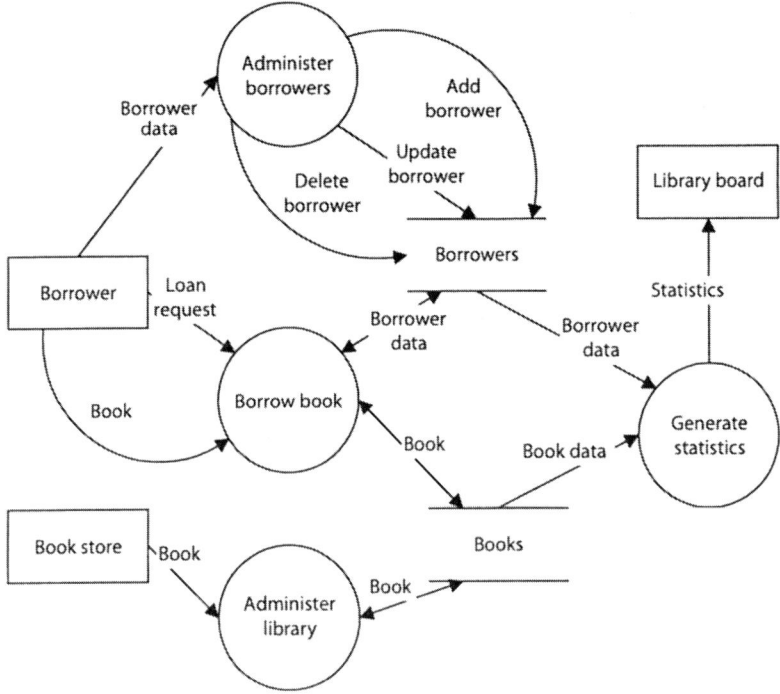

Fig. 4.8 Data flow diagram.

When modelling the legacy system, you can use DFDs to identify the functionality which you intend to reuse in the target system. They are also useful for identifying the mapping of processes onto data. For target system modelling, you should use them to consider the relative merits and drawbacks of different functional decompositions.

4.1.3   Structural Viewpoint

The structural viewpoint focuses on a system's software architecture and data structures. This is an important viewpoint which you subsequently develop into a technical model to support target system design. You should use the results from functional modelling as inputs to structural modelling.

Data stores in DFDs represent high-level data objects. In some cases they contain sufficient information, and you can defer decomposing them until technical modelling. In other cases, where you require a better understanding of them, you should use entity relationship diagrams (ERDs) as part of your context model.

ERDs are particularly suited to data modelling. You should use them to create an overview of legacy system data structures and to model the target system's data requirements. You can use entity relationship models to compare the advantages and

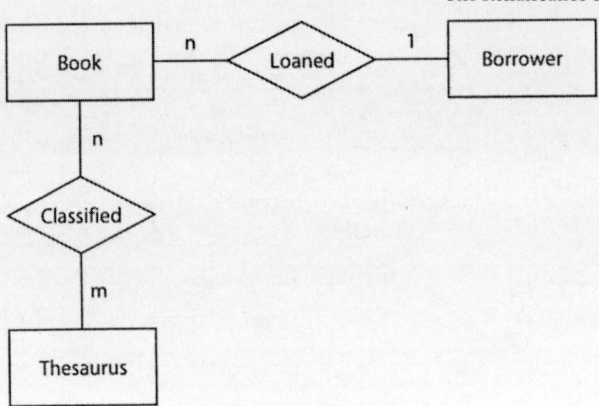

Fig. 4.9 Entity relationship diagram.

disadvantages of different data models. In many cases, you have to migrate legacy data to the target system. You should concentrate on them during data modelling.

Figure 4.9 shows a simple ERD. The basic elements of ERDs are entities, attributes and relationships. Over the years, these have been extended with generalization/ specialization relationships, weak entities, roles and cardinalities. Collectively, they define extended entity relationship diagrams (EERDs).

You should use block diagrams to model a system's software architecture. Block diagrams capture two complementary structural views:

- *Logical.* This view represents groupings of logically related components and their dependencies. Typical examples include user interface components, data management and input/output control.

- *Physical.* The physical view shows the physical relationships between software components. Blocks represent components such as processes and files. You can use this view to map software components onto hardware and network devices.

You should develop the logical view to gain an understanding of how a system's functionality is implemented at a high level. It helps you to identify coarse-grained components to reuse in the target system. In many cases, the legacy system's architecture is the starting point for developing the target system. The physical view is particularly useful when you assess the hardware and network requirements of the target system.

You can use the UML's component diagrams and packaging features to realize block diagrams. For documenting inter-component relationships, such as "use", you can use the UML's stereotype construct. Figure 4.10 shows a package diagram. Figure 4.11 decomposes the "Acquisition" package into its constituent components. In this manner, you can build decomposition hierarchies until you have a sufficient understanding of the system's structure. To supplement UML diagrams you can use an informal notation, which may be more appropriate to non-technical audiences. We use this notation later for Fig. 4.16.

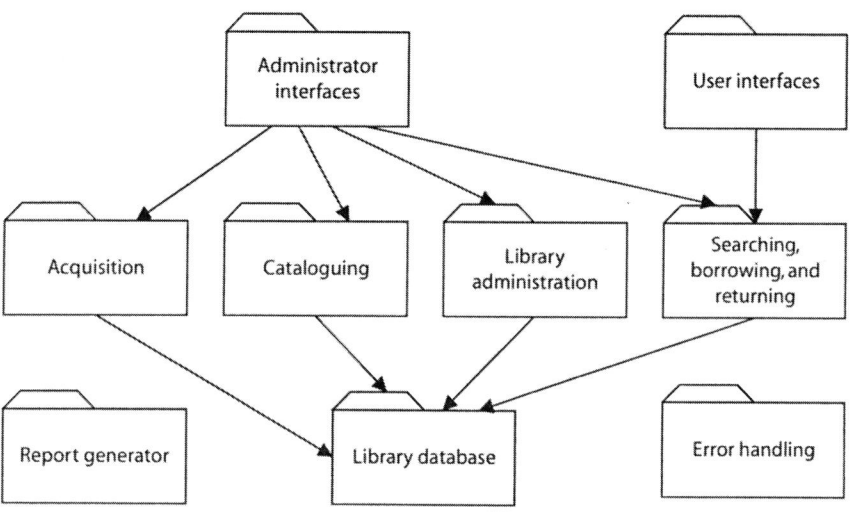

Fig. 4.10 Block diagram.

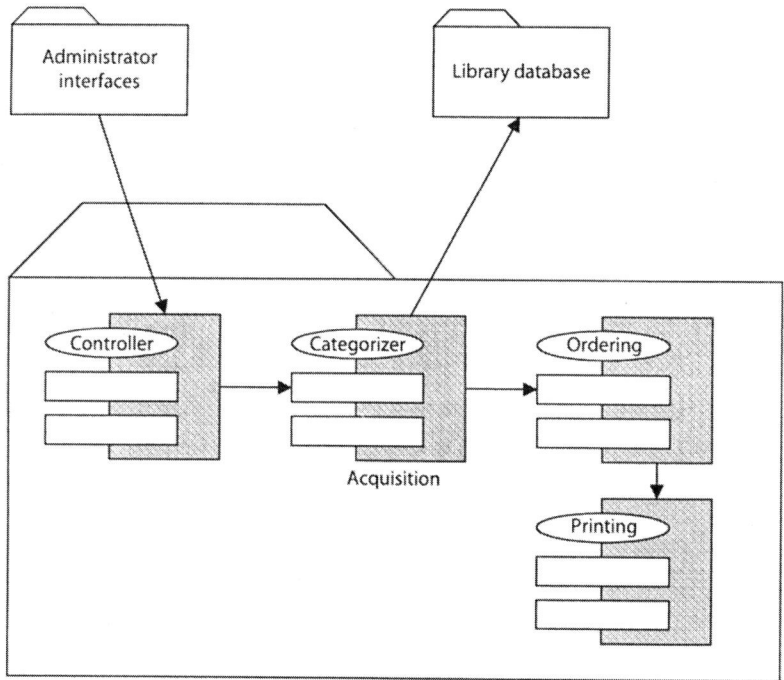

Fig. 4.11 Component diagram.

4.1.4   Environment Viewpoint

The environment viewpoint includes the communication, network and hardware aspects of a system. You should use this viewpoint to document and understand the environment in which a system exists, or in which it will be implemented. Communication includes external interaction with other systems and inter-process communication.

During environment modelling, you may develop models to understand the legacy system and to support target system design. In both cases, you can describe the mapping of software components onto hardware components. Where your target system uses a distributed infrastructure, you should develop a model for it. This is because modern distributed architectures are more complex than centralized legacy environments. You should also model the relationship between legacy and target system hardware components.

The UML provides deployment diagrams for modelling hardware components and communication links. These diagrams are particularly suited to modelling distributed systems and mapping software components onto processing elements. Figure 4.12 shows a simple deployment diagram with three executable components. You should represent executable files and dynamic link libraries as processes and allocate them to a processor.

Deployment diagrams are standardized in the UML, but their graphical notation is dull. You may want to consider using more interesting "polished" diagrams (Fig. 4.13). Polished diagrams do not contain as much detail as deployment diagrams. In particular, they do not show the mapping of software components to processors. Instead, they emphasize the physical composition of a system. You should use polished diagrams when you present the system to non-technical personnel. Polished diagrams are particularly suited to conveying the current and future organization of hardware resources.

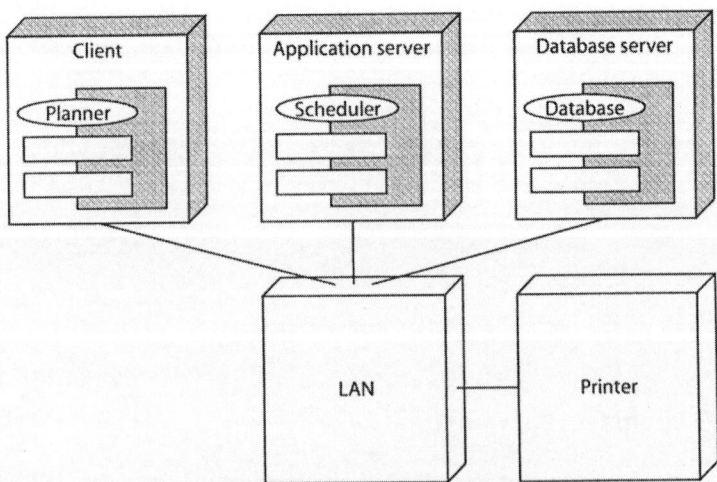

Fig. 4.12 Simple deployment diagram.

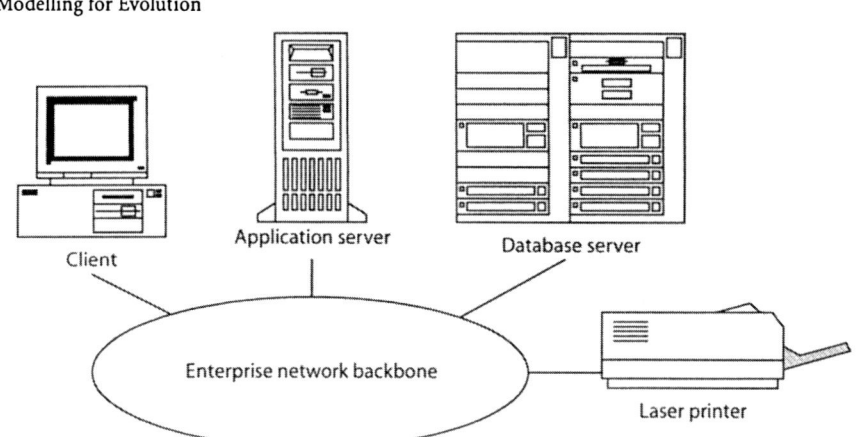

4.2   Technical Modelling

During technical modelling, you should decompose context models which capture the structural and environment viewpoints of both the legacy and target systems. You can build technical models by refining context models and adding detail to them. Figure 4.14 summarizes the objectives of technical modelling.

You should build technical models of legacy components which you intend to reuse in the target system. It is pointless to focus on components which are to be discarded. The degree of modelling for reusable components is dependent on the level of understanding you require. In cases where you do not need to modify a component, you do not need to understand how it works. In this case you are concerned with how to use it, and should model its interface. In other situations, which involve changing a

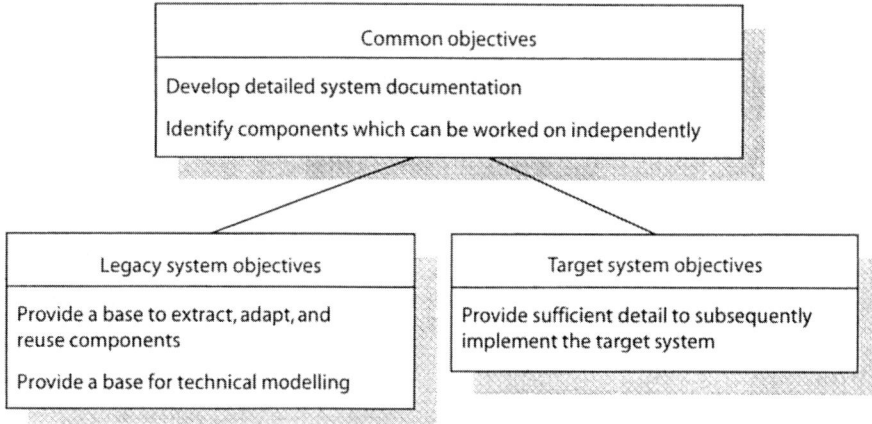

Fig. 4.14 Technical modelling objectives.

component, you should model its implementation too. In either case, you can use reverse engineering tools to help develop the models.

For target system modelling, you should use as much detail as you would in any development project. Models of the target system constitute design documents and contribute to the system's documentation.

4.2.1 Technical Modelling for 3GL Applications

Modelling an existing 3GL application is a two-step process. First, you should build "static" models. This involves elaborating the structural context models with details of the system's composition. When you have developed the static model you should proceed with "dynamic" modelling. Here, you reveal how the static model's elements interact.

To begin with, you should develop an inventory of files which define the system's configuration. You may have identified some of these files during context modelling. You may know that some files are redundant, but you should still catalogue them in order to identify all system components. Particularly good sources of information for doing this include makefiles and library definitions.

You should use the files to develop models which elaborate the earlier abstract models. For large systems, reverse engineering tools are essential. Where they are not available, in cases involving proprietary programming languages for example, you should consider writing simple source code analyzers using widely available parsing tools. Simple analyzers offer semi-automated support for building models by retrieving useful information from source code.

You should not develop technical models for components which do not feature in the target system, or which are to be treated as black boxes. The value of technical modelling is in understanding those components which you want to integrate with the target system. For these components, you should use as much detail as is necessary to understand them.

Dynamic modelling is more difficult than static modelling. It involves tracing paths of execution through system components which you identified during static modelling. Execution information is often distributed across the system. In general, tools do not support dynamic modelling very well.

To help you develop a dynamic model, you should adopt a top-down approach where you begin by following paths of execution through high-level subsystems. You should proceed incrementally by decomposing these subsystems into lower-level components and observing the flow of control. You may gain sufficient understanding without too many iterations of decomposition.

You should reserve detailed dynamic analysis for components which are critical to the target system. For components which are to be reused "as is", you do not need to understand their flow of control. In other cases, where you intend to reengineer a component, you must understand how its elements interact.

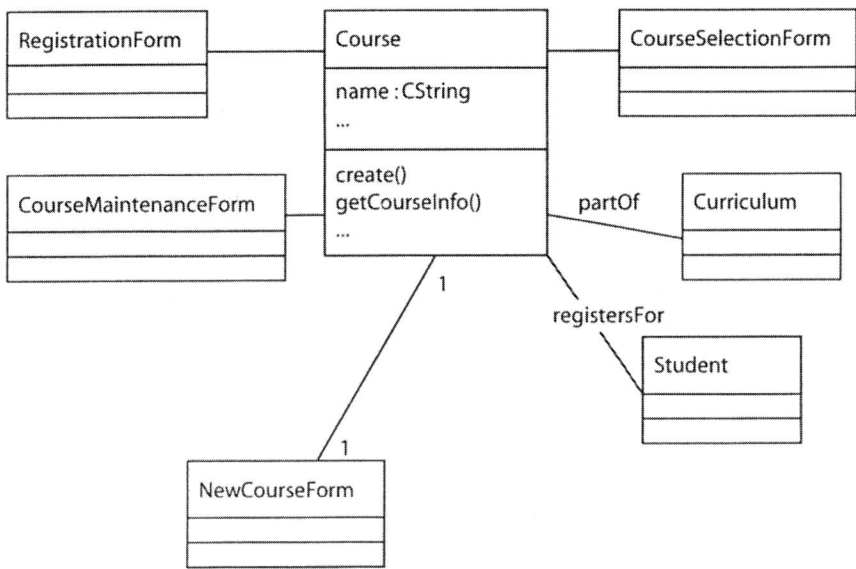

Fig. 4.15 Class diagram.

We suggest that you use the UML for both static and dynamic modelling. Class diagrams are suitable for developing static models. For dynamic modelling you should use object, sequence and collaboration diagrams. An object diagram is an instance of a class diagram which shows a snapshot of some part of the executing system. Figure 4.15 shows a UML class diagram. It shows the class structure for a component and the relationships between classes. Each class has three sections. The top section holds its name. The centre section contains a set of attributes, which collectively realize its state. The bottom section describes its interface in terms of methods.

Table 4.3 describes the mapping of 3GL elements onto the UML. We have defined these mappings based on studies of both functional and object-oriented 3GLs, which include COBOL, FORTRAN, C and C++, in addition to several scripting languages.

4.2.2   Technical Modelling for 4GL Applications

Many recent data processing applications have been implemented using 4GL technology. While they may not be as old as 3GL systems, many have legacy problems. When you tackle projects involving 4GL applications, you should understand how to model them. You should also structure any target 4GL system according to sound architectural principles.

Initially, modelling 4GL applications appears difficult because of the array of 4GLs on the market. There are many 4GL vendors, each seemingly with their own language constructs, elements and notation. These are, however, superficial distinctions,

Table 4.3 3GL modelling in the UML

	3GL property	UML diagram	UML element
Files	Source file	Component	Component
	Executable file	Component Deployment	Component
	Object file	Component	Component
	Logical file	Object	Utility
	Physical file	Deployment	Component
	Subsystem	Component	Package
Function-oriented	Function/routine	Object	Utility
		Sequence Collaboration	Message
	Data type declaration	Class	Utility
	Variable	Object	Utility
Object-oriented	Class	Class	Class
	Object	Object	Instance object
	Attribute	Class	Attribute
	Method	Class	Method
		Sequence Collaboration	Message

which are analogous to syntax variations for 3GLs. For example, FORTRAN and C programs look very different, but conceptually they are based on similar ideas, which include functions, data declarations and file types. Despite the varied appearance of 4GLs, they are fundamentally similar.

Modern 4GLs incorporate client/server technology. They are particularly suited to providing GUI "front ends" to databases. 4GL applications are typically clients which connect to database servers. Client/server systems differ from centralized architectures in that functionality is not implemented by a single server (a mainframe computer), but is distributed, either logically or physically, across many clients and servers. We elaborate and discuss variations on this architectural model in Chapter 5.

In addition to adopting the client/server model, most 4GLs are partially object-oriented. They embody the object-oriented principles of abstraction and encapsulation with language constructs for classes, objects, attributes and methods. Similarly to object-oriented 3GLs, 4GLs also provide constructs for implementing relationships, such as inheritance, use and aggregation.

The modelling conventions described in Table 4.3 are generally applicable to modelling 4GLs. You should use hardware/network diagrams to capture the client/server hardware, and deployment diagrams to map the software architecture onto the hardware. For building technical models of the software structure, you should use the UML's component, class, object and sequence diagrams.

Table 4.4 4GL modelling in the UML

4GL property	UML diagram	UML element
Database interface	Class	Class
Extended attribute	Class	Attribute
External function	Class	Stereotyped method
Function	Class	Stereotyped method
	Sequence Collaboration	Message
Global constant	Class	Stereotyped attribute
Internal data model	Class	Stereotyped classes
Message	Class	Stereotyped method
	Sequence Collaboration	Message
Named menu	Class	Stereotyped method
Resource	Class	Stereotyped attribute
User interface	Object	Instance object

To provide for rapid application development (RAD), 4GLs provide abstractions for GUIs and database manipulation. Windows elements include resources, menus and messages. Database abstractions include tables, views and stored procedures. You can use the UML to model these 4GL elements. Table 4.4 describes the mapping of 4GL-specific properties onto UML diagrams.

You should complement UML models with textual descriptions. By using the UML alone, for example, you cannot capture the rationale for a class or document fine details such as the parameter interface for a function. When using the UML to model 4GL applications, you should:

- Use class diagrams as the fundamental notation. You can use them for modelling 4GL classes, but also for other elements including subsystems, menus and database interfaces.

- Annotate classes with "stereotypes" to indicate the class type. For example, to document all global constants, you should use a class and stereotype it "Global constants". In it, you should declare one attribute for each global constant. You can model functions, messages and menus in a similar way.

- Use sequence or collaboration diagrams to capture snapshots of the dynamic interaction between objects. For the functions and messages in Table 4.4 you should use these diagrams for common interaction scenarios.

- Model dependencies between files using component diagrams.

- Document subsystems using package diagrams when dealing with large applications.

Modern 4GL development environments are visual and support a graphical approach to developing and changing applications. Often, you can create and make changes to data schemas, user interfaces and the application's structure using "drag and drop" techniques. While visual development contributes to RAD, it does not encourage systematic analysis and design prior to implementation. To be an evolutionary system, you should ensure that any 4GL application that you evolve conforms to a sound architectural model.

Figure 4.16 illustrates a generic and scalable architecture for evolutionary 4GL applications. It makes a clean separation of data and procedural concerns and has a clear hierarchical structure. You can map it onto two-, three- or multi-tier architectures, which we introduce in Chapter 6.

The first layer comprises data objects. Basic constraints include domain constraints, not-null constraints and referential integrity rules for relational databases. You can use stored procedures to implement more complex constraints. Layer 2 provides some abstraction over the data objects layer. You should define data views and use stored procedures to implement table manipulation functions, such as insert, update and delete. For large systems, you should use layers 3 and 4 for data-oriented business services, which are application-independent.

The procedural components are insulated from the database part by the database interface subsystem (layer 5). You should ensure that all database access from 4GL objects is via this subsystem. You should use a separate subsystem (layer 6) to implement common business functions. By using a separate subsystem for them, you can reuse them in other applications. The user interface is the top-level layer, which you should structure in terms of generic and application-specific components.

You may want to integrate COTS components, such as CORBA or DCOM objects, with the target system. These components are often generic. In this case, you can use a wrapper subsystem to tailor them to the needs of your application. You should use layer 8 to encapsulate COTS components behind simplified interfaces. You should use the final layer for reusable classes and functions. This includes components which you have developed for your organization and components supplied by others.

4.3   Traceability in System Modelling

Traceability means that you should be able to identify and follow links between different but related system models. Models can be related in three ways:

1 *Multiple views.* During context modelling, you may model the same system from different viewpoints. You should be able to identify, for example, how a business process is implemented by the system. Where you model the former using a use case diagram and the latter with a data flow diagram, you should document the relationship between them. Table 4.5 describes how different diagrams relate to each other.

2 *Refinement.* You may refine some context models into technical models. In cases where you decompose the data stores of a data flow diagram into entity

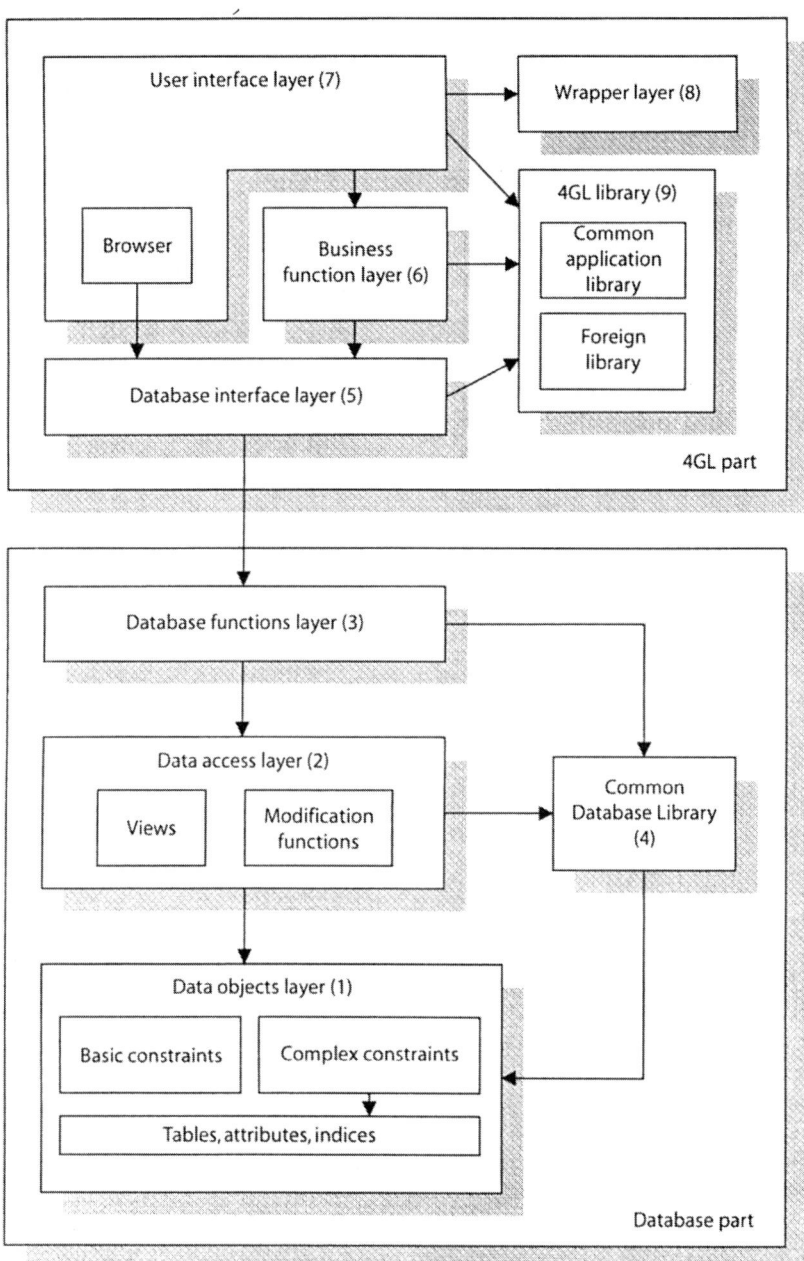

Fig. 4.16 Evolvable 4GL application architecture.

relationship diagrams, for example, you should record that the latter is an elabo-
ration of the data store.

3 *Transition.* Where you use a legacy system as the basis for the target system, you
   may reuse much of the legacy system. You should capture the relationship

Table 4.5 Traceability across context diagrams

	Use-case	Sequence/ collaboration	DFD	ER	Block	Deployment
Deployment			(node, process)		(block, process)	
Block			(node, block)			
ER			(datastore, entity)			
DFD	(actor, terminator) (use case, node) (link, dataflow)	(message, dataflow)				
Sequence/ collaboration	(actor, actor)					
Use case						

between legacy and target system models. This serves to document which components are to be reused and in what form.

You should use a configuration management programme to manage the models and their relationships. Many case tools provide configuration management functionality, but not all case tools support the complete set of techniques we have presented in this chapter. You may need to use a separate tool or manual system for configuration management.

Traceability is important for the following reasons:

- It supports change impact analysis by enabling you to study a component's dependencies. You can, for example, consider scenarios where you need to determine the effects of making a change to a particular component.

- Where you have several individuals involved in modelling, traceable models assist the team to understand other parts of the system relatively quickly.

- Similarly to design documents, traceable models provide a base for understanding and communicating about a system.

- Collectively, the above reasons, coupled with the increase in system comprehension, enable you to reduce evolution costs.

The result of refining context models to technical models is a model hierarchy. Abstract context models are at the top, with detailed representations of data schemas and procedural code at the bottom. To navigate up and down the hierarchy, you can use a hierarchical numbering scheme.

To capture how a system is to evolve, you should trace legacy system models through to target system models. In cases which involve much reuse of the target system, you should use the legacy system models as the basis for target system models, but highlight changes on the target system's models. In particular, you should use use case diagrams to make explicit the new processes which the target system will support. You should develop block diagrams to show how legacy system components are to be integrated with target system. To show how legacy and target hardware are to be connected, you should use deployment diagrams.

References and Further Reading

Batini C., Ceri S. and Navathe S.B. (1991) *Conceptual Database Design: An Entity-Relationship Approach*. Benjamin/Cummings, Redwood CA.

Booch G. (1998) *Unified Modelling Language User Guide*. Addison-Wesley, Reading.

Parnas D.L. (1994) Software aging. *Proceedings of the 16th International Conference on Software Engineering*, Sorrento, Italy.

RENAISSANCE Consortium (1998) *Architectural Modelling*. Consultancy report, http://www.comp.lancs.ac.uk/projects/renaissance/.

Robertson J. and Robertson S. (1994) *Complete System Analysis*. Dorset House.

Key Points

- Evolution modelling supports the process of system understanding. You should build models to help you assess legacy systems, to choose a suitable evolution strategy and to design target systems which may integrate legacy components.

- Context modelling captures a system at a high level of abstraction and from four viewpoints: business, functional, structural and environmental.

- Technical modelling elaborates context models. Static models capture a system's software composition; dynamic models document the interaction of compositional units.

- The degree and content of modelling are dependent on a particular evolution project. In general, you should focus on legacy components which are to be integrated in the target system.

- The UML is appropriate for modelling both 3GL and 4GL applications. You may supplement UML diagrams with other diagrams, which include data flow diagrams and entity relationship diagrams.

- Traceability is important because it allows you to navigate through related models. You should cross-reference diagrams across multiple views, from context to technical models, and from legacy system models to target system models.

5 Migration to Distributed Architectures

Objectives

- To explain why distributed architectures are appropriate for evolutionary systems.
- To introduce architectural models for distributed systems. Each model has a physical configuration onto which you can distribute software components.
- To describe system integration models. An integration model describes how to integrate software layers and how to incorporate parts of a legacy system with a distributed architecture.

Contents

Changes in business needs have contributed to the development of distributed computing solutions. They range from PC-based local area networks for small workgroups to enterprise-scale solutions which may be globally distributed. Distributed architectures have many advantages over centralized legacy structures, but at the expense of increased complexity. In most cases, however, their complexity is manageable and is dwarfed by the benefits they offer.

Distributed architectures provide a sound basis for hosting evolutionary systems. They are evolvable and you can integrate parts of a legacy system with them during reengineering. In addition, there is much scope for incremental evolution. For example, you can provide remote access to a system using Internet-based user interfaces prior to restructuring the application in preparation for migrating it to a distributed object-based architecture.

The strengths of distributed systems lie in their ability to present a virtual machine abstraction over a network of heterogeneous hardware and software resources. Their benefits, of which the first two are particularly significant to evolutionary systems, include:

- *Scalability.* Modern distributed systems can grow to meet changes in users' needs. They are naturally loosely coupled architectures, which enable you to upgrade or introduce new resources without affecting other parts of the system.

- *Openness.* In contrast to the proprietary interfaces found in centralized solutions, distributed systems promote standards to ensure interoperability between their components. Widely adopted standards are in place to provide for platform independence and for integration of several software technologies.

- *Communication transparency.* A distributed application is composed of several processing units which may be physically distributed over a network. Communication transparency provides for one processing unit to communicate with another using a uniform communication primitive. From the sender's perspective, the primitive is the same for both local and remote communication.

- *Location transparency.* In many cases, you should be able to use a distributed system's resources regardless of their location on the network. For example, where an application needs access to a data manager component it is often of no concern to the application where the component is located.

- *Availability.* Distributed systems enable you to provide sufficient resources to applications and users. Where a service is in heavy demand, you can use techniques such as replication or migration to improve its availability. Replicating a service often introduces complexity, because you may have to maintain consistency between replicas. In other cases, you can migrate a service to a processor which is under-utilized to improve its availability.

- *Fault tolerance.* Failure of one processor does not necessarily cause the whole system to fail. If the failed machine does not contribute to the processing of a particular application, users of that application will not be affected by the fault. In addition, you can design distributed systems with explicit requirements for fault tolerance. For example, you can replicate parts of an application on physically separate processors to reduce the risk of losing system service in the event of a hardware fault.

- *Resource sharing.* In principle, you can use any resource which is provided by a distributed system. In practice, however, you should impose access restrictions in the interests of security and practical considerations.

In Section 5.2, we introduce a number of integration models which rely heavily on "middleware". Middleware is any technology which enables heterogeneous components to interact. More specifically, middleware enables interoperability between different software technologies and across heterogeneous hardware. It is a fundamental contributor to the virtual machine abstraction of distributed systems.

Middleware enables different software technologies to communicate with each other by providing an interface between them. To illustrate this, consider an application which needs access to a particular database. You can use a middleware "driver" to provide the interface between the application and database.

Middleware plays an important role in evolutionary systems. If you subsequently replace the database, in many cases you will need to change the application because the old and new databases may use different versions of SQL. If, however, you use a middleware driver which conforms to a standard, such as Open Database Connectivity (ODBC), the degree of change to the application is minimized. This is because the driver provides applications with a database-independent interface and converts database requests to the particular version of SQL used by the database.

Middleware encapsulates the details of several network protocols, processors and operating systems which may host a distributed system. For example, distributed object technology, which we introduce later, enables you to develop object-based applications where the objects may execute and communicate over heterogeneous hardware. Using technology such as Common Object Request Broker Architecture (CORBA), you can develop these applications without regard for the underlying hardware.

5.1 Distributed Architectural Models

Architectural models describe both the "physical" configuration of a system's hardware and how software layers can be deployed on it. They have evolved from simple monolithic structures, through client/server models, to complex and highly distributed architectures.

Software architectures, also known as "logical" system models, describe a system's composition in terms of software layers and the relationships between them. A common software model comprises a three-layer hierarchy (Fig. 5.1). The top layer, "presentation", manages the user interface and uses services provided by the "application" layer. This layer, in turn, uses the services exported by the bottom layer, "data management".

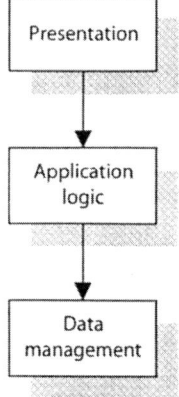

Fig. 5.1 Simple logical model.

Software architectures are independent of physical architectures. You can deploy a multi-layered software structure onto a centralized platform, such as a mainframe host, or on a physically distributed architecture. You cannot, however, distribute a monolithic logical architecture over a physically distributed environment.

Table 5.1 introduces four distributed architectural models. We introduce them starting with the more primitive in terms of their support for physically distributing logical layers.

Table 5.1 Distributed architectural models

Two-tier	Two-tier models are simple client/server architectures which employ a server to manage data. Application-logic is tightly integrated with either presentation or data management.
Three-tier	Three-tier architectures separate presentation, application logic and data management. You can distribute each of these layers independently.
Multi-tier	Multi-tier models extend three-tier architectures by decomposing the application logic layer into further distributable units.
Distributed object	Distributed-object architectures are based on collections of cooperating objects. An object is the unit of configuration and distribution. Using distributed object technology, you can develop applications which comprise several fine-grained objects.

Early two-tier models were constrained to distributing an application's presentation layer. During the 1980s, tools such as the X-Window system allowed user interfaces to be deployed on desktops. These first generation client/server architectures employ clients, which have very limited functionality, to manage remote presentation. The vast majority of processing is performed by the server, which typically integrates application logic and data management. Figure 5.2 illustrates a simple two-tier architecture.

More recently, 4GL development tools, such as Visual Basic and SQLWindows, have emerged which move application logic to clients. In this case, application software executes on clients, which are typically hosted by PCs. Each client is connected to a centralized server which is responsible for data management. This model, often referred to as a "fat client" because the client integrates presentation and application, characterizes second generation two-tier architectures (Fig. 5.3).

Figure 5.4 shows a variation of the two-tier model which distributes application logic over both the client and the server. Modern database management systems make this possible by their support for stored procedures. You can use this model to separate enterprise functions from application functions. You should implement enterprise functions on the server and application-specific rules on the client, since the former are common to all applications while the latter refer to a particular application.

Two-tier models satisfy most requirements for workgroups and small-scale applications. You can develop and evolve these systems cost-effectively, since modern 4GLs integrate the necessary technical components, such as database connectivity and communication middleware.

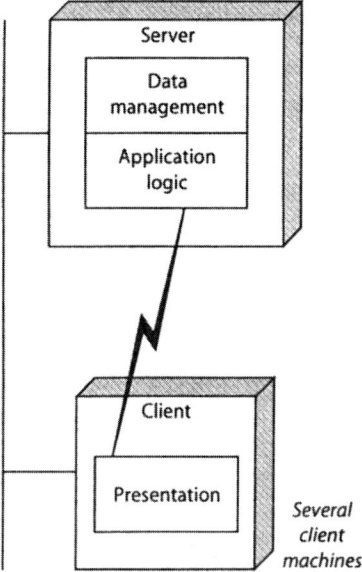

Fig. 5.2 Remote presentation two-tier architecture.

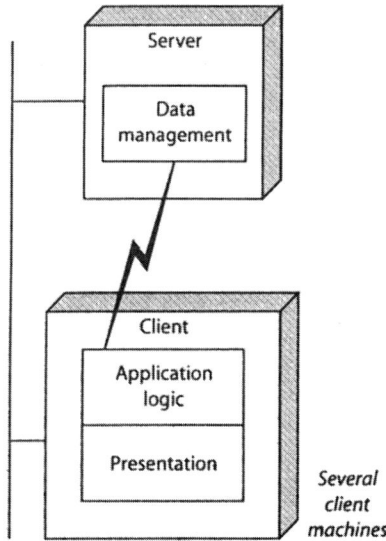

Fig. 5.3 Remote data management two-tier architecture.

Two-tier models do, however, suffer from limited evolvability because of:

● *Scalability constraints.* The centralized database server may become a serious bottleneck in cases where there are several users or large volumes of traffic. You can upgrade server hardware and network bandwidth, but these are likely to be short-term solutions. You may consider replicating servers, but typical development tools do not manage the resulting complexity.

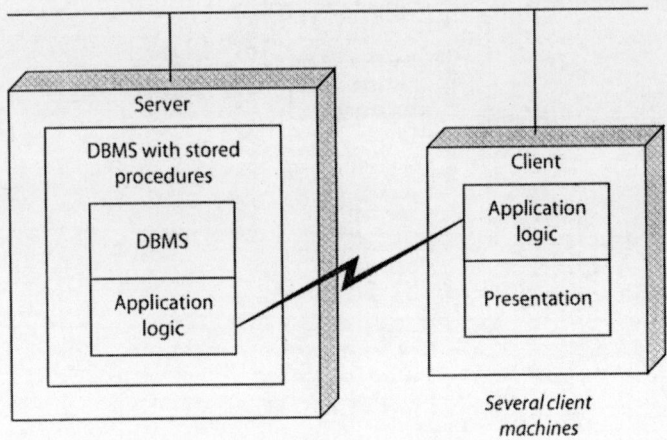

Fig. 5.4 Distributed logic two-tier architecture.

- *Tool vendor dependencies.* 4GL applications are tied to their development environments and vendors. In some cases, particularly with early 4GLs, you cannot avoid investing in the vendor's proprietary programming language, middleware and database access model. This is a particularly undesirable situation if the vendor ceases to support its product.

You should consider a three-tier architecture for medium to large applications. Two-tier systems are particularly inappropriate for these applications because they integrate application logic with either presentation or data management. This tight coupling means that application logic is difficult to isolate and change. Figure 5.5 shows that three-tier systems decouple application logic from presentation and data management.

You can physically distribute the three logical layers of a three-tier architecture using two or three processors. In either case, you should use clients for presentation and a server for data management. For a two-tier system, you can deploy the application layer on either the clients or the server. With three tiers, you should use an application server to host the application logic.

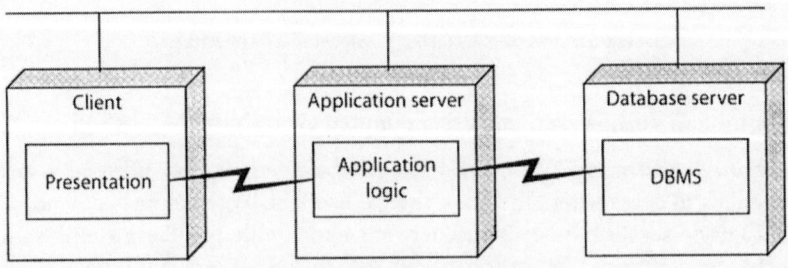

Fig. 5.5 Generic three-tier architecture.

A variation on the three-tier model is a multi-tier architecture, which decomposes the application layer into sub-layers. You can physically distribute the logical layers on multiple application servers or deploy them on a single server.

The main benefit of three- and multi-tier systems is their evolvability. You can scale these architectures to meet users' changing needs. In addition, they are generally less proprietary than two-tier models, since interfaces between layers are usually compatible. Where this is not the case, gateways that comply with popular standards such as ODBC and CORBA are often available. Three- and multi-tier systems also provide more potential for improving resource availability and fault tolerance than two-tier models.

Three- and multi-tier development environments are, however, relatively expensive and technically immature. This is in contrast to the 4GLs which have emerged for developing two-tier applications. Developing three-tier applications requires experience and specialist skills to manage their increase in complexity.

Communication in distributed object architectures (Fig. 5.6) is not hierarchical as in preceding models; instead, objects request the services of one another. Objects plug into a software bus, which supports basic services, such as transparent inter-object communication and finding other objects which are plugged into the bus.

For application logic, distributed objects promote reuse of "business" objects rather than "technical" objects. Business objects are loosely coupled and completely define some part of the business process. They are responsible for their own presentation and data management. In practice, distributed objects interact with other layers.

Of all the distributed architectural models introduced here, the distributed object architecture is technically superior. However, the supporting technology lacks stability and has not yet been used on a wide scale. Distributed object technology also results in complex applications; fine-grained object solutions require substantial design effort to ensure that they are not a performance bottleneck. A popular basis for distributed object technology is Internet-based systems. We discuss the relationship between Internet technology and distributed objects later in this chapter.

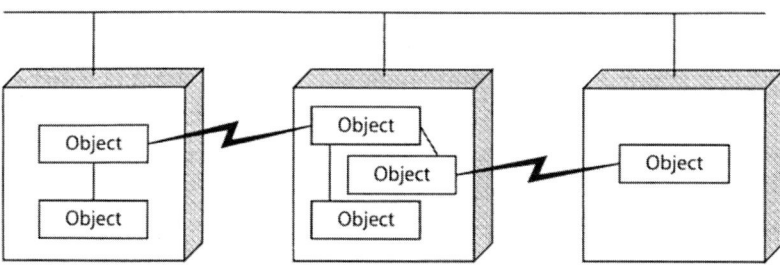

Fig. 5.6 Distributed object architecture.

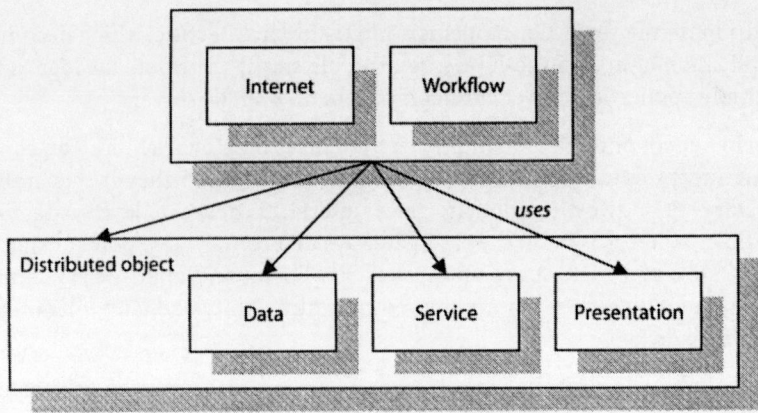

Fig. 5.7 Integration models.

5.2   System Integration Models

Systems are typically built from a combination of software layers. Legacy systems are often data-centréd and service-oriented. They use functions or programs to implement the application logic which manipulates shared data resources. You can integrate these layers using several "integration models". Each model defines a logical structure and describes how you can integrate it with parts of a legacy system.

Figure 5.7 identifies these models and shows the relationships between them. System integration models are thus complementary. The workflow model uses the services of more primitive layers, such as service and presentation. In cases where you use distributed object technology, it is often appropriate to use it to encapsulate lower-level models.

Table 5.2 shows which integration models you should use to implement a particular evolution strategy. We only include reengineering strategies because continued maintenance and system replacement offer no integration of legacy components with a target system. The workflow model does not support a particular reengineering strategy, but it may be useful in cases of business process reengineering.

Table 5.2 Reengineering strategies and integration models

Integration model	Reengineering strategy			
	Revamp	Restructure	Rearchitecture	Redesign with reuse
Data		✓	✓	✓
Service		✓	✓	✓
Presentation	✓		✓	✓
Internet	✓		✓	✓
Distributed object			✓	✓

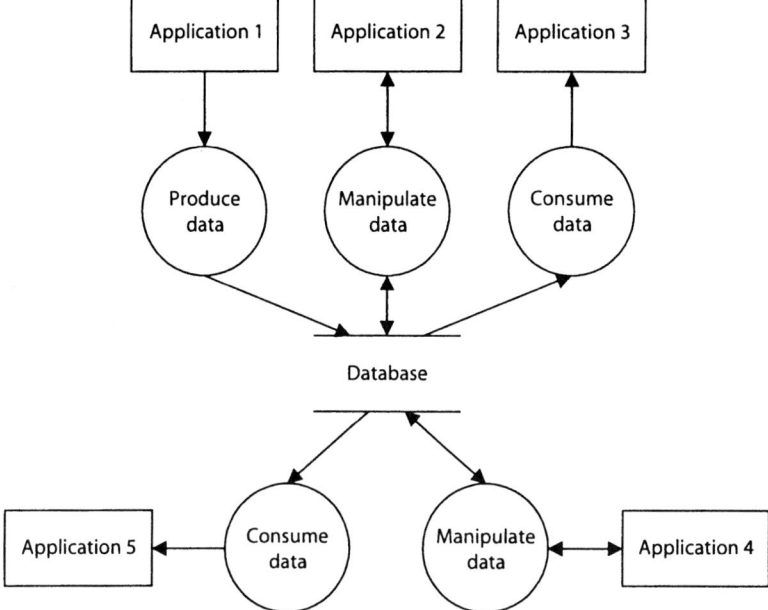

Fig. 5.8 Enterprise data dependencies.

5.2.1 Data Integration

Many legacy systems are data-centric. Communication is based on systems which manipulate shared data. We use the term "system" to mean a program or a complete application. The data may be stored in files, a database or a combination of each. Figure 5.8 shows how one application may capture and store data in a database, which is subsequently manipulated and consumed by other applications. Each application contributes to the global consistency of its enterprise's data.

Data-centric models result in a tight coupling between applications and the database, and between applications themselves. This may cause a number of problems during system evolution. In particular, you should consider:

- *Data schema dependencies.* If you change a data schema, it will impact all programs or applications which access its data content. Although database management systems shield applications from the implementation details of a data structure, any semantic changes to the schema will ripple across procedural units.

- *Data dependencies.* Where you have many applications which share a common base of data, it may not be possible to extract one of those applications and reengineer it. This is the case where reengineering involves migrating part of the system's data to new technology. If other applications need to access that data, but cannot do so because of the technology change, you should choose a reengineering strategy which precludes data migration. Otherwise, from a global perspective, your enterprise's data will become inconsistent.

- *Application logic dependencies.* In cases where you intend to restructure an application, you should first develop a model which captures the data flow across all systems that share common data. You can use this to identify the data dependency relationships between applications. For example, a particular application may be responsible for manipulating existing data which is subsequently used as input to others. After reengineering, you should ensure that the restructured application manipulates the shared data in the same way that it did before it was evolved. If it doesn't, applications that depend on its behaviour may be presented with erroneous data.

- *Scattered data integrity rules.* Where you introduce a new application which accesses legacy data, you should be aware of integrity rules that apply to that data. Many legacy applications embed integrity rules in their application logic. You may have to model other applications which manipulate the shared data to extract them. Failing to understand these rules may mean that you develop an application which violates the data's consistency.

Where you need to preserve data on legacy storage technology, you should consider one of the following solutions:

1 *Direct access.* This solution, shown in Fig. 5.9, allows reengineered applications to access a range of legacy data models and sources. The direct access method does not hide the legacy data's implementation from the reengineered application. In particular, you need knowledge of the legacy data's location and format when developing the reengineered application.

2 *Meta-data encapsulation.* In this approach, you can develop a meta-schema which defines the legacy system's data model. This solution encapsulates details of the legacy data. The reengineered application need not distinguish between data which is maintained on old technology and data which is managed using a new database. A middleware component refers to the meta-schema and maps legacy data to the reengineered application's native data format. Figure 5.10 illustrates this solution.

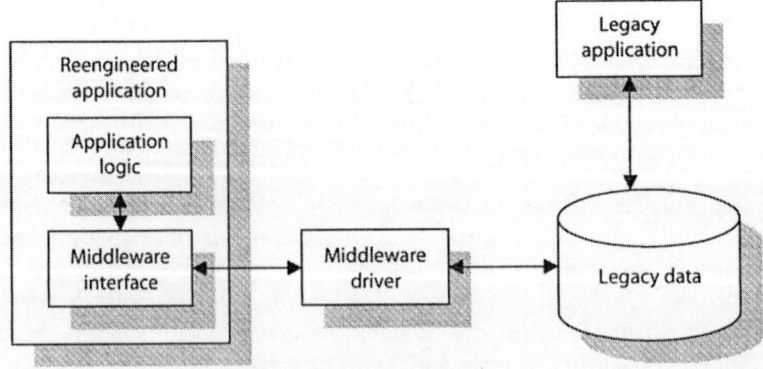

Fig. 5.9 Direct access to legacy data.

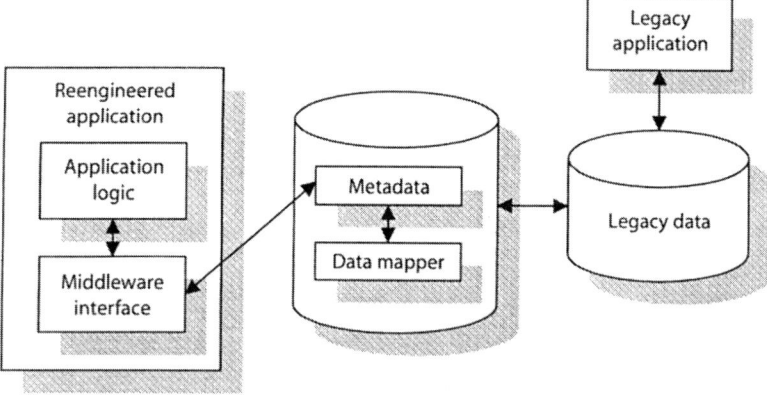

Fig. 5.10 Meta-data encapsulation of legacy data.

Both data management approaches support the coexistence of legacy and reengineered systems which share legacy data. In either case, middleware exists to bridge the differences in hardware and software architectures. The simpler solution, direct access, requires that, as part of reengineering, you implement the mapping between legacy data and the native format of the reengineered application. In the second solution, middleware automates this by referring to the meta-schema.

Where you intend to reengineer only a few applications within a large enterprise, you should select the direct access approach for the reengineered systems. You should also select this solution when you have no plans to migrate the enterprise's data to a different hardware platform. In these cases, it may not be cost-effective to use the meta-data solution.

In other cases, you should consider encapsulating legacy data to reduce the risks involved in migrating critical data to new technology. Where you intend to abandon the legacy system's operational environment, but need to maintain legacy data, you should use the meta-data encapsulation method to provide for seamless manipulation of both legacy and target system data.

Meta-data encapsulation is well-suited to incremental evolution strategies which involve data migration. Where you rearchitecture application programs before you migrate data, you should use the meta-data approach to interface reengineered programs with legacy data. This prepares the application programs for the rearchitectured data. Where you know that you will migrate data, it is pointless to use the direct access approach because you would subsequently need to reengineer the application programs to remove the data mappings embedded in their source code.

5.2.2 Service Integration

Before the adoption of object technology, software systems were often structured as a set of services. Consequently, the application logic of many legacy systems is implemented using routines, procedures and functions.

Figure 5.11 shows a generic service-oriented model. Traditionally, services are tightly integrated in one executable program. Service-based legacy systems are thus constrained to centralized architectures. The services are bound statically using linkers at application generation time

In distributed systems, you can distribute services over a network of machines (Fig. 5.12). A client program can request a service regardless of whether it is hosted locally or remotely. There are two mechanisms which support communication-transparent distributed services:

1 *Remote procedure call (RPC)*. RPCs support synchronous communication between application programs. RPCs have the same semantics as procedure calls in languages such as C, but the procedure may execute on a remote machine. RPC development tools use an interface description language (IDL) to specify a service's interface in a language neutral way. To create a service, you can use a

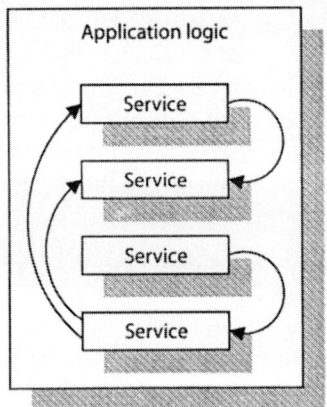

Fig. 5.11 Centralized service-based model.

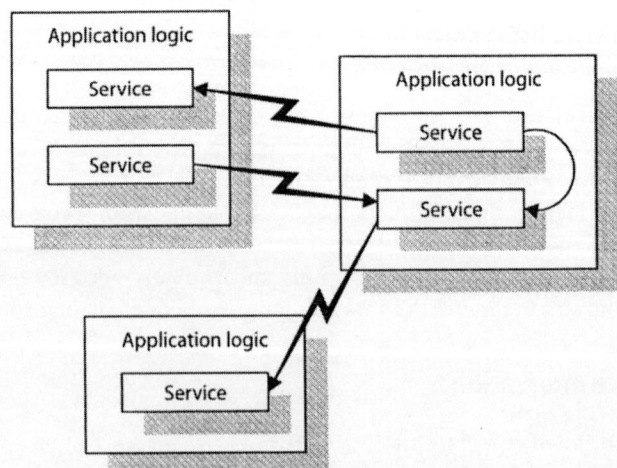

Fig. 5.12 Distributed service-based model.

pre-compiler to generate the interface in a particular programming language, and then develop its corresponding implementation. The separation of interface from implementation allows the call to be made over a network. Figure 5.13 shows the structure of a RPC service.

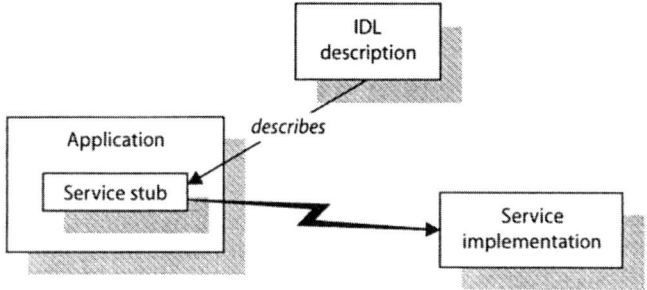

Fig. 5.13 RPC communication.

2 *Message-oriented middleware (MOM)*. This mechanism provides for asynchronous communication between applications by message passing. Communication is indirect via an intermediate queue. MOM supports a very loose coupling between applications. Figure 5.14 shows the structure of MOM-based communication. MOM is a relatively new mechanism which has been used to provide for safe and guaranteed communication between applications. In general, it has not been adopted as a mechanism to distribute the services of a single application.

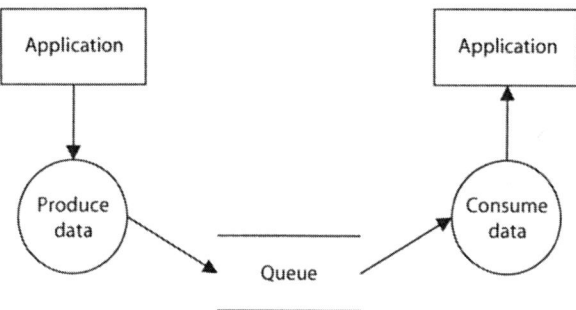

Fig. 5.14 MOM communication.

You can distribute a legacy application, using either technique, without resorting to extensive reengineering strategies. RPCs and MOM enable you to provide remote access to a legacy system for use by other applications. In either case, however, you may need to restructure the system first to identify independent services which can be distributed.

Services are procedural abstractions which encapsulate and enforce their own integrity rules. Other applications can use these services without the risk of compromising system consistency.

RPC tools and MOM products are widely available for several hardware environments and operating systems. Many vendors adhere to a common interface across multiple platforms. This means that little effort is needed if you migrate an application to a new platform.

A particular vendor's tools are usually interoperable across heterogeneous systems, but they are generally incompatible with other vendors' products. The Distributed Computing Environment (DCE) defines a standard for RPC, but it has not been widely adopted. Products that are available on multiple platforms have generally defined *de facto* standards. The current (1998) lack of a common standard, however, means that application interoperability based on RPCs and MOM cannot be guaranteed.

Distributed service technology is technically mature and stable, but you should consider distributed object technology when you select a target system. Distributed object technology provides more powerful abstractions than RPC and MOM, but you can use it to distribute services. It is supported by two dominant standards which are converging to be interoperable.

5.2.3   Presentation Integration

Typical centralized legacy applications interact with users through character-based terminals. These terminals do nothing more than present data. In most cases, they communicate with application logic using a proprietary protocol.

The revamp evolution strategy is concerned with improving a system's presentation. To revamp a system, you must first understand its presentation protocol. You can then analyze the flow of data from the application to terminals and prepare the data for presentation in an alternative format. There are several tools, known as "screen scrapers", which automate much of this process. Figure 5.15 illustrates the essence of this approach.

You should consider revamping a system when you want to change the appearance of its user interface. For some classes of system user, you may want to present the application to them using GUI capabilities. To do this, you should replace dumb terminals with PCs, workstations or graphical terminals.

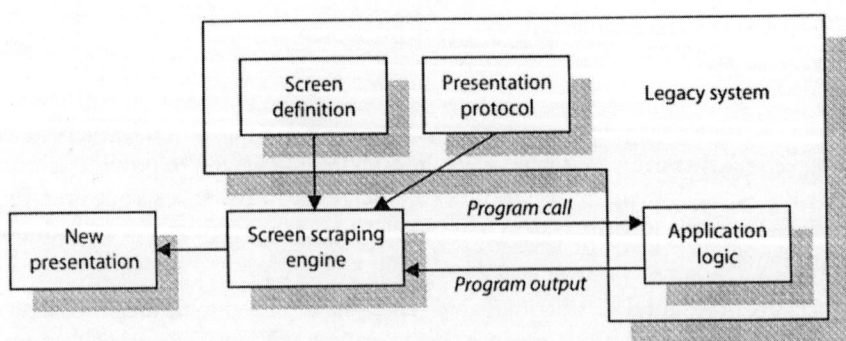

Fig. 5.15 Screen scraping.

PCs are often the most cost-effective solution because you can use them to host software packages in addition to legacy system presentation. This solution is often appropriate for middle to senior personnel who want to use productivity packages, which are generally cheaper and in many cases only available for modern PC-based systems.

When you extract data from a legacy application, you can use it as input to some processing before you present it. For example, you may use the data as a row of data for a database query, or as a variable for a script.

Despite the above benefits of changing a legacy system's presentation, the application retains any deficiencies it had prior to being revamped. We identified the benefits, limitations and risks of this strategy in Chapter 4. In many cases, revamping is a short-term solution and more extensive reengineering effort is necessary. Revamping is often, however, a good first step in an incremental evolution strategy.

5.2.4   Internet Integration

You can use Internet technology to revamp a legacy system in a similar way to presentation-based integration, but using World-Wide Web (WWW) browsers rather than GUI technology. Use of Internet technology in this way is, however, subject to the risks and limitations associated with revamping.

In addition to the benefits of presentation-based integration, you can gain further value from using Internet technology. In particular, a system with a WWW interface offers:

- *Remote access over the Internet*. You can open a legacy system to access from the Internet using WWW browsers for presentation. In many cases you may not want public access, but you can still use Internet technology to provide a closed "intranet", which contains access within an organization.

- *Uniform access from multiple platforms*. Classical distributed technology fails to encapsulate the problems of interoperability inherent in a heterogeneous environment. Internet technology is a simple yet extremely effective solution for presenting users on different machines with a common user interface. WWW browsers are available on several platforms.

Figure 5.16 shows the basic WWW architecture. The browser is a client which sends a request, a Universal Resource Locator (URL) for a particular page to the server. The server locates the page and returns it to the client for displaying. Pages are structured according to a simple language, Hypertext Markup Language (HTML). This model is static; it does not allow the server to query a database to generate a page's content. Instead, it can return only existing pages.

To resolve the deficiencies of the basic model, a number of variant models have emerged. Figure 5.17 shows the Common Gateway Interface (CGI) architecture. This model extends the static model with support for dynamic page creation. The server can execute a program to generate a new page. Part of the script may involve access to

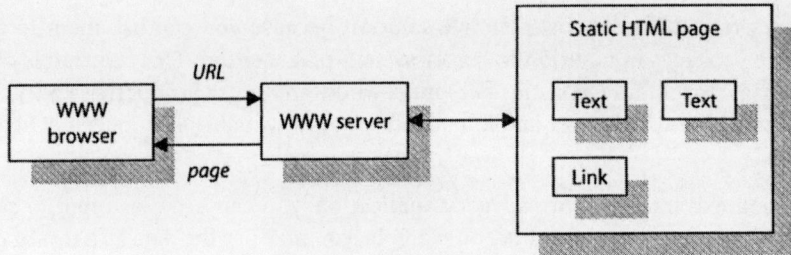

Fig. 5.16 Basic WWW architecture.

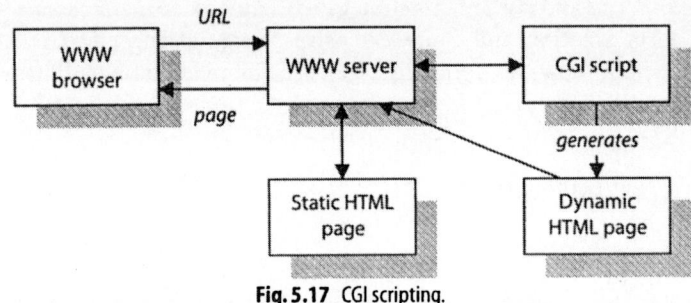

Fig. 5.17 CGI scripting.

a database, in which case you can present the results of a query using a WWW browser.

There are, however, a number of drawbacks with the CGI model. Most importantly for database applications, there is no concept of "session". A new database connection is made for each page request. Performance also suffers in this model because the server creates a new process to manage each request. While you can develop scripts using high-level scripting languages such as Perl relatively quickly, they are difficult to evolve because they integrate application logic with presentation.

A variation on the CGI model is the Dynamic Page Generation model, which aims to improve the CGI model's performance. It employs an engine to execute the scripts embedded in HTML pages.

The basic WWW architecture is generally inadequate for commercial applications, since they require more than the ability to display static pages. The CGI and dynamic page generation models can manage relatively simple data-oriented systems. You can use them to revamp a legacy system and provide remote access using a uniform user interface across many platforms. They do not, however, scale to transaction-based systems or systems which involve complex database queries.

Figure 5.18 shows a more recent architecture which is based on distributed object technology. This model creates a shortcut between the client (browser) and an application by using a separate communication channel. The client uses the server initially, but only to start the dialogue and install components on the client which are necessary to support communication between itself and the application.

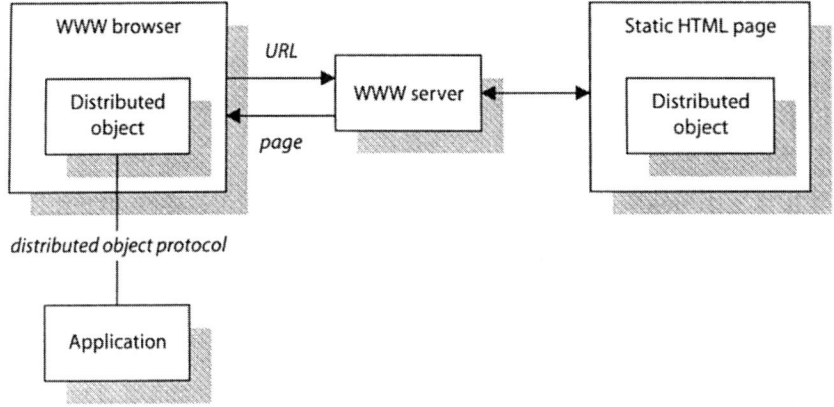

Fig. 5.18 Object-based model.

There are two implementations of this model:

1 *Java applets.* An applet is an object which executes in a WWW browser. It communicates with the application using CORBA's distributed object technology and
   Netscape's IIOP protocol.

2 *ActiveX components.* An ActiveX object is conceptually similar to a Java applet,
   but it communicates with an application based on Microsoft's DCOM technology.

In both cases the application must be built using object technology, since communication between the browser and application uses an object-based protocol.

Object-based architectures are technically superior to the preceding Internet models.
In addition to support for distributed and platform-independent solutions, they offer
the potential to build complex applications. They are, however, subject to frequent
change and lack a stable standard. Problems such as security and performance are
obstacles which prevent these architectures from being more widely used today.

If you choose the object-based model, you will probably have to rearchitecture your
legacy system because of the model's dependency on distributed object technology.
In many cases this may not be cost-effective.

You can use Internet technology within an incremental evolution strategy. For
example, you can replace or reengineer legacy components which relay services to
WWW browsers. You may be able to pick individual components and evolve them
transparently to system users. Similarly to revamping a system using GUI
technology, migrating from text-based presentation to Internet browsers is often a
good first step in an incremental strategy.

5.2.5   Distributed Object Integration

You can realize all the benefits of distributed systems, introduced at the start of this
chapter, using distributed object technology. The cost of achieving these benefits is

extensive reengineering, but there is much potential for reusing parts of a legacy system in a distributed object architecture.

Distributed object architectures support an approach to software development based on assembling loosely coupled configurations of objects. They support the notion of "system families" presented in Chapter 1.

Where traditional object-oriented technology failed to meet expectations of wide scale reuse, distributed object technology is likely to succeed because it defines a binary standard for object reuse. "Componentware" markets have emerged which offer reusable objects for sale. In many cases it is more cost-effective to procure a suitable component than it is to develop it from scratch.

At the heart of this technology is an Object Request Broker (ORB), which is responsible for implementing the virtual machine abstraction (Fig. 5.19). It supports object interaction in a communication- and location-transparent manner. In addition, it provides a set of basic objects to support distributed application development. In particular, they include support for replication, transaction processing and security.

Distributed objects are programming language-independent. An object can invoke another's methods without regard to its programming language. Similarly to RPCs, ORBs use an IDL to define an object's interface in a language neutral way. Many ORB vendors provide language bindings for popular languages, such as C and COBOL.

There are currently two mainstream standards for distributed object technology: CORBA and Microsoft's Distributed Component Object Model (DCOM). The former is a product of the Object Management Group (OMG), whereas Microsoft's proposals

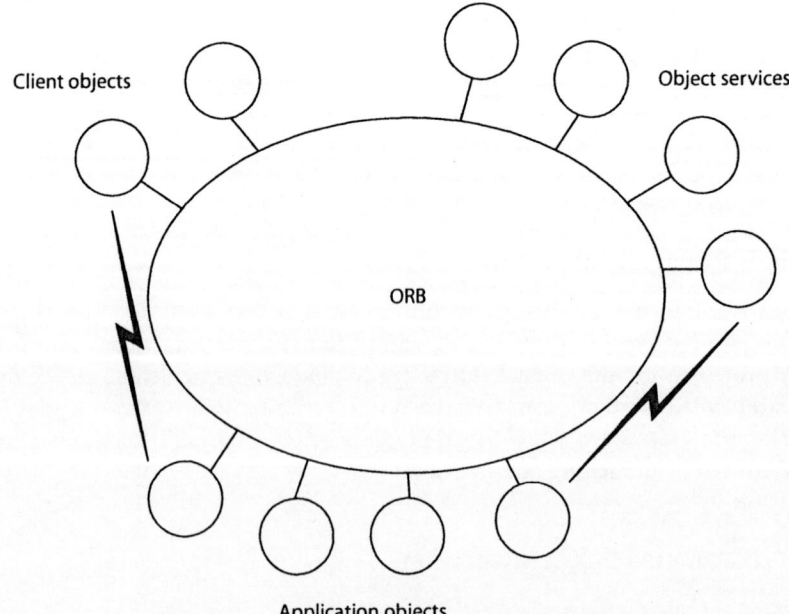

Fig. 5.19 Logical view of a distributed object architecture.

simply reflect the widespread use of its products. Both standards have been well adopted. They are not necessarily mutually exclusive, since middleware products have emerged to bridge them.

Where you follow a rearchitecturing or redesign-with-reuse reengineering strategy which involves distributed object technology, you may reuse legacy components using a technique termed "wrapping". Wrapping is essentially the process of encapsulating a legacy system component inside a distributed object. To wrap a component, you should identify the operations you want to expose and map them onto entry points in the legacy component.

You can wrap a component at several levels of granularity. You may want to encapsulate an entire application as a distributable object so that other objects which are connected to the ORB can communicate with it. In this case, you should identify operations that the legacy application should export and develop an object interface for them. At the other extreme, you may decompose an application into several fine-grained objects.

Component wrapping is a particularly useful technique for system reengineering. It provides a safe yet rapid approach to system rearchitecturing. It is safe because you reduce the risk of losing critical business rules which may be embedded in legacy system components. Rather than discard legacy code, you simply package it in one or more distributed objects. In many cases, you can use wrapping to rearchitecture a system with less effort than would be required to replace it.

You can migrate a system to distributed object technology by following an incremental evolution strategy. Often you will have to restructure a system to identify components which make suitable objects. After restructuring, you can package and distribute legacy abstractions as part of the target system. Subsequently, you can focus on particular object implementations and evolve them according to evolution requirements.

There are several solutions for integrating legacy resources in a distributed object architecture. Two general solutions include:

1 *Direct access.* The simplest approach is to maintain direct access between legacy components, which may or may not be wrapped as distributed objects, and the resource. The resource cannot be accessed through the ORB. You should adopt this solution when access to the resource is not required by other applications.

2 *Encapsulation.* You can package the resource as a distributed object. The resource is accessible both to legacy applications and to other objects which are connected to the ORB. This approach enables you to encapsulate additional behaviour such as replicating the resource, for example. Where all access to it is through the ORB, a distributed object is essentially the resource's manager, and is responsible for ensuring consistency between the replicas.

5.2.6   Workflow-Based Integration

Many of today's organizations need to compete globally, reduce operating costs, and develop new services and products rapidly. To address these requirements, you may

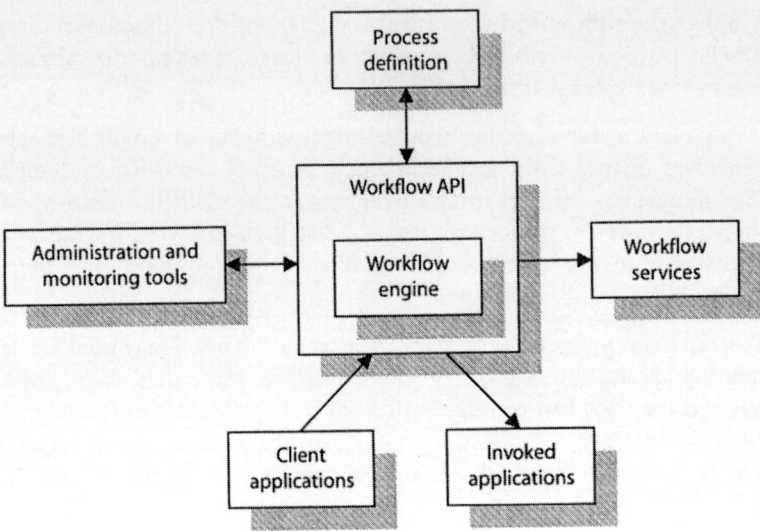

Fig. 5.20 Workflow reference model.

need to improve the way your organization works. This in turn may generate a need to change information systems which support the business. Using workflow technology, you can support, control and improve your business processes.

The Workflow Management Coalition has defined a standard architecture for workflow enabled systems (Fig. 5.20). At the heart of this model is a "workflow engine", which is responsible for distributing work (tasks) to actors. An actor may be a person or application. Tasks may be manual, partially automated or fully automated. The interface with "invoked applications" is the basis for integrating applications within a workflow system.

You can use workflow technology to:

1 *Simplify complex interactions between legacy applications.* A task may involve a series of transactions which span many applications. In this case, the workflow solution provides, as part of its user interface, a service which encapsulates the transactions in one service. Rather than make the sequence of transactions on each system, users simply invoke the single service provided by the workflow solution. Figure 5.21 shows how you can use workflow technology to automate a process which involves three applications. When used in this way, workflow technology presents users with the illusion of a single and coherent application, but which is actually realized by a collection of often disparate systems.

2 *Generate task descriptions.* During business process reengineering, you can map new processes onto interactions with information systems. The workflow engine generates task descriptions, which explain how to use existing information systems to complete the process. This is a lightweight approach for integrating legacy systems with a new business process. It does not, however, remove the need for users to use several applications to perform the new process.

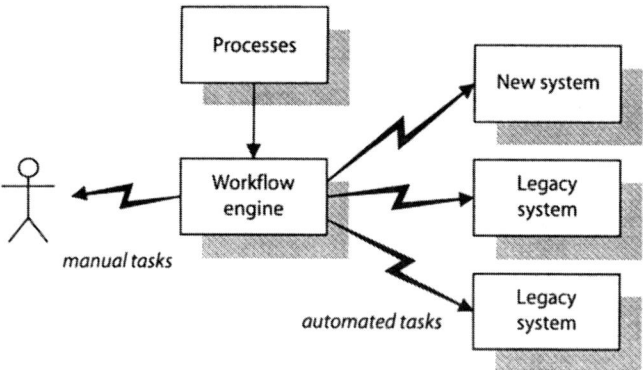

Fig. 5.21 Application automation.

Table 5.3 Integration model summary

Integration model	Strength	Weakness
Data	Little impact on legacy system architecture No modification of legacy source code	Tight coupling between data and applications Conversions to and from legacy data format may be necessary
Service	Safe access to legacy system functionality Loosely coupled application logic	No common standard
Presentation	No impact on application logic	No improvement in evolvability
Internet	Uniform system access across many platforms	Competing standards for technology
Distributed object	Encapsulation of services and data Potential for legacy component reuse	Target system complexity Immature enabling technology
Workflow	Business process driven Can be based on other integration models	Requires an investment in understanding business processes Tools do not comply with standards

You can use workflow technology to provide for incremental evolution. By adopting the workflow paradigm, you should identify clearly defined processes. You can migrate task support from a legacy system to a target system.

Where you use workflow systems to coordinate legacy applications, you can use service-based integration models to provide the workflow engine with entry points to legacy applications. As we discussed earlier, you may need to restructure an application before you can identify services which you can expose.

To involve a legacy system in a workflow solution, you should document the business processes which legacy applications support. You can use the modelling techniques introduced in Chapter 4 to do this. Once you have understood these processes, you may modify and document them using the workflow architecture's "process definition" tools. You should then map any new, often more abstract, processes onto those processes supported by legacy applications.

The architectural model, defined by the Workflow Management Coalition, supports some interoperability between the many workflow products on the market. However, vendors' interoperability is limited. Different vendors use their own standards and develop workflow products based on different behavioural models. In addition, most workflow tools lack support for analyzing, validating, testing and debugging processes.

Table 5.3 summarizes the strengths and weaknesses of the workflow model in addition to the other models which we have discussed in this chapter.

References and Further Reading

Coulouris G. and Dollimore J. (1994) *Distributed Systems – Concepts and Design*, 2nd edn. Addison-Wesley, Reading.

Pope A. (1998) *The CORBA Reference Guide: Understanding the Common Object Request Broker Architecture*. Addison-Wesley, Reading.

RENAISSANCE Consortium (1998) *Client/Server Migration*. Consultancy report, http://www.comp.lancs.ac.uk/projects/renaissance.

Serain D. (1998) *Middleware*. Springer-Verlag, London.

Wijegunaratne, I. and Fernandez, G. (1998) *Distributed Applications Engineering*. Springer-Verlag, London.

Key Points

- Architectural models have evolved from monolithic structures to complex, object-based architectures. Later models offer much potential for distributing software layers.

- A system integration model describes a logical structure of software layers. Each model supports reengineering by integrating legacy system components within a distributed framework.

- You can integrate legacy data components with a target system using either direct access or encapsulation techniques.

- You can distribute a legacy system's services without changing its architecture using RPC and MOM technology. This enables you to open an otherwise closed system to remote access from other applications.

- In many cases, you can change a legacy system's presentation layer to GUI technology without modifying its application logic.

- In addition to using Internet technology to revamp a system, you can provide remote access to it using the WWW.

- Where you rearchitecture a system using distributed object technology, you can package legacy code as distributable objects.

- Workflow technology enables you to support business process reengineering by coordinating the operation of several legacy applications.

6. Case Study 1: Evolution of a Legacy System

Objectives

- To show how you can use Renaissance to develop an evolution strategy for a legacy system.
- To demonstrate how to manage an evolution project using Renaissance.
- To show how you can customize Renaissance according to project and organizational needs.
- To show the impact of technical, organizational and business factors on system evolution.
- To illustrate the guidelines presented in Chapters 3–5: evolution planning, system modelling and migrating to distributed architectures.

Contents

6.1 Background
6.2 Scenario 1: Evolution Strategy Development
6.3 Scenario 2: Evolution Strategy Implementation

In this chapter, we present a case study based on our experiences with reengineering legacy systems. The system's technology typifies many data processing systems that were developed in the 1970s and remain in service today. This case study provides the foundation for two scenarios. Each scenario extends the case study with additional technical, business and organizational characteristics. Table 6.1 summarizes each scenario according to the characteristics of legacy systems which we introduced in Chapter 1.

The first scenario demonstrates the value of good software engineering. In this case, the system has been maintained by a technically mature organization. The system has been subjected to a preventative maintenance program as part of the agreement between the development and operational organizations. Consequently, the system is in good technical condition. From a business viewpoint, the system generally supports the operational organization's business process, and its business goals are not radical. We demonstrate how you can use Renaissance to determine a suitable evolution strategy for the system.

Table 6.1 Scenario characteristics

Characteristic	Scenario	
	1	2
High maintenance costs		✓
Complex software		✓
Obsolete support software		
Obsolete hardware		
Lacking technical expertise		✓
Business critical	✓	✓
Backlog of change requests		✓
Poor documentation		✓
Embedded business knowledge	✓	✓
Poorly understood by maintainers		✓

In contrast to Scenario 1, the second scenario is more negative. The system is in poor technical condition since it has been maintained according to an *ad hoc* process. Rather than invest in a quality maintenance program, the operational organization has procured the services of many software houses to make changes to its system. Its policy of reducing maintenance costs has, however, resulted in a system which is difficult and expensive to maintain.

Scenario 2 also involves radical business goals. Furthermore, the operational organization mandates a particular target system. We show how you can use Renaissance to manage the transition between the legacy and target systems. Table 6.2 summarizes the parts of Renaissance we illustrate in this chapter.

Table 6.2 Demonstration of Renaissance

Renaissance	Scenario 1	Scenario 2
Method	Used to develop a suitable evolution strategy	Used to manage an evolution project with a mandated target system
Process	Phase 1	Phases 1 to 4
Customization	Responsibilities Document repository	Process model Responsibilities Document repository
Evolution planning	Legacy system assessment Evolution strategy development Cost estimation and risk assessment	Evolution project planning Risk assessment
System modelling	Context modelling	Context modelling Technical modelling
Migration to a distributed architecture	Consideration of a distributed architecture for the target system	

6.1 Background

Build It Better (BIB) is a wholesale/retail organization which deals with building materials. Examples of stock handled by BIB include bricks, concrete, stone, plumbing materials, electrical products, insulation and timber. BIB was established in 1975 with the purpose of providing the building trade of a small region with supplies. The initial region, A, encapsulated three outlets. Figure 6.1 shows how the organization has grown from conception to present day.

The increased size and physical distribution of BIB's operation overloaded the original manual practices. In particular, BIB began to experience difficulties in its accounting operations and maintaining accurate stock records. Such difficulties caused BIB's management team to procure the services of a business consultancy firm which advised BIB to introduce automated support for its business.

Figure 6.2 shows key events in the evolution of BIB and its supporting information system.

Figure 6.3 uses a DFD notation to provide a high-level context diagram for BIB's enterprise. Functions correspond to physical sites which process information. Data flowing between the sites comprises electronic data (the "warehouse inventory" for example), physical entities (such as "stock"), and manual communications ("stock enquiry").

A single warehouse is located centrally to the outlets. Its location is critical for providing an effective distribution channel to outlets. All suppliers of BIB deliver exclusively to the central warehouse, from where stock is transferred to outlets. Head

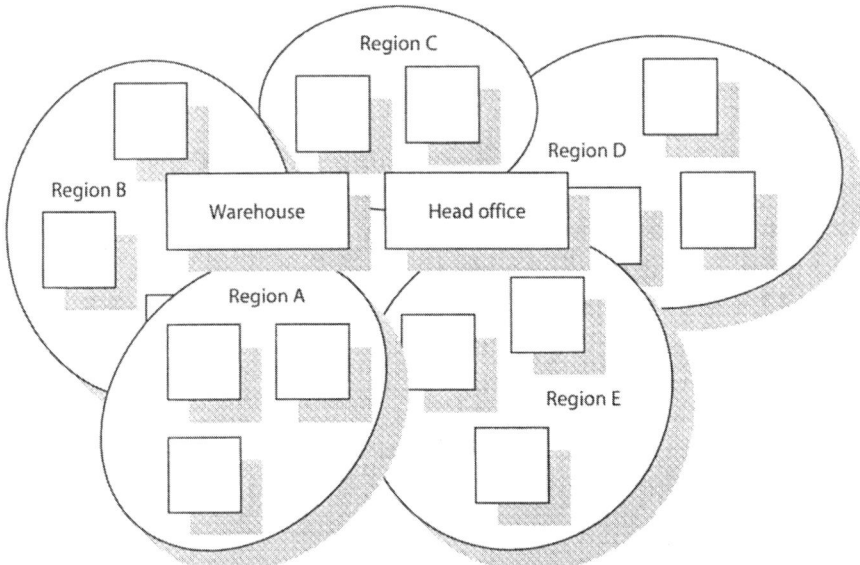

Fig. 6.1 Geographic growth of BIB.

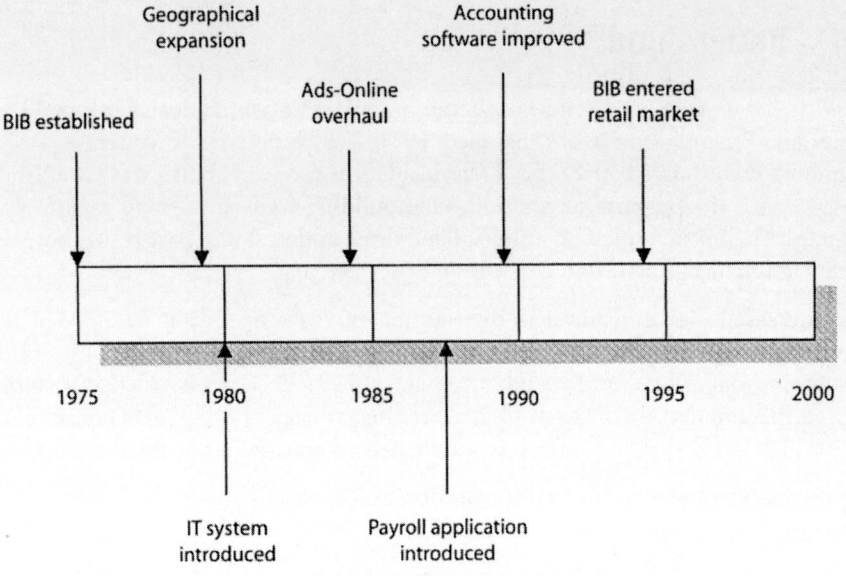

Fig. 6.2 Timeline for BIB.

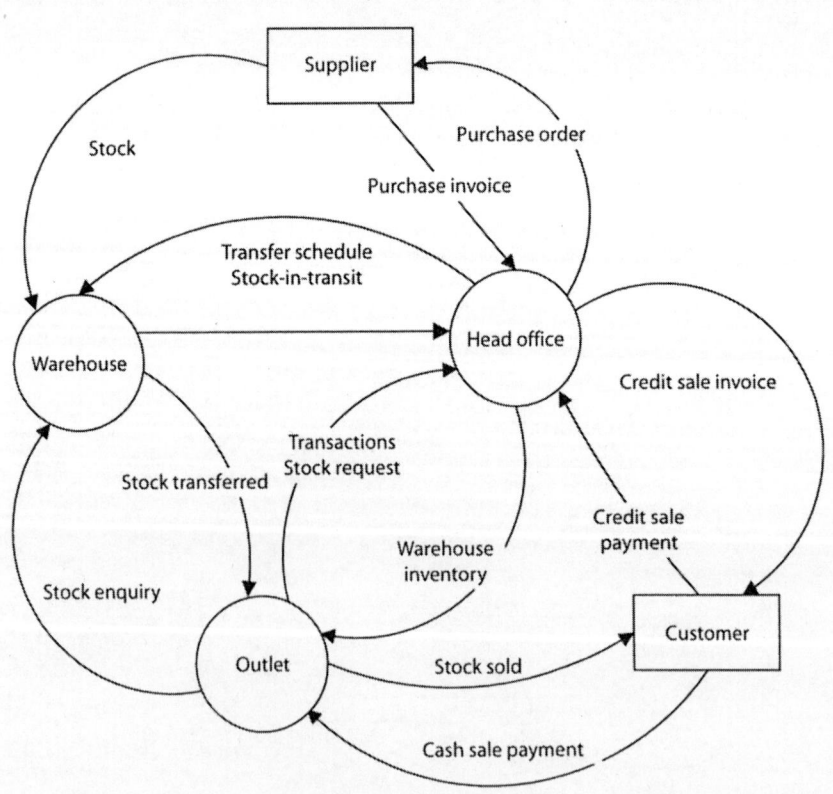

Fig. 6.3 Context diagram for BIB.

office, responsible for BIB's operation and management, is located near to the warehouse.

Head office is responsible for five functions:

1 *Accounts receivable.* Outlets may offer wholesale customers credit, so head office deals with these accounts. This involves debiting accounts for credit sales, crediting accounts when payments are received, generating account statements and dispatching invoices.

2 *Accounts payable.* Accounts payable is responsible for managing accounts held with suppliers. Suppliers send purchase invoices to head office which are only paid if the stock being invoiced has actually arrived at the warehouse.

3 *Buying.* Buyers are responsible for buying stock for the warehouse and outlets. They monitor stock levels in outlets and the warehouse, and decide which suppliers to order stock from. Buyers are also responsible for assessing the market-place and ordering new stock lines when appropriate.

4 *Transport.* The transport function transfers stock from the warehouse to outlets. The geographic operation of BIB is subdivided into regions where particular day(s) of the week are allocated to a particular region.

5 *Financial management.* This is a senior management function which coordinates the other functions. Particular activities include strategic planning, accounting management and general decision-making.

The warehouse maintains a stock of popular products. Ideally, the warehouse should always be able to meet requests for stock from outlets. Obtaining stock from suppliers should only be necessary for maintaining the warehouse's stock levels. Warehouse staff physically organize stock according to its status: warehouse stock or stock-in-transit. The former is stock which has not been allocated for transfer to any outlet; the latter is stock which has been reserved for transfer to a particular outlet.

Head office notifies the warehouse of warehouse stock which is to be made stock-in-transit, and supplies the warehouse with stock transfer schedules. A transfer schedule specifies stock to be transferred to outlets on a particular day. When stock is delivered to the warehouse from suppliers, warehouse staff advise head office of the deliveries in order for head office personnel to pay purchase invoices.

Outlets are the interface between BIB and its customers. All sales made by an outlet are recorded and sent to head office for processing. Head office uses this information to update wholesale accounts, and to update its records of outlet inventories. The latter is necessary for head office to calculate which stock to tag stock-in-transit, to determine what stock must be ordered from suppliers and to prepare stock transfer schedules.

On occasions when outlets cannot satisfy customer requirements for stock, the outlet generates a stock request and sends it to head office. This should rarely occur, except for specialist products which are particularly expensive or for products which are in little demand. Head office arranges to transfer the required stock from the warehouse, if it is available, or orders the stock from a supplier.

There are of course additional activities which form part of BIB's business model, such as processing miscellaneous expenses, returning damaged stock to suppliers, auditing, bad creditor management and so on. In this chapter, however, we have deliberately presented a simplified view of BIB's operation because superfluous detail would obscure this case study.

Towards the end of the 1970s, the management team of BIB acted on the advice to install automated support for their business by introducing a computer system. Some of the original system's hardware remains in service today. The mainframe and minicomputers have been upgraded over the years, but the underlying technology remains unchanged. The hardware comprises:

- *One IBM mainframe.* This machine, located at head office, stores and processes the vast majority of BIB's data.

- *Several IBM minicomputers.* Each outlet uses a minicomputer to store local inventory data, and accumulated stock requests and sales data. In addition, these machines manage a copy of the warehouse inventory, which they download periodically.

- *Several character terminals.* Each outlet has a small number of terminals which are connected to the local minicomputer. The warehouse has a collection of terminals which are connected to the mainframe remotely via a dedicated communication line. Head office hosts many mainframe terminals.

- *Communications, printers and secondary storage.* All minicomputers are connected to the mainframe. There is at least one printer at each site. Mainframe data is stored on disks and is archived onto tapes.

The initial system was entirely batch-oriented. Software included a suite of COBOL programs which manipulated structured (Virtual Storage Access Method (VSAM)) files. In essence, data was collected and recorded in transaction files for subsequent batch processing. During batch processing, the transaction files were merged with master files. Processing was scheduled at times when the system was not in use.

The computerized solution met expectations of increased efficiency and reduced error, but it soon became apparent that its data was often inconsistent with reality. For example, on receipt of stock from suppliers, warehouse personnel entered delivery details into a transaction file. When scheduled, this file was merged with the warehouse master file. During the time between deliveries and updating the master file, the master file was an inaccurate representation of the stock actually held at the warehouse. Head office buyers found themselves resorting to written notes about expected or recent deliveries.

The problem of inconsistent data was a major contributing factor to the 1984 overhaul. The mainframe's COBOL/VSAM combination was replaced with an Ads-Online/IDMS configuration. Ads-Online is a 4GL, designed primarily for use with the IDMS network database. Some of the COBOL programs were retained to supplement the Ads-Online solution. This revised online solution provides head office personnel with up-to-date information.

The system, however, retains a batch mode of communication between the mainframe and minicomputers. Outlets continue to record sales data and stock requests in transaction files which are batched and sent to the mainframe overnight every working day.

In addition to the Ads-Online overhaul, BIB's system has evolved in a number of other ways. Minor modifications have been necessary to comply with changing legislation and tax rate changes. The IDMS data schemas have been changed to respond to new product types. Occasionally, adding a new product caused difficulties because it is available in units not previously recognized by the system. One example involved the introduction of paint as BIB's first liquid product, where the system had to deal in litres.

As a consequence of expansion, head office personnel found their manual processes for calculating salaries and wages to be particularly time-consuming. Moreover, producing year-end accounts and auditing became a complex and error-prone activity. Payroll and additional accounting programs, developed in Ads-Online, were introduced the late 1980s.

Recently, BIB entered the retail market. Retail customers typically require smaller quantities of products than wholesale customers. They also need different types of products and services. The implications of supporting retail customers incurred additional data and procedural changes.

6.2 Scenario 1: Evolution Strategy Development

In this scenario, we extend the case study with additional characteristics which further define its technical, organizational and business properties. This scenario demonstrates how you can use the method to develop a suitable evolution strategy for BIB's system.

A quality software house, MIS (Management Information Systems), performed the earlier transformation to 4GL and database technology. MIS has been responsible for maintaining the system since and does so according to a well-defined and practised change management process. In addition to managing BIB's change requests, MIS actively pursues a preventative maintenance program as part of its agreement with BIB. Consequently, the system is in good overall technical condition.

MIS recognizes that in the software industry in particular, quality personnel are essential for producing quality products. MIS trains its staff in emerging technologies and encourages valued individuals to stay with the company. This means that MIS maintains a body of individuals who have developed a sound understanding of BIB's application.

BIB and MIS enjoy a good working relationship. MIS typically deals with change requests promptly and without having to employ excessive effort. BIB is satisfied with the maintenance costs, but is a little sceptical of the return on its investment in preventative maintenance. BIB was, however, persuaded to enter the scheme by a convincing argument from MIS, based on reduced long-term costs, rapid incorporation of change requests and increased reliability.

Recently, as part of its continuing efforts to improve product and service quality, MIS has discovered the Renaissance method. Naturally, MIS is reluctant to replace its existing practices with a completely new method, but realizing that Renaissance can be tailored to its needs, the team at MIS has decided to use it as the basis for a new service.

The result of MIS's service is a consultancy report which identifies how a particular information system should evolve, or in other words, a "system evolution strategy". MIS markets the service based on the need for change in business and the consequent need for those changes to be computer-supported.

BIB is interested in this service for four reasons. First, it is concerned about the Year 2000 problem's impact on its existing information system. Second, BIB wants to know whether its system can support its business strategy. The third reason concerns the introduction of the European single currency. Although its impact on BIB is currently unclear, BIB's management team is anxious to know whether the system will have difficulty in trading with the new currency. Finally, BIB is worried about the age of its hardware. Despite servicing and upgrades, the mainframe machine and several of the minicomputers have been in operation for over twenty years.

6.2.1   Method Customization

Renaissance provides guidance from project conception through to deploying the target system in its operational environment. In this scenario, however, MIS requires only the Plan Evolution phase (Fig. 6.4) of the method to support the new service.

You can tailor Plan Evolution to offer a cost/risk trade-off, where more effort reduces the risk of error in selecting an inappropriate evolution strategy. MIS exploits this and provides the service at two levels:

1 *Quick and approximate.* MIS offers the service at relatively low cost, using little effort, to assess the system at a high level. The result is an indication of a suitable evolution strategy for BIB's system.

2 *More expensive, but more accurate.* In this case, MIS employ additional effort to assess the legacy system at a greater level of detail.

MIS recommends the first option initially, as there is little point in procuring an expensive service when it is clear from a quick study that reengineering is unnecessary. MIS appreciates that the method's process is iterative and that any information it captures during a quick service may be used as input to a more thorough investigation.

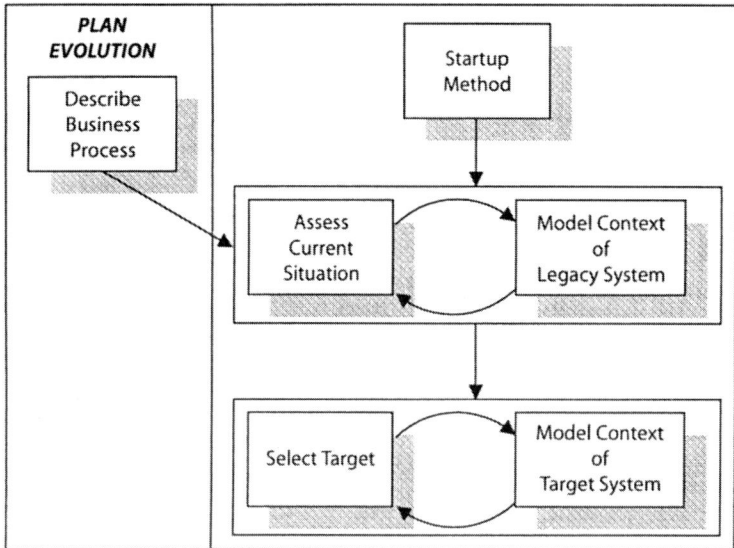

Fig. 6.4 The Plan Evolution phase.

In Chapter 2, we introduced the idea of a document repository, which manages information throughout the course of the method. MIS does not need all the repository's folders and documents. Project Plan, for example, is created during the Implement phase of the complete method and so does not feature in MIS's constrained version of Renaissance. Figure 6.5 shows the repository's contents following the Startup Method activity.

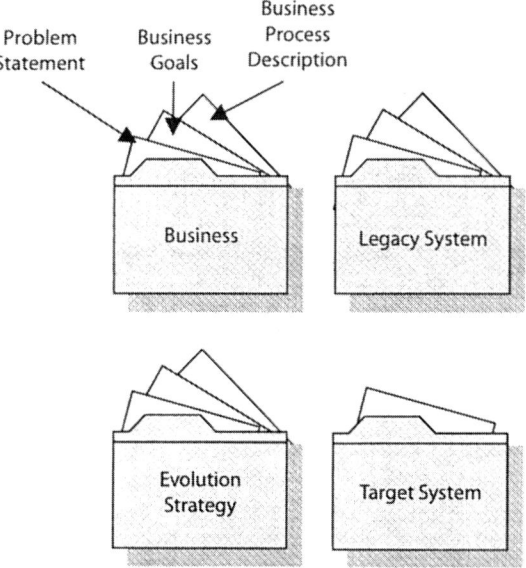

Fig. 6.5 Repository contents after activity Startup Method.

Table 6.3 BIB's business goals

1	*To maintain the existing market.* BIB intends to retain its stronghold over existing regions.
2	*To expand geographically.* Opportunities for growth lie to the immediate North East of BIB's outlets. Expansion, however, is constrained in that all outlets must be no more than 220 kilometres from the warehouse.
3	*To attract further retail customers.* BIB's management team believes that the retail market offers great potential. Initial thoughts on attracting more retail customers include:

    (i)   *Introducing accounts and credit schemes for retail customers.*

    (ii)   *Introducing a delivery service for retail customers.*

    (iii) *Providing expert services.* Do-It-Yourself (DIY) has become a popular activity, but many potential customers are deterred by a lack of knowledge and practical skills. The BIB team thinks that making experts available for consultation would transform potential customers into real customers.

MIS fills the Business folder initially with three documents:

1 Business Goals. A prerequisite of MIS's service is that BIB describes its business goals. They enable MIS to determine the degree of change to BIB's system which is necessary to support them. Table 6.3 shows BIB's business goals. They are open-ended statements and can be implemented in many ways. In the Assess Current Situation activity, MIS develops them into more precise requirements to better understand the needs of a target system.

2 Business Process Description. MIS also requires a description of BIB's business process to assess how well the system supports it. MIS develops a similar description to that which we presented in Section 6.1. Given the relationship between MIS and BIB, MIS expends little effort on this task.

3 Problem Statement. There is no specific problem as such. We described how BIB's interest in the service grew from concerns over hardware age, the Year 2000 issue, the European single currency and whether the system can meet BIB's business strategy. Any solution is, however, constrained by cost. BIB is reluctant to spend vast sums of money on its support system. BIB's concerns and budget constraint form the problem statement.

The remaining repository folders are placeholders for information which BIB produces during subsequent activities. Figure 6.6 shows the documents which MIS aims to develop over the course of its service. We return to these documents as necessary when describing subsequent activities.

Finally, MIS identifies personnel from both organizations who are involved in providing the service. Using the service to develop a quick and approximate evolution strategy requires experts who can contribute to the Assess Current Situation activity. MIS brings in an external consultant, who has a sound understanding of the wholesale/retail industry, to meet the responsibility of Application Business Expert.

Table 6.4 shows BIB's responsibilities. In this scenario, it is convenient for the managing director to meet the responsibilities of Client Representative and Legacy

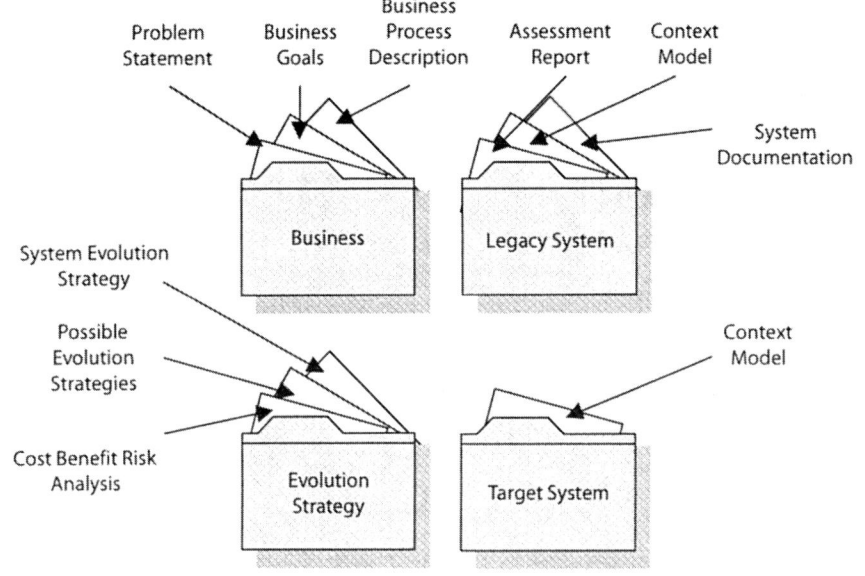

Fig. 6.6 Repository contents upon completion of the method.

Table 6.4 BIB's responsibilities

Responsibility	BIB individual					
	Managing director	Warehouse worker	Outlet clerk	Head office clerk	Outlet manager	Head office manager
Client Representative	✓					
Legacy System Functional Expert	✓				✓	✓
User		✓	✓	✓	✓	✓

Table 6.5 MIS's responsibilities

Responsibility	MIS individual		
	Software Engineer	Software Engineer	Senior Software Engineer
Software Project Manager			✓
Estimator			✓
Modeller		✓	✓
Legacy System Developer	✓	✓	✓

System Functional Expert. Users are taken from several areas of work and from several positions within the organization. Three individuals from MIS are involved in providing the service (Table 6.5). MIS define a new responsibility, Estimator, to support accurate cost estimation by an experienced engineer.

6.2.2 System Assessment

MIS performs Assess Current Situation to determine whether BIB's system is a candidate for evolution. This involves assessing technical, business and organizational factors. MIS records the results of this exercise in the Assessment Report. Where assessment reveals that the system is no longer required to support BIB's business, there is no point in following the method further. MIS, however, expects to identify a number of possible evolution strategies.

You can assess the current situation at a number of levels of detail, where more thorough assessment requires more effort. Figure 6.7 summarizes the technical and business assessment scales, introduced in Chapter 3, and shows that MIS selects a relatively high level for both. This is in keeping with the quick service procured by BIB and is based on the opinions of the knowledgeable individuals included in Table 6.4 and Table 6.5.

Renaissance suggests that you should perform Assess Current Situation and Model Context of Legacy System iteratively. The point of context modelling is to support the assessment activity. Modelling promotes an understanding of the system which is vital for effective assessment. Where assessment is based on a poor understanding of the system, the results are at best loosely approximate, and at worst wholly inaccurate and misleading. The degree of modelling required is thus dependent on how well the system is understood. In this scenario, MIS does little modelling because of the availability of documentation and experienced technical personnel.

The Application Business Expert works with MIS's software engineers and BIB personnel to develop a model which shows how BIB's system supports its business

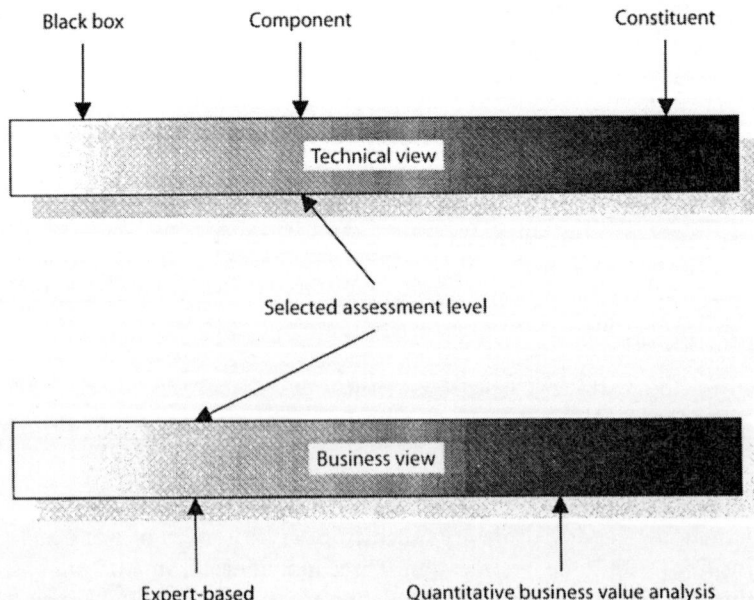

Fig. 6.7 Assessment levels.

process. User manuals, change history documents and requirements documents contribute to a description of what the system does, but do not expose any differences between that and what it "should" do.

In Chapter 4, we introduced use case diagrams as a means of modelling a system from a business perspective. Use case diagrams are particularly suitable in this case since business analysts, software engineers and system users readily understand them. The Application Business Expert develops these models by collaborating with Users, Legacy System Functional Experts and Legacy System Developers. In addition, she studies how the system is used in practice. She finds this technique particularly useful as users do not always point out system failings because they have changed how they work to compensate for them.

The Application Business Expert finds it convenient to introduce a number of roles within BIB's organization which include: head office clerk, outlet operator, warehouse operator and manager. Any one individual may fill several roles. For each role, she produces a use case diagram to show how the role interacts with the system. Figure 6.8 shows the use case diagrams for the outlet operator and warehouse operator roles. Underlined use case names are cases which are not supported by the system.

The use case diagrams reveal a small number of functions which are poorly supported by the system. One problem in particular is where outlet staff enquire about the availability of warehouse stock. This may be necessary when an outlet has insufficient stock to satisfy a customer's order. In this case, outlet staff view their local copy of the warehouse inventory. In many cases, it is clear that there is enough stock in the warehouse to guarantee transfer of stock to the outlet. In this case, outlet staff simply create a new stock request to be batched and sent to head office overnight. The stock should arrive at the outlet on the next scheduled stock-transfer day.

On other occasions, however, browsing the warehouse stock file reveals that sufficient stock exists to satisfy the customer's order, but that the level of warehouse stock is low and so may already have been allocated for transfer to another outlet. In this case, outlet staff telephone the warehouse and attempt to reserve the stock. Warehouse staff notify head office to prepare the stock-transfer schedule. This

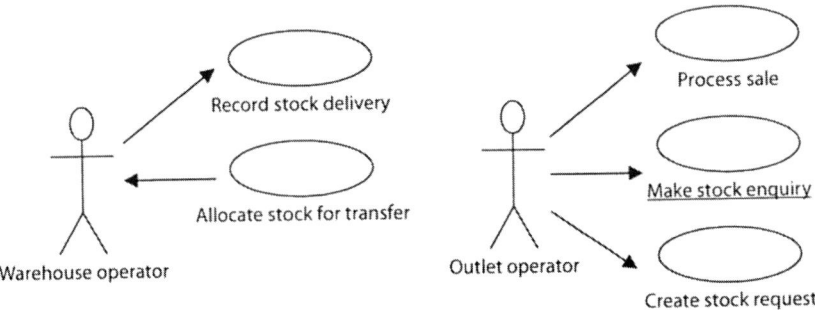

Fig. 6.8 System services.

approach is error-prone and sometimes results in dissatisfied customers where stock fails to arrive at the outlet.

Generally, the system does support the business process very well. The Application Business Expert finds that it is vital to BIB's continued operation. This has been borne out in BIB's experience, since automated support has been necessary to manage problems of scale. The Application Business Expert adds that BIB's industry is in a period of growth and endorses BIB's plans to continue to expand and enter new markets.

Having established that the system has a high business value "today", the Application Business Expert considers whether it will retain its value in the foreseeable future. She works with the software engineers to derive a set of high-level requirements from the business goals. Table 6.6 shows these evolution requirements which the Software Project Manager and Legacy System Developer consider, from a technical perspective, for accommodation by BIB's system.

Table 6.6 Evolution requirements

1	The system provides services to manage retail customer accounts
2	The system provides services to manage a customer delivery service
3	The system provides services to manage expert consultation
4	The system is able to accommodate new product types
5	The system is Year 2000-compliant
6	A WWW information service is accessible to customers

Requirements 1–3 are functional implementation-independent requirements. Requirement 1 involves providing a similar set of accounting services for retail customers to those currently supported for wholesale customers. Requirement 2 means that the system should manage an electronic diary for coordinating and booking customer deliveries. The third requirement necessitates another electronic diary for managing appointments with experts.

The first three requirements are abstract and can be implemented using several solutions. For example, experts could be available at outlets, or customers could book them for home visits. At this stage, however, MIS is concerned with the nature of the requirements and whether they can be integrated with the existing system. The software engineers anticipate that they can develop further programs and data structures to accommodate these requirements. They point out, however, that an online interface between the outlets and head office would enable the requirements to be implemented more effectively. This would also solve the main problem with BIB's system, revealed by the Application Business Expert earlier.

Requirements 4 and 5 are non-functional requirements. The former concerns the system's evolvability. It must be able to manage new products which BIB introduces to meet the needs of retail customers. The software engineers believe that both requirements can be accommodated by the existing system.

The final requirement is generated from the Application Business Expert's belief that BIB should raise its profile by marketing itself on the WWW. Her suggestions for exploiting the Internet include:

- *Advertisement.* BIB could use the WWW to publicize information about itself, including outlet locations, trading hours and product information.

- *Transaction processing.* Customers could use the Internet to order products and arrange for payment and delivery. In addition, a WWW server could manage expert services.

To assess the technical quality of BIB's system, MIS engineers decompose it into application software, support software and hardware. They view each of these parts as a black box and do not differentiate, for example, between Ads-Online functions, COBOL programs and IDMS schemas when assessing the application software. Rather, they derive representative measures for each part at an abstract level.

The software structure and environment are well documented. Figure 6.9 shows the software architecture for the minicomputer installations. This model contains sufficient detail for high-level assessment. Figure 6.10 shows the hardware for BIB's installation. We use the UML's package diagram to present the former, and a hardware/network diagram for the latter.

The software engineers choose a number of system attributes, from those introduced in Chapter 3, on which to base their assessment (Table 6.7). MIS selects these attributes because they can be readily valued using expert opinion. For example, the

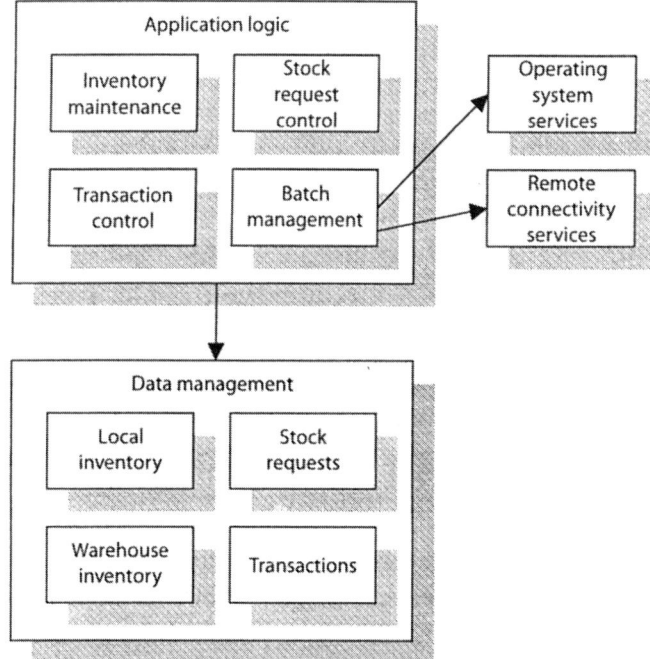

Fig. 6.9 Software structure for outlets.

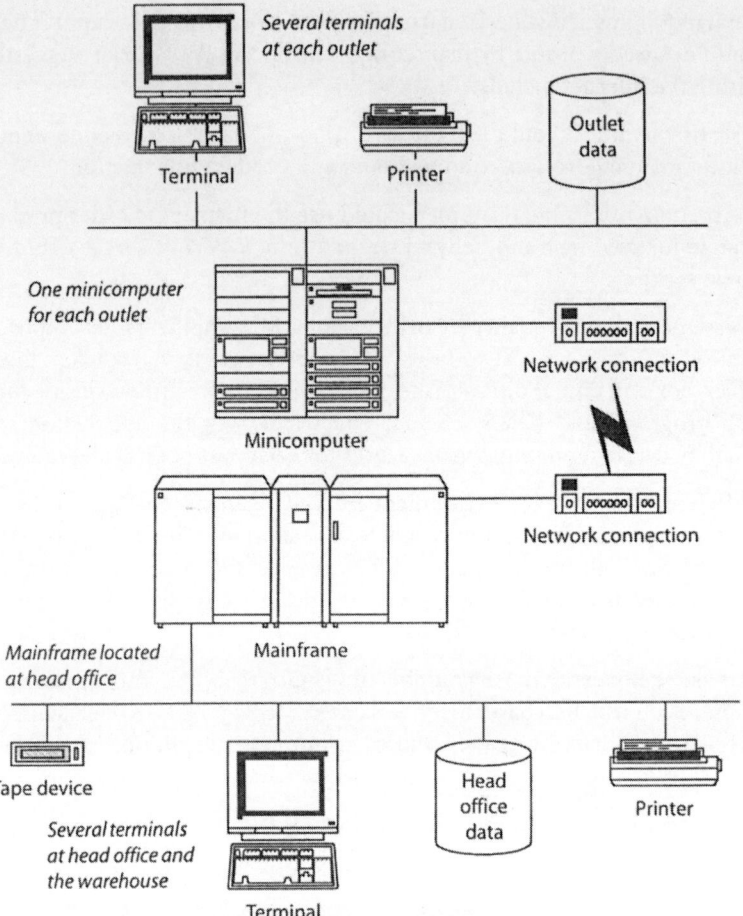

Fig. 6.10 Hardware architecture.

engineers can provide a value for "maintenance record" based on their knowledge of dealing with change requests. They know which requests have been implemented and the effort required to implement them.

MIS uses the simple attribute-rating scheme which we described in Chapter 3. It involves assigning each attribute a value in the range 1–4, where 1 is a low score. MIS considers that a total score that is less than the maximum possible score divided by two indicates a problem with the system's evolvability.

The change history of the application demonstrates that MIS has maintained the system at reasonable cost. MIS is rarely unable to accommodate change requests and the majority of them have been dealt with to BIB's satisfaction. MIS thus assigns the "maintenance costs" and "maintenance record" attributes high scores.

The system is clearly aging. The US National Bureau of Standards suggests, as a guideline, that when a system is over seven years old further investment in it may be

Table 6.7 Technical quality assessment results

	Attribute	Score
Application software	Age	1
	Documentation	4
	Performance	3
	Maintenance costs	3
	Maintenance record	4
	Complexity	3
Support software	Age	1
	Documentation	3
	Performance	3
	Failure rate	4
	Vendor/supplier	4
	Frequency of fixes	3
	License costs	2
Hardware	Age	1
	Documentation	3
	Performance	3
	Maintenance costs	2
	Failure rate	4
	Vendor/supplier	4
	Total	55/76

unwise. Much of BIB's system is well over seven years old. Consequently, MIS assigns "age" a low score.

MIS rates "performance" high because the system provides services to its users with satisfactory response times. The Application Business Expert accounts for the functional deficiencies in BIB's system in her assessment of business value.

As a consequence of MIS's technical maturity, the application's complexity has been controlled. Documentation is unusually good in this scenario. The software engineers understand the system and can determine the impact of proposed changes with little effort. MIS assigns "complexity" a value of 3, however, because some early minicomputer programs are more difficult to understand.

The "vendor/supplier" attribute for both support software and hardware is particularly important for system evolvability. Where 4GLs, for example, form part of a system's support-software, its evolution is constrained by the support available for these products. Ads-Online is currently supported on mainframe systems, and MIS expects that this will continue in the immediate future. IBM also continues to support its hardware products. MIS therefore rates "vendor/supplier" with a high score.

Mainframe and minicomputer installations incur high servicing and maintenance costs. Given BIB's plans for continued expansion, the costs of introducing additional minicomputers would further increase these costs. MIS also considers Ads-Online's licensing costs to be expensive. This is reflected in the scores for "license costs" and hardware's "maintenance costs".

Having gathered information for both business value and technical quality, MIS and the Application Business Expert examine their findings. The Application Business Expert finds that BIB's business process does not require significant change. There are a small number of processes which could be better supported by the system. The system can largely meet BIB's evolution requirements. These factors collectively constitute a high business value. Without employing considerably more effort in a thorough business value analysis, it is difficult to quantify business value. It is clear, however, that the system is critical to BIB's continued prosperity.

The result for technical quality, 72%, gives an early indication that the application is technically sound. Figure 6.11 plots the results on the quadrant map, which we introduced in Chapter 3. According to the map, the application falls in the category of low-priority reengineering. MIS realizes, however, that this measure of technical quality cannot be taken at face value, so it carries out further analysis.

The Year 2000 date change problem is a risk factor which is guaranteed to occur. The cost of not dealing with the problem before 2000 can be fatal for the organization concerned. The software engineers involved in providing MIS's service consider that BIB's system can be made Year 2000-compliant without any reengineering.

Where the Year 2000 problem is well defined and understood, the impact of the single European currency is uncertain. Given the proven maintainability of the system, MIS does not anticipate difficulties in addressing the problem, subject to reasonable time constraints. However, MIS urges BIB to review this issue when further information is available.

MIS has assigned "age" a noticeably low value. Despite the system's age, rigorous hardware maintenance and servicing policies ensure that the system operates

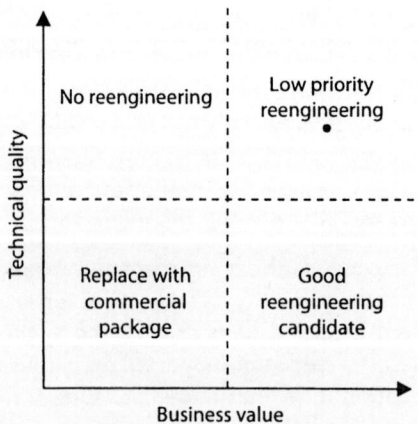

Fig. 6.11 Assessment results.

reliably and with satisfactory performance. This, coupled with the high scores for both the hardware and support software "vendor/supplier" ratings, suggest that the system's age is not actually cause for alarm.

Finally, MIS considers organizational factors which have an impact on the success of any proposed reengineering effort. MIS's technical maturity is a critical success factor. In this scenario, MIS has proven that it is sufficiently mature to tackle a reengineering project by its effective change management program. BIB must have a positive attitude to change in order for any reengineered system to be successful. Based on its experience with BIB, MIS is satisfied that BIB would effectively manage the introduction of any new system.

One organizational factor which may be cause for concern is that until recently, MIS has specialized in providing business solutions using mainframe technology. MIS has, however, tackled a number of small projects using modern GUI and Internet technology to provide database front ends. MIS is confident that it has acquired adequate skills in this technology.

MIS concludes that low-priority reengineering is appropriate for BIB's system, but work should start on the Year 2000 problem. The team understands that BIB's system must continue, in some form, to support BIB in the future. The system can evolve according to either continued maintenance or a reengineering strategy. Table 6.8 summarizes the motivation for reengineering. Organizational factors, in this case, do not appear to constrain reengineering. However, MIS should conduct a more detailed assessment before making any critical decisions.

Table 6.8 Motivating factors for reengineering

Reduced hardware maintenance costs
Reduced support-software licensing costs
Provision of Internet access for customers
Improved business process support
Effective implementation of new services

6.2.3   Evolution Strategy Development

During the Select Target activity, the MIS team considers a number of target systems and develops an evolution strategy to transform BIB's system to one of those target solutions. Similarly to the Assess Current Situation activity, Select Target involves some modelling. Model Context of Target System assists MIS to understand the candidate target systems and to assess how each system meets the evolution requirements.

The MIS team briefly examines each of the evolution strategies introduced in Chapter 3 with the intention of eliminating those which are clearly unsuitable.

- *Continued maintenance.* Likely to be the cheapest strategy, continued maintenance appears appropriate given the combination of technical and business factors in this scenario.

- *Revamp.* Changing the appearance of BIB's system is of no interest to BIB. GUIs are overkill for all but BIB's managerial functions. In fact, a GUI would introduce unnecessary complexity and inefficiency for operations such as entering details of stock received.

- *Restructure.* Restructuring involves improving the internal workings of an application without changing its functionality. MIS's assessment revealed that the application is in good technical condition, so there is no need to restructure it.

- *Rearchitecture.* Migrating to a distributed architecture is a relatively expensive and radical form of reengineering. Part of the problem statement is a budget constraint. MIS think that rearchitecting the system would be too expensive.

- *Redesign with reuse.* Some redesign of the application would allow BIB's system to address the shortfalls of its business process support. MIS views this strategy as an enabling mechanism for an online interface between the outlets and head office.

- *Replace.* A drastic strategy which is fraught with risk. MIS rules out replacing the system because its good technical condition means that it can be maintained or reengineered. Either option is likely to be much cheaper than replacement.

MIS reduces the above strategies to two Possible Evolution Strategies. For each of these, it performs a cost/benefit/risk analysis exercise and documents its findings in the Cost Benefit Risk Analysis report. MIS uses this document as the basis for developing the System Evolution Strategy.

Continued maintenance has a number of prerequisites which span technical, business and organizational factors. Technically, the system must be in good condition and well documented. It must be easy to understand, and change requests must be accommodated at reasonable cost with little impact on other parts of the system. From a business perspective, the system should support the current business process and be able to accommodate evolution requirements. The organization which is responsible for maintaining the system must have a body of engineers who are familiar with it.

In this scenario, the majority of these prerequisites are satisfied. The cost items involved in continued maintenance are few, because unlike other strategies, there are no additional software life cycle activities to perform. For example, you do not need to do any data analysis to prepare for data migration. In BIB's case, the costs are predictable and constitute software and hardware maintenance. Neither cost would change greatly in the short term.

MIS looks beyond the current situation and assesses the long-term impact of continued maintenance on BIB's system. MIS observes three drawbacks:

1 *High long-term costs.* BIB's continued investment in a system which is composed entirely of legacy technology will incur high costs. This is not only because of the running costs associated with mainframe and minicomputer installations, but because over time, the system will become a specialist concern. Personnel with legacy skills will become rare and may command high rates of pay.

2 *Lack of support for BIB's business process.* Continued maintenance will not address the system's deficiencies in supporting BIB's business process. To address these failings, the system should be partially redesigned to provide a complete online solution.

3 *Lack of support for evolution requirements.* Continued maintenance cannot accommodate all evolution requirements. Requirement 6, introduction of a WWW server, requires some reengineering. In addition, requirements 3 and 4 would be more effectively implemented if outlets had online access to the electronic diaries.

In Chapter 3, we introduced a generic set of risk factors which pertain to particular evolution strategies. MIS filters these factors and identifies three which are relevant to this strategy. Table 6.9 shows these factors with the class and condition which MIS's engineers award them. The condition reflects the engineer's opinion of the degree of threat that the risk poses to maintaining BIB's system.

Table 6.9 Risk factors for continued maintenance

	Risk factor	Class	Condition
1	Experienced maintenance staff leave	Unavoidable	No risk
2	System will not meet evolution requirements	Unavoidable	Moderate
3	Obsolete operational environment	Unavoidable	Moderate

MIS can reduce the probability of risk factor 1 occurring by maintaining its good working environment. In the unlikely event of this factor becoming a reality, continued maintenance could be expensive, ineffective and error-prone. These effects can, however, be mitigated by the existing documentation, which would enable new maintainers to understand the system. MIS does not see this risk factor as a critical success factor for continued maintenance.

Risk factors 2 and 3 cannot be avoided. Continued maintenance cannot accommodate all evolution requirements. If BIB selects this strategy, it will trade new functionality for relatively cheap software costs. Possible effects of risk factor 3 include system failure, difficulties in supporting the system in the long term, and difficulties in accommodating future business requirements.

Having considered continued maintenance, MIS moves on to possible redesign-with-reuse solutions. A target system which provides outlets with online access to head-office data would effectively implement evolution requirements 1–5. In addition, it would better support BIB's business process. MIS considers two such target systems:

1 *A centralized monolithic system.* The cheapest solution is to retain the fundamental legacy software and hardware architectures, but to decommission the minicomputers and connect outlet terminals directly to the mainframe. The mainframe would be responsible for hosting all application logic and data.

2 *A distributed solution.* BIB could replace each minicomputer with a server which hosts an outlet's inventory. Figure 6.12 uses the UML's deployment notation to

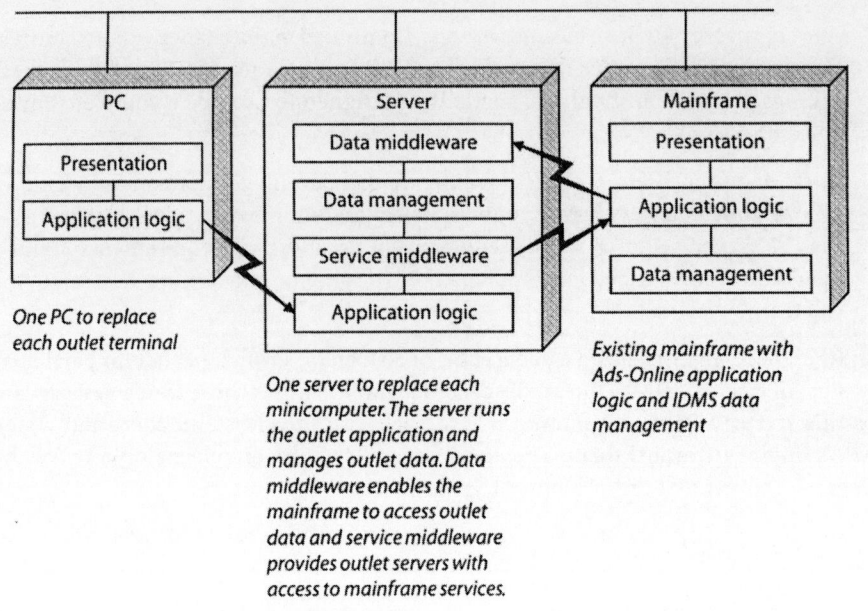

Fig. 6.12 Architecture for target system 2.

show the hardware architecture for this system and the mapping of software layers onto it.

Target system 2 is the more interesting solution. According to the classification scheme for distributed architectures, introduced in Chapter 5, it is a multi-tier system. The mainframe would continue to host head office data and application logic using IDMS and Ads-Online. Each server would be responsible for managing an outlet's local inventory, relaying mainframe services to outlet PCs, and providing the mainframe with access to its local inventory.

If the server platform supports VSAM tools and appropriate middleware, MIS can use either of the data integration techniques introduced in Chapter 5 to make the data accessible to PC applications. It may, however, be more sensible to migrate the VSAM data to a relational database. This would simplify access from outlet PCs, but would necessitate a middleware driver to interface between the new database and the mainframe application.

In addition to integrating data, MIS should use a service-based integration technique to provide outlet servers with access to mainframe services. MIS might have to restructure parts of the Ads-Online application to provide entry points to particular services.

Target system 1 is the cheaper of the two online systems. This is largely due to its relatively simple hardware requirements. Both strategies, however, incur many of the cost items introduced in Chapter 3. In particular, they include the software development costs to analyze, design, implement and test the new software. Target system 1 involves migrating outlet functionality and data to the mainframe. For target system

2, MIS's engineers must implement outlets' application logic and data using new technology. This, coupled with the use of new middleware products, means that target system 2 may also incur training costs.

To support a WWW publicity server, MIS suggests that it should be implemented independently of BIB's current system or either target system. A publicity server simply raises BIB's profile by advertising BIB using the Internet, and does not need access to the organization's data.

To support transactions across the Internet, for ordering products and booking experts and deliveries for example, the server needs access to BIB's data. In this case, MIS expects to use a data-based integration technique to provide the server with access to data, which would reside on new servers and/or the mainframe. In any case, the transactions are simple and MIS believes that the CGI WWW model is sufficient to implement them.

MIS performs a risk analysis exercise similar to that for continued maintenance. Table 6.10 shows relevant risk factors for the redesign-with-reuse strategies. Risk factor 1 exists because of the scope for error in transforming the existing system to an online solution. This is particularly true for target system 2 because of the use of new technology. The impact of this factor could be a system which fails. MIS's sound understanding of the existing system, coupled with its recent experience with new technology, leads it to believe that the probability of this factor occurring is very low.

Table 6.10 Risk factors for redesign with reuse

	Risk factor	Class	Condition
1	Errors introduced during evolution	Avoidable	No risk
2	Unpredictable target system performance	Avoidable	Moderate
3	Lack of skills for target technology	Unavoidable	Moderate

Risk factors 2 and 3 require some action. MIS believes that the mainframe can manage online accesses from outlets in addition to providing existing services to head office and the warehouse. MIS would simulate the increased load on the mainframe to ensure that the target system would perform adequately. A mainframe upgrade may be required to mitigate this risk. Despite the learning curve associated with distributed system development, some MIS personnel have gained experience with distributed technology. MIS would, nevertheless, respond to this risk factor by further training.

To complete its service, MIS selects the most appropriate System Evolution Strategy. The team has continued maintenance and two redesign-with-reuse strategies to choose from. Table 6.11 summarizes these strategies. Based on the following discussion, MIS recommends strategy 3, subject to BIB's budget constraint.

Continued maintenance loses its initial appeal because it is associated with relatively high costs over both the short and long terms. This is due to BIB's continued investment in legacy technology.

Table 6.11 Possible evolution strategies

	Strategy 1 Continued maintenance	Strategy 2 Redesign with reuse Target system 1	Strategy 3 Redesign with reuse Target system 2
Costs			
Strategy	Low	Low-medium	Medium
Short-term	Low-medium	Low	Low
Long-term	High	Medium	Low-medium
Critical risk factors	Dated operational environment Support for evolution requirements	Target system performance	Target system performance Lack of skills for target technology
Benefits	Strategy costs Adequate support for business process	Good support for business process Reduced operational costs	Good support for business process Reduced operational costs First stage of rearchitecturing
Evolution requirements satisfied	1, 4, 5	1–6	1–6

Strategies 2 and 3 lead to a reduction in short-term costs because they decommission the minicomputers. MIS expects strategy 3 to bring the lowest long-term costs because it involves a significant departure from legacy technology. The use of modern distributed technology for outlets means that outlet software would be relatively cheap to procure, license and change. For example, MIS could implement the application logic for outlets using a current 4GL, such as Microsoft's Visual Basic. Rather than build the application from scratch, engineers could exploit the Componentware market which has emerged for COTS DCOM objects.

Strategies 2 and 3 also offer better support for BIB's business process and evolution requirements than the first strategy. Strategy 1 maintains the current level of support for the business, which although adequate is not ideal. The root cause for these functional drawbacks is that outlets do not have online access to head office data. Implementation of evolution requirements 2 and 3 may actually be better managed by manual procedures if the system is not reengineered.

BIB operates in an industry which, according to the Application Business Expert, is forecasted to grow. It would be wise for BIB to invest in its system to exploit forthcoming opportunities. While it is difficult to look beyond the current evolution requirements, a system which is built using modern technology is likely to be more able to evolve and integrate tomorrow's requirements than BIB's legacy system.

Strategy 3 offers an incremental path for system rearchitecturing which enables BIB to spread the costs and risks of system evolution. The mainframe installation could subsequently be migrated to servers running a relational database/4GL solution. The system would retain and integrate the PC/server combination for outlets with the reengineered head office solution. The ultimate result of rearchitecturing would be an open system, able to interoperate with others if necessary to exploit future opportunities.

Having completed the service, BIB should consider MIS's recommendations. If BIB is interested in either strategy 2 or 3, MIS should perform another iteration of Plan Evolution to build on the first. In particular, the MIS team should carry out a more detailed assessment to validate the evolution strategy.

At the end of the second iteration of Plan Evolution, BIB should make a commitment as whether to proceed with reengineering. Should BIB choose to continue, MIS should customize the remaining phases of the method to manage the implementation of the strategy. During any subsequent iterations of the method, material gathered in earlier iterations can of course be reused.

6.3   Scenario 2: Evolution Strategy Implementation

In this scenario, we show how you can use Renaissance to manage an evolution project which has fundamentally different technical, business and organizational characteristics from the first scenario. In this case, BIB's senior management mandates a package solution to support a radically changed business process. In addition, MIS has not built up a wealth of knowledge of BIB's system. MIS's first contact with BIB is the acquisition of a contract to replace BIB's system with the proposed package.

BIB's management team has operated a policy of minimizing short-term IT costs and has not understood the need for quality software engineering practice. Consequently, MIS has selected several software houses, based on cost alone, to maintain its system.

BIB's IT policy has, paradoxically, resulted in a system which is very expensive to maintain. The lack of continuity in maintenance personnel and poor change management means that the system is poorly documented and suffers from structural decay. MIS has little understanding of the system's internal workings and, from initial studies, engineers have not been able to identify the impact of change scenarios.

Recently, BIB procured the services of a business analyst to discuss the organization's future. The analyst developed two business goals:

1   *Expand geographically.* In this scenario, opportunities exist for BIB to expand far beyond its current regions. Similarly to Scenario 1, the DIY industry is growing and the analyst expects this growth to be sustained in the future. Expansion is, however, constrained by the single warehouse located near head office, so the business analyst suggests that BIB introduces a second warehouse in the North.

2   *Provide just-in-time delivery services to customers.* Currently, customers order products from outlets and return to collect them once the goods have been

transferred from the warehouse. The analyst suggests that when a customer orders products from an outlet, BIB should offer to deliver them directly to the customer instead of the outlet. Not only does this solution provide a customer delivery service, but it provides a faster and more direct route between the warehouse and customer.

The business analyst points out that the idea behind shortening the warehouse–outlet–customer chain can also be used to provide a direct distribution channel from suppliers to outlets and customers. It may be possible for suppliers to deliver directly to outlets rather than the warehouse. Similarly, suppliers could deliver to BIB's customers directly, bypassing both the warehouse and outlets. Just-in-time delivery schemes may not always be appropriate, and in any case they require cooperation from suppliers. However, where BIB can exploit them they provide BIB with an advantage over competing organizations.

Distributed warehouses and just-in-time delivery services change BIB's business process substantially. The analyst stresses that before BIB implements either business goal, its system should be able to support the necessary functionality. Both business goals introduce new complexity, which can only be managed effectively with an information system.

Once a suitable system is in place, the analyst recommends that BIB implements the business goals incrementally. Initially, BIB should introduce the just-in-time delivery service to provide a direct path between the warehouse and customers. BIB should delay introducing other just-in-time services which involve suppliers until it has spoken with its suppliers.

The business analyst recommends the use of a software package to support BIB's reengineered business process. The package is designed explicitly for the wholesale and retail industry. It defines a generic business process model which developers tailor to the needs of a particular organization. Development involves completing logical forms and assigning values to parameters instead of writing more imperative instructions in a 3GL or 4GL. The business analyst recommends the package because it offers:

- *An evolutionary product*. The package is subject to continuous improvement. Its vendors respond to changes in the wholesale/retail industry by revising the package regularly. Recently, they released a version with support for building applications with WWW user interfaces. Currently, they are examining the impact of the European single currency on the industry.

- *Modularity*. The package is modular and modules share information stored in a relational database. MIS can select and license only those modules which are necessary for BIB's enterprise. Modules include sales, purchasing, inventory, logistics, accounting, payroll and forecasting.

- *Support for rapid application development*. Assuming engineers are suitably trained, they can develop an application relatively quickly. Package abstractions manage much of the wholesale/retail industry's complexity. Development and evolution costs are thus low.

- *High vendor quality.* The package vendor's future looks assured. Over the last five years, it has been widely used for wholesale–retail organizations. The vendor has experienced substantial growth in recent years.

- *Reduced operating costs.* The package runs on PCs and servers, which are considerably cheaper to maintain than mainframe technology.

6.3.1 Method Customization

MIS tailors the method so that it supports the task of replacing BIB's current system with the proposed solution. Figure 6.13 shows that the team selects all phases of the method. MIS does not, however, perform the Assess Current Situation or Select Target activities, since BIB mandates the target solution. It is pointless to examine the costs, benefits and risks of the package because the business analyst has carried out a similar exercise.

One constraint which bears heavily on the project is that MIS should minimize disruption to BIB's trade when it deploys the system. MIS makes a number of adjustments to Renaissance's process to satisfy this constraint:

- In this scenario, Plan Evolution is concerned with managing the implementation of an evolution strategy. Activities Plan Deployment and Plan Evolution Project are brought forward to phase Plan Evolution.

- The team expects to migrate the majority of the current system's data to the new system. In MIS's experience, much data in commercial data processing systems remains largely invariable. This constitutes "static" data, which we introduced in Chapter 2. To migrate static data early and in parallel with other activities, MIS moves Migrate Data from phase Deliver and Use to Implement.

- BIB requires that its employees are trained and ready to use the system before it is deployed. Consequently, MIS moves Train Operators from phase Deploy to Deliver and Use.

At this stage, MIS adds three documents to the repository:

1 Business Goals. MIS records the business goals generated by the business analyst.

2 Business Process Description. MIS structures this document in three parts:

   (i) *Current business process.* MIS elaborates on the description we presented in Section 6.1 and uses it to help it to understand the current situation.

   (ii) *Revised business process.* This part describes the revised business process, which includes the just-in-time warehouse to customer service and online access to head office's system from outlets. Initially, the target system will support this process.

   (iii) *Proposed business process changes.* This section documents the business analyst's suggestions for distributed warehousing and additional just-in-time services. MIS expects to implement these changes as part of subsequent improvements to BIB's system.

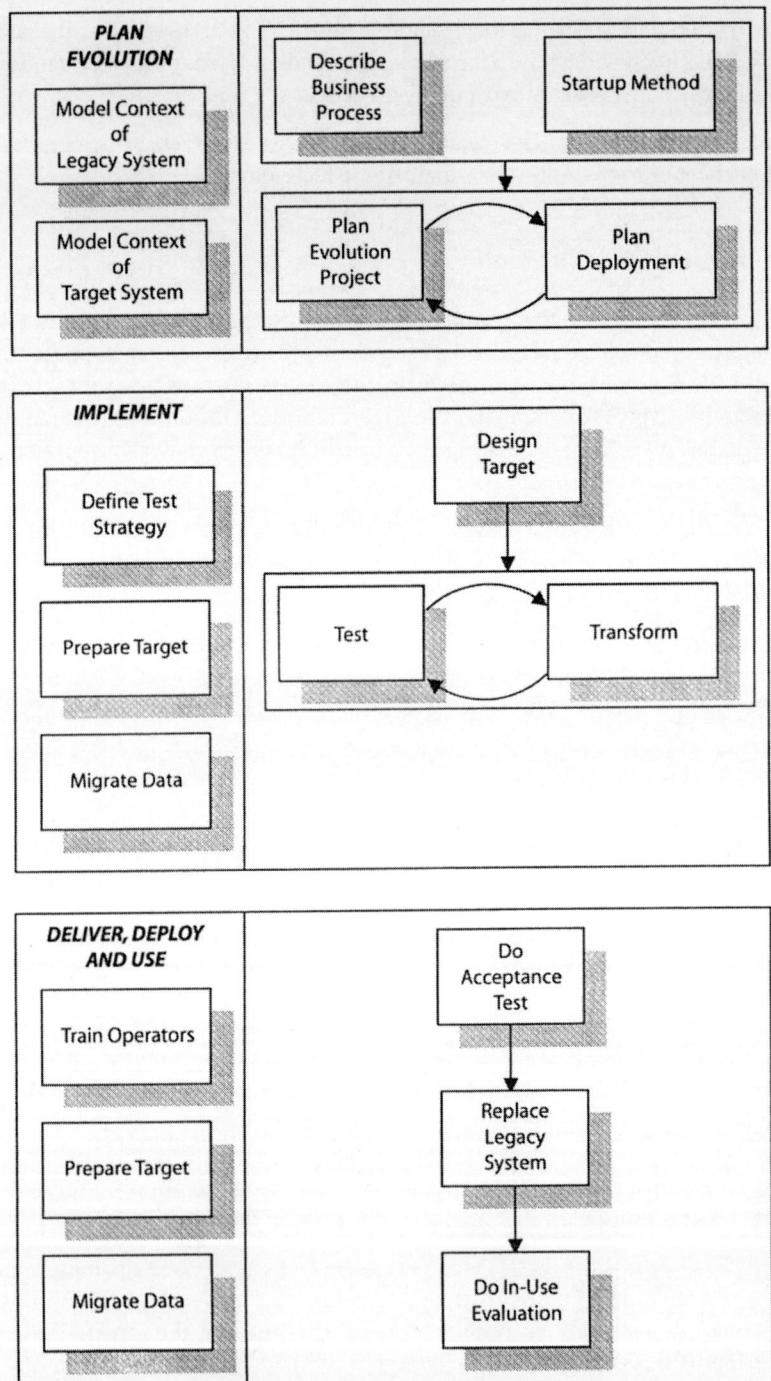

Fig. 6.13 Customized process model.

3 *Problem statement.* The problem in this case is clear – to make the transition from BIB's current mainframe system to the distributed package solution. The MIS team documents the deployment constraint for minimal disruption to BIB's operation.

Figure 6.14 shows the documents which MIS develops during the course of the project. MIS selects them from the repository introduced in Chapter 2. Noticeable omissions include the Assessment Report for both the legacy and target systems, and the Evolution Strategy documents. These are not necessary in this scenario because of the prescribed solution.

To complete the customization process, MIS identifies project responsibilities. Table 6.12 shows the responsibilities for MIS personnel. Renaissance defines the Legacy System Developer responsibility, which requires individuals who have a good technical knowledge of a legacy system. In this scenario, MIS cannot meet this responsibility, but it needs to understand parts of BIB's system. Data is particularly important, since MIS expects to migrate much of BIB's data for use by the target application. To address this need, MIS assigns the Modeller responsibility to suitable engineers who will construct data models.

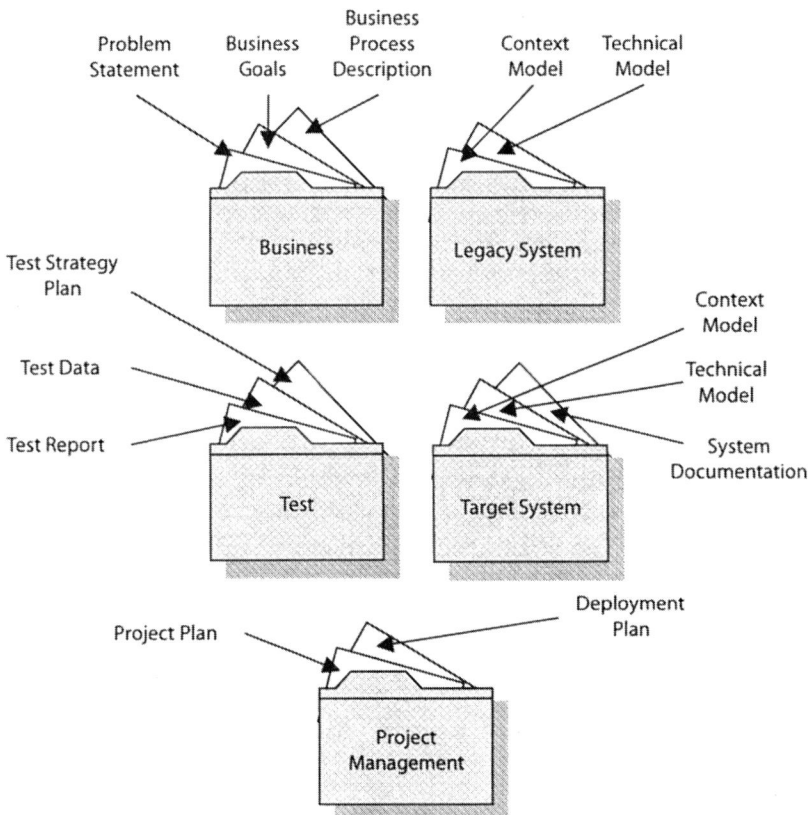

Fig. 6.14 Repository contents on completion of the method.

Table 6.12 MIS's responsibilities

Modeller
Network Engineer
Quality Engineer
Software Engineer
Software Project Manager
Package Expert

Table 6.12 also introduces two new responsibilities: engineer and Network Engineer. Renaissance does not define them since they are project-specific. The former requires an expert in WARIS application development who can advise other project members on appropriate use of the technology. The latter is necessary to install and configure the hardware infrastructure which hosts the WARIS application.

BIB's responsibilities are unchanged from the first scenario. A critical responsibility which neither MIS nor BIB can meet is organizational change management. To succeed, this project requires commitment and cooperation from all levels of BIB personnel. A project may fail if system users are divorced from the evolution process. BIB introduce a Change Manager to liaise with MIS and BIB to ensure that tasks which are dependent on BIB's staff are appropriately addressed from a human perspective.

6.3.2   Evolution Project

The evolution strategy in this scenario is a hybrid strategy which involves replacing the majority of the system, but reengineering its data. During Plan Deployment, MIS considers how it can deploy the target system while minimizing disturbance to BIB.

Of the deployment approaches introduced in Chapter 2, incremental deployment is the preferred approach because you can gradually reengineer a system without any significant loss of service. In this case, however, the extent of evolution means that incremental deployment is unsuitable. The business process changes, coupled with the shift in implementation technology, mean that MIS cannot evolve BIB's legacy system to the target system in a series of increments.

The two coexistence approaches to system deployment support more extensive reengineering strategies than incremental deployment. The first approach involves replacing legacy system components with target system components. Throughout deployment, there are two operational systems and the services they provide are mutually exclusive. As you deploy a target system component which implements services, you should decommission the component(s) of the legacy system which provide those services. Depending on the services they need, system operators use either the legacy or target system. The second coexistence approach results in two separate systems running through the deployment period.

In Chapter 2, we pointed out that both coexistence approaches are suited to service oriented systems. MIS, however, classifies BIB's system as data-oriented. The MIS team sees the first coexistence approach as unworkable because both legacy and target components need access to the system's data during the deployment period. MIS could replicate the data for each system, but maintaining consistency between the replicas would be complex and error-prone. MIS rules out the second coexistence approach for similar reasons.

MIS cannot avoid the Big Bang approach to deployment, which incurs some loss of system service. With thorough planning, however, MIS can minimize the period over which the system is unavailable. MIS performs activities Plan Deployment and Plan Evolution Project, and schedules as many tasks as possible for completion before shutting down BIB's current system. This means that, during deployment, MIS should only have tasks remaining which cannot be performed prior to deployment. Figure 6.15 shows project milestones which reflect MIS's project and deployment planning.

Deployment tasks include shutting down BIB's current system, migrating dynamic data, and inspecting the target system before it is used. MIS's Project Manager estimates that 20 person days are required to perform these tasks, and (subject to resource constraints) they can be completed within one working week. Based on initial project planning, MIS develop a Deployment Plan. Table 6.13 shows the main points of this plan.

Outlets will remain open throughout deployment, but they will only sell customers what they have in stock. They will not be able to order stock or make stock enquiries since all head office functions will be unavailable. Outlet staff will keep manual records of transactions.

According to BIB's research, the third week of January is statistically the quietest week for trade throughout the year. Consumers tend to overspend over the Christmas and New Year period, which results in a drop in retail activity afterwards. There are fewer wholesale customers during January because of cold weather and because their trade is also affected by consumer spending.

Table 6.13 Deployment plan summary

BIB operates in reduced form throughout the deployment period.

Deployment is scheduled for January, with contingency periods in February and October.

MIS gives BIB one month's notice of deployment. During this time, MIS prepares itself, its customers, and its suppliers for deployment.

MIS rehearses deployment in a simulated environment with real data.

All tasks which can be completed before deployment will be. These include:

- Migrating static data.
- Acceptance testing.
- Installing the target system's infrastructure.
- Training operators.

The deployment period will be one working week.

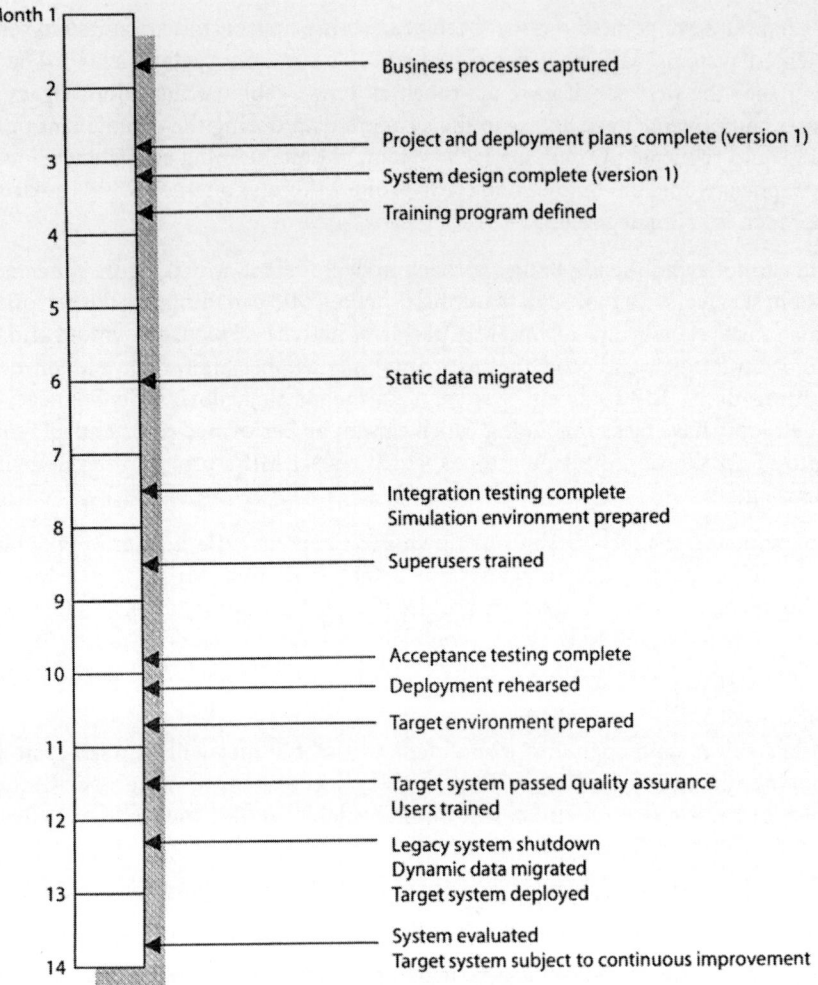

Fig. 6.15 Project milestones.

BIB addresses the possibility of delayed deployment with an alternative period set in late January or February. Although trade picks up in February, it is still a relatively quiet time of year. Beyond February, BIB enjoys busy trade until October, where there are usually a couple of quiet weeks preceding the run-up to Christmas. To handle the worst-case scenario, where deployment is delayed beyond February, BIB suggests a fortnight in October.

The Change Manager assists BIB to plan for deployment during the one month notice period. BIB wants to reduce the volume of dynamic data to migrate over deployment, so the Change Manager advises BIB to order products from suppliers during this period only if the supplier can deliver the goods and invoice BIB before deployment. This reduces the number of unpaid transactions which need to be carried forward to the target system. The Change Manager suggests similar techniques for reducing other dynamic data.

MIS identifies the risk factors, introduced in Chapter 3, which are present in this project (Table 6.14). The first factor is associated with evolution strategies which involve replacing legacy system components. In this case, MIS engineers discard the legacy code which implements BIB's application logic, and reimplement much of it using new technology. MIS thus faces the risk of losing business knowledge during this transformation. To manage this risk, the engineers develop context models of the existing system to ensure that they have a sound understanding of the legacy system's behaviour. In addition, MIS talks to BIB individuals who have been assigned the User and Legacy System Functional Expert responsibilities.

Table 6.14 Project risk factors

1	Loss of embedded business rules
2	Lack of system knowledge
3	Operational organization not committed to staff training
4	Errors introduced during evolution
5	Inadequate or inconsistent documentation

MIS responds to risk factors 2, 4 and 5 in a similar way to the first factor. Gaining a sufficient understanding of the legacy and target systems can control all these factors. MIS has developed a sound base of skills in using the proposed package technology to develop applications, so the team does not need to train further to combat risk factor 4.

The Change Manager is responsible for managing risk factor 3. Since the project incurs both business process changes and technology changes, it requires commitment from BIB personnel. To improve the chances of project success, BIB personnel should understand how their new system impacts their jobs and how they should use the system. Table 6.15 summarizes the Change Manager's involvement in the project.

Table 6.15 Change Manager responsibilities

Define system user procedures
Manage training of BIB personnel
Disseminate information to BIB individuals
Assist BIB to prepare for deployment
Develop documentation for system users

The Change Manager handles information dissemination throughout the project by writing a short monthly magazine which keeps BIB personnel informed of project progress. The magazine describes the motivation and benefits of the target system in a way that users can understand. In addition, it explains how jobs will change and informs readers of project tasks which affect them.

MIS's Modellers develop models of the target system, planned iterations of the target system and selected parts of the legacy system. They focus on the legacy system's behaviour and data, because much of these form part of the target system. It is unnecessary to build models of other legacy system components, such as software and hardware architectures, since they are redundant in the target system.

MIS develops a series of use case diagrams to capture the behaviour which is common to both the legacy and target systems. For data modelling, they use reverse engineering tools to help extract logical models from VSAM structures and IDMS schemas. Tool support is essential in this case because of the absence of documentation and suitable technical individuals. Figure 6.16 shows part of the output from the reverse engineering tool. It is an ER diagram which captures part of BIB's system's logical data model. These data models support data migration and provide a starting point for developing target system data structures.

For the target system, modellers focus on its behaviour, data and architecture. The modellers extend the earlier use case diagrams to include the just-in-time customer delivery services and online stock reservation. Figure 6.17 uses a UML deployment diagram to show how the package solution is deployed on the target architecture.

In addition to modelling the legacy and target systems, MIS considers subsequent evolution requirements and builds models of future versions of the target system.

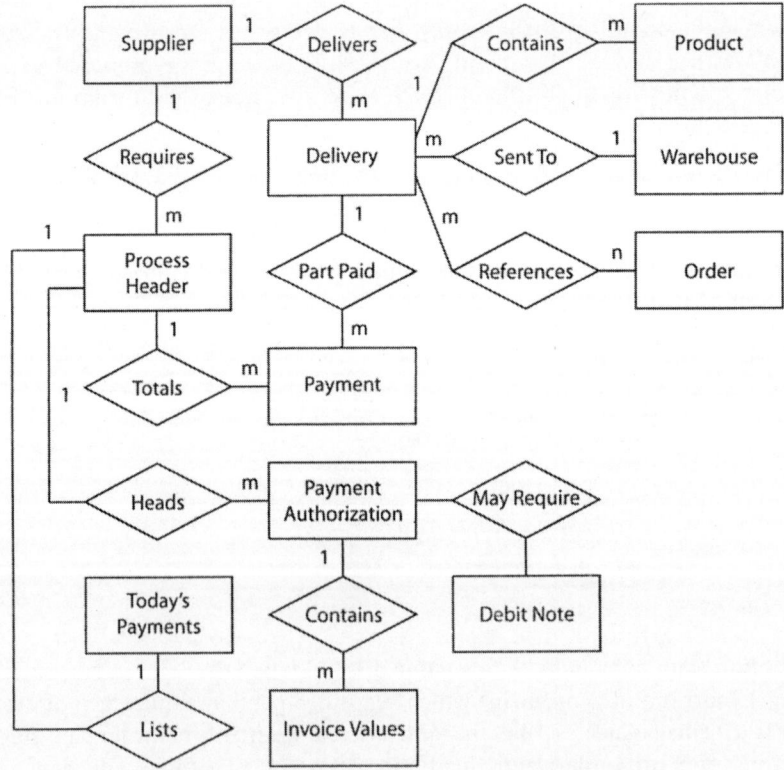

Fig. 6.16 Technical model extracted from BIB's legacy system.

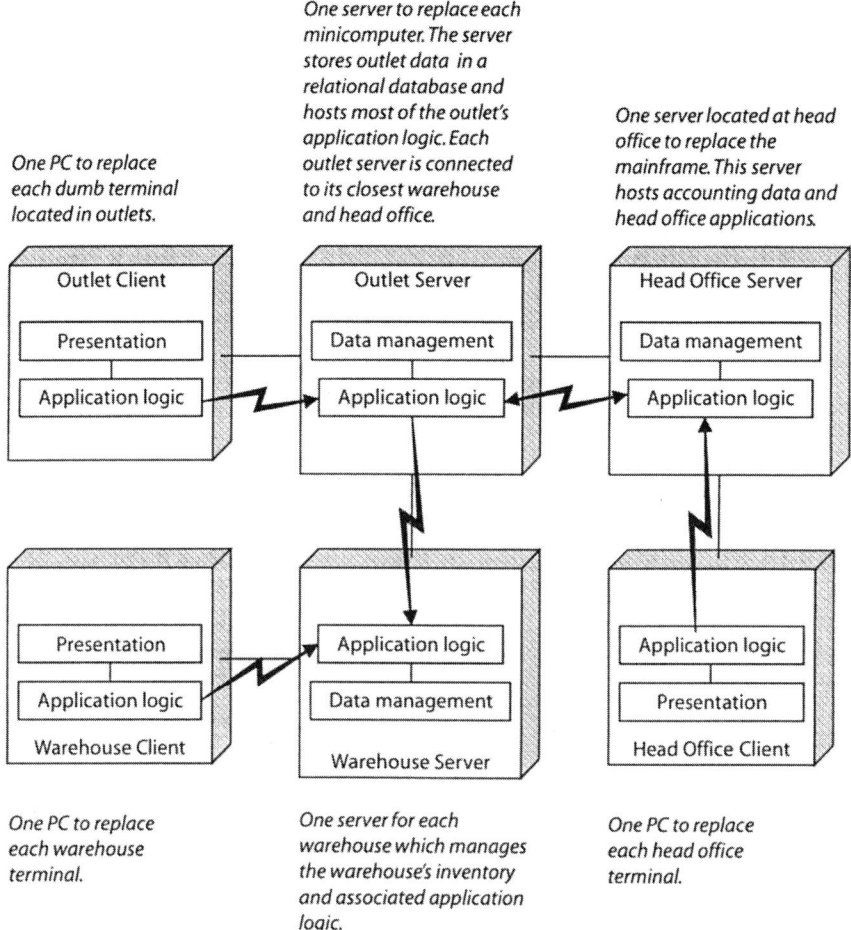

Fig. 6.17 Target system architecture.

The team anticipates that the target system will evolve to support multiple warehouses and additional just-in-time services. An objective of MIS's design of the target system is to develop a system which is able to accommodate these requirements without subverting its structure. This contributes to pre-planned product improvement, which we introduced in Chapter 1.

MIS engineers start the Implement phase with activity Design Target and develop earlier context models of the target system into a system design. They use the technical modelling techniques, introduced in Chapter 4, to contribute to the design process. By building more detailed models, MIS finds that the IDMS structure can be improved. Several years of maintenance mean that the data's logical structure is overly complex.

MIS reengineers the logical data model not only to improve its structure, but also to integrate the future data requirements. With the aid of tool support, engineers generate relational schemas from the reengineered data model. MIS defines data mapping rules which the tool uses to automate much of the transformation process. The volume of BIB's data means that a manual transformation would be impractical. Nevertheless, engineers validate the resulting data by manual inspection to ensure that integrity rules have been preserved. MIS employs a similar approach for migrating VSAM data to the relational database.

The MIS team distinguishes between static and dynamic data. The former is data which remains largely invariable, and the latter generally equates to transaction data. In BIB's case, static data includes supplier, customer, product and personnel information. BIB's dynamic data corresponds to outstanding orders, unpaid invoices and customer accounts.

In Migrate Data, MIS engineers migrate BIB's static data, which, in effect, creates a replica of legacy data on the target system. MIS controls this replication by a configuration management programme. Whenever BIB personnel change data which MIS has replicated, MIS updates the relational database. Although changes are infrequent, it is vital that MIS manages them so that the target system can be loaded with accurate data.

In parallel with data migration, other MIS engineers work with the Quality Engineer during Define Test Strategy. The absence of documentation means that there are no original test cases or test data which MIS can use to test parts of the target system. MIS develops new test cases and test data which are largely based on the earlier context models. The Test Strategy Plan comprises:

- *Unit testing*. MIS develops artificial test data for each module and uses it to test modules once they have been implemented.

- *Integration testing*. When all modules have been implemented, MIS uses the data which it used for unit testing to test the complete system. Prior to integration testing, software engineers and the Network Engineer prepare a simulation environment which they use to test the interfaces between outlets, the warehouse and head office.

- *Acceptance testing*. At this stage, MIS uses a copy of the "real" data which has been migrated to the target system. BIB operators use the simulation environment throughout acceptance testing. The Change Manager ensures that those operators who are involved in acceptance testing have been suitably trained beforehand.

- *Stress testing*. MIS manage stress testing similarly to acceptance testing, but in this case, all operators use the system simultaneously. MIS stress test the system to reveal potential performance problems. MIS aims to resolve any problems by scheduling particular system tasks, such as management report generation, to times when the system is not heavily loaded.

MIS practises migrating dynamic data as part of rehearsing deployment. Engineers find that some data mapping rules can be improved to better exploit the tool's automation capabilities. Engineers strive to get the most out of the tool to reduce the time they spend on data migration and validation during deployment.

Prepare Target involves two tasks: preparing the simulation environment for acceptance and stress testing, and laying the target system's foundations at head office, outlets and the warehouse. The simulation environment consists of several PC clients (one for each area of BIB's business), servers and the network. With the simulation environment in place, MIS engineers install and configure the hardware infrastructure at BIB's sites. They install support software such as the relational database, remote connectivity middleware and the package's run-time environment. The Change Manager ensures that the latter task does not disrupt BIB by installing the target system outside of BIB's normal trading hours.

The Change Manager prepares an operator training program for the Train Operators activity of phase Deliver and Use. He splits BIB personnel into two classes: "superusers" and "users". Superusers are approachable individuals who have a sound understanding of their role within BIB and can communicate well. These qualities make them suitable for being involved in acceptance testing and for training other users. The Change Manager takes one superuser from each area of BIB's business and trains them before acceptance testing. After acceptance testing, superusers train other users.

Once MIS deploys the target system, BIB evaluates it. The reengineered system satisfies its users, since much of the legacy system's data has survived and is used by the package solution. Although the original application source code has been discarded, MIS has extracted its behaviour using modelling techniques. The target system is well documented and is prepared for an extended evolutionary life. MIS should manage the system according to the evolutionary paradigm to prevent the legacy phenomenon from reoccurring.

References and Further Reading

RENAISSANCE Consortium (1998) *Renaissance Method Handbook.* http://www.comp.lancs.ac.uk/projects/renaissance/.
RENAISSANCE Consortium (1998) *Evolution Planning.* Consultancy report, http://www.comp.lancs.ac.uk/projects/renaissance/.
RENAISSANCE Consortium (1998) *Architectural Modelling.* Consultancy report, http://www.comp.lancs.ac.uk/projects/renaissance/.
RENAISSANCE Consortium (1998) *Client/server migration.* Consultancy report, http://www.comp.lancs.ac.uk/projects/renaissance/.

Key Points

- Renaissance supports both long-term evolution planning and evolution project management.

- An evolution strategy depends on technical, business and organizational factors. The method provides guidelines for selecting an evolution strategy based on these factors.

■ Evolution projects involve activities not found in development projects. Renaissance provides guidance for these activities, which include migrating data, deploying the target system, incremental reengineering and integrating legacy system components with a target solution.

■ System modelling supports many evolution activities by enabling you to gain a good understanding of legacy and target systems. The degree of modelling you should do depends on factors such as the availability of maintenance staff and documentation.

■ Scenario 1 shows the benefits of a technically mature approach to system evolution. Systems which are well documented and which retain sound structures are more responsive to change.

■ Once reengineered, you should manage a system according to the evolutionary paradigm to prevent legacy problems from reoccurring.

7. *Case Study 2: Evolution of a Modern System*

Objectives

- To show that evolution problems are not constrained to dated legacy systems written in 3GLs.
- To show how you can customize Renaissance to the needs of a 4GL evolution project.
- To illustrate how you can use modelling techniques to support the development of evolvable 4GL systems.

Contents

This case study complements Chapter 6, whose material was based on a combination of legacy systems and evolution scenarios which we have experienced. We took this approach in Chapter 6 to demonstrate much of Renaissance. We also discussed, in some detail, the motivation and rationale for carrying out particular activities. In this chapter, we present a less detailed account of one particular evolution project which we managed using Renaissance. Table 7.1 summarizes those parts of Renaissance which we illustrate in this chapter.

This project involved a five-year-old client/server system. Despite its relative youth and the use of modern implementation technology, the system suffered from some of the legacy system characteristics introduced in Chapter 1. In particular, some of its components were complex and its documentation inconsistent. From the users' point of view, the system's performance was unsatisfactory.

We include this particular case study because it illustrates that modern technology, by itself, does not guarantee evolvable systems. Organizational factors, such as the availability of engineers who have experience with relevant implementation

Table 7.1 Demonstration of Renaissance

Method	Used to develop a suitable evolution strategy and to manage implementing a target system
Process	Phases 1 and 2
Customization	Process model Responsibilities Document repository
Evolution planning	Legacy system assessment Evolution strategy development Cost estimation and risk assessment
System modelling	Context modelling Technical modelling to support target system design
Migration to a distributed architecture	Consideration of a suitable logical architecture to improve the target system's performance and evolvability

technology and others who understand the system from technical and functional perspectives, affect system evolvability. In this chapter, the root cause of the system's poor performance was that it was originally implemented as a pilot project for a new technology.

The system, Cost Computing System (CCS), is one of many systems that collectively provide a set of services to a health insurance company. Figure 7.1 shows the structure of these applications. The applications are classified into two groups: operational systems and management information systems. The former provides services such as customer administration and payment management, while the latter supports managerial and strategic functions.

CCS is a medium-sized application and has been implemented in Centura's SQLWindows. SQLWindows is a modern 4GL which is well suited to developing two-tier client server systems. All operational systems have been implemented using Uniface, which is another 4GL, but is more suited to enterprise-scale applications.

As part of its long-term strategy, our client intends to integrate the management information systems with the operational systems. Both types of systems are independent and our client requires that they become more interoperable. Of all the management information systems, CCS has a relatively high business value, so our client requested that we start with this application.

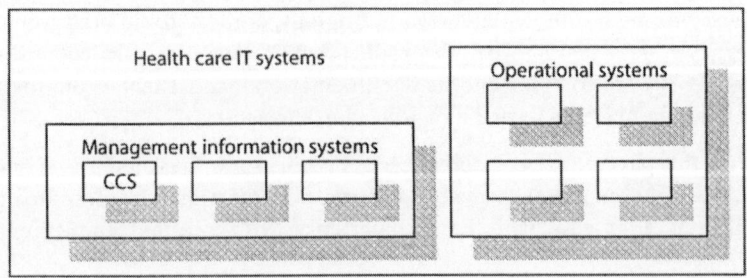

Fig. 7.1 Health insurance applications.

Before we reengineered CCS, our client's industry started going through a period of extensive change. Our client expected that this would generate significantly more data for CCS to process. Since CCS struggled to provide satisfactory response times with its original load, the anticipated increase in load further contributed to the need for reengineering.

7.1 Overview

To manage reengineering CCS, our engineers tailored the method's process model according to our organization's processes and the needs of this evolution project. In addition, we aimed to minimize the overhead of adopting Renaissance. In particular:

- We have well-established system delivery and deployment procedures, so we did not use Renaissance's Deliver and Deploy and Use phases.

- We brought the Plan Evolution Project activity forward from phase Implement to Plan Evolution. Similarly to the second scenario in Chapter 6, we did not need to do much long-term planning, since our customer had defined clear objectives for its systems. We thus used phase Plan Evolution to manage the reengineering project.

- Software design is as important for 4GL as it is for 3GL applications. To address this, we created an explicit Design phase from decomposing Renaissance's Design Target activity into more detailed tasks. Since developing CCS, we have gained experience with 4GL and client/server technology. We used this experience to reengineer CCS according to a well-designed software architecture which aims to improve CCS's performance and evolvability.

- Similarly to the Design phase, we changed the Implement phase so that it is made up of less abstract activities. In particular, the Implement phase reflects our process for system testing.

- We integrated our method for business process reengineering (Business Process Optimization (BPO)) with Renaissance. Although there was no need for business process reengineering in this case, we used BPO to perform the Describe Business Process activity.

In this chapter, we use data flow diagrams to describe the customized process model. Data flow diagrams complement the static diagrams used in Chapters 2 and 6 by showing which activities produce and use particular documents. We use nodes to represent activities and tasks, and data stores for documents and other deliverables. Figure 7.2 shows the three phases of the modified process.

In Plan Evolution, we gained an understanding of CCS and created an abstract model of the target system. We then developed an evolution strategy for making the transition between CCS and the target system. During Design, we built technical models of both systems which helped us to identify and integrate reusable components. In phase Implement, we built and tested the target system.

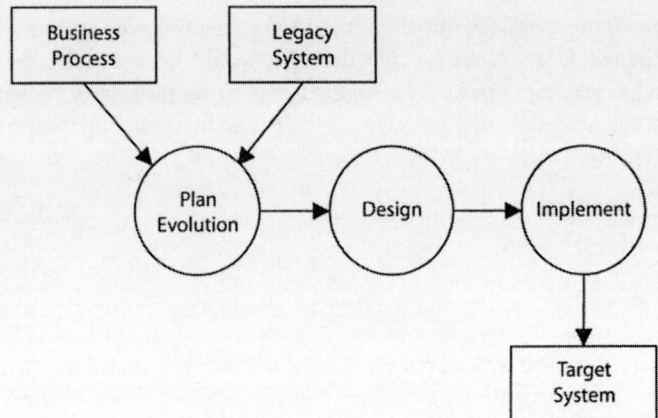

Fig. 7.2 Customized process model.

Figure 7.3 shows the data flow diagram for phase Plan Evolution. We had five objectives for this phase:

1 *To assess the legacy system.* We developed a context model of CCS to support the Assess Current Situation activity. Once engineers had a sufficient understanding of CCS, they were able to assess it effectively.

2 *To document the business process which the target system should support.* In parallel with the assessment activity, we performed Describe Business Process. We used BPO to capture the existing business process and considered minor improvements which the target system could support.

3 *To describe the target system at an abstract level.* During Model Context of Target System, we extended and refined CCS's Context Model into a model for the target system. This model captured new functional requirements and provided a high-level view of its software and hardware architectures. At this stage, we modelled two possible target systems.

4 *To develop an evolution strategy.* For each target system, we identified possible evolution strategies. We then considered their relative costs, benefits and risks which we used to select the most appropriate target system and evolution strategy.

5 *To prepare a project plan.* When we completed the above activities, we had sufficient information to construct a project plan to implement the evolution strategy. Since we had our own procedures for system delivery and deployment, project planning was similar to planning development projects. We used our own techniques and processes to define milestones, develop work packages, manage resources and perform other project planning tasks.

Figure 7.4 introduces a number of new activities. During Analyze Requirements we generated a set of requirements for the target system based on the Business Process Description and Context Model documents.

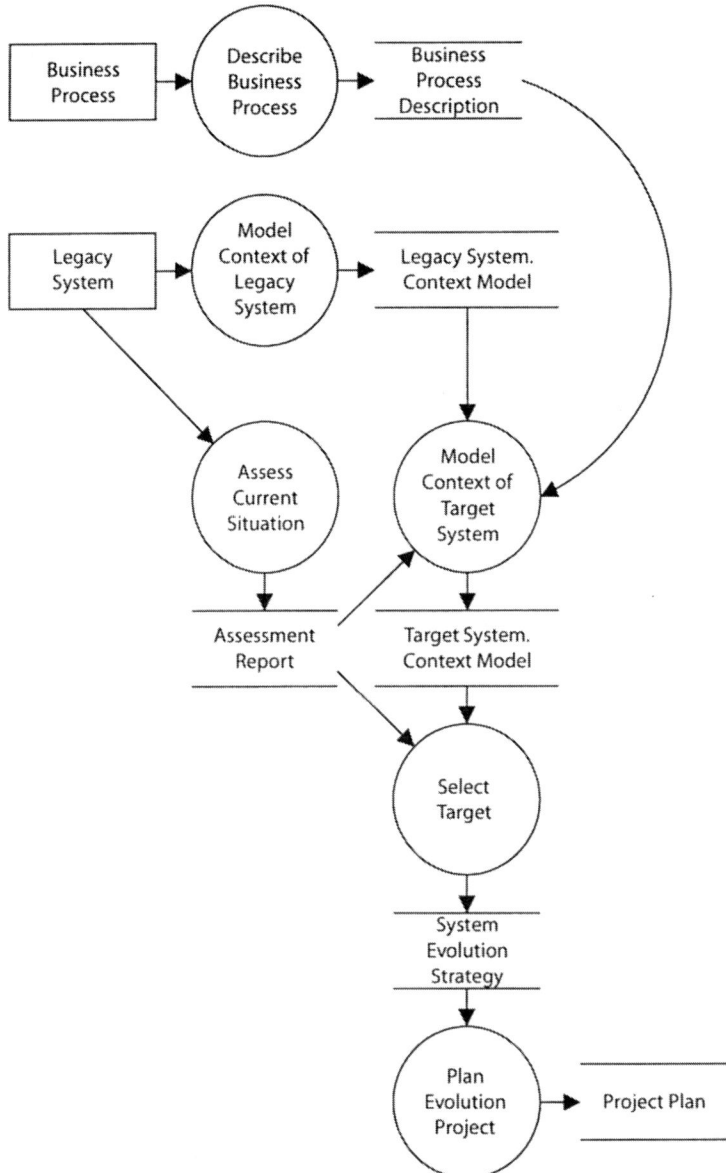

Fig. 7.3 The Plan Evolution phase.

While engineers were involved in documenting requirements, others built technical models of the legacy system. The aim of Build Technical Model of Legacy System was to identify those components of CCS which could be reused in the target system. We focused on only those components which looked promising for reuse since it was pointless to develop detailed models of components which clearly did not feature in the target system.

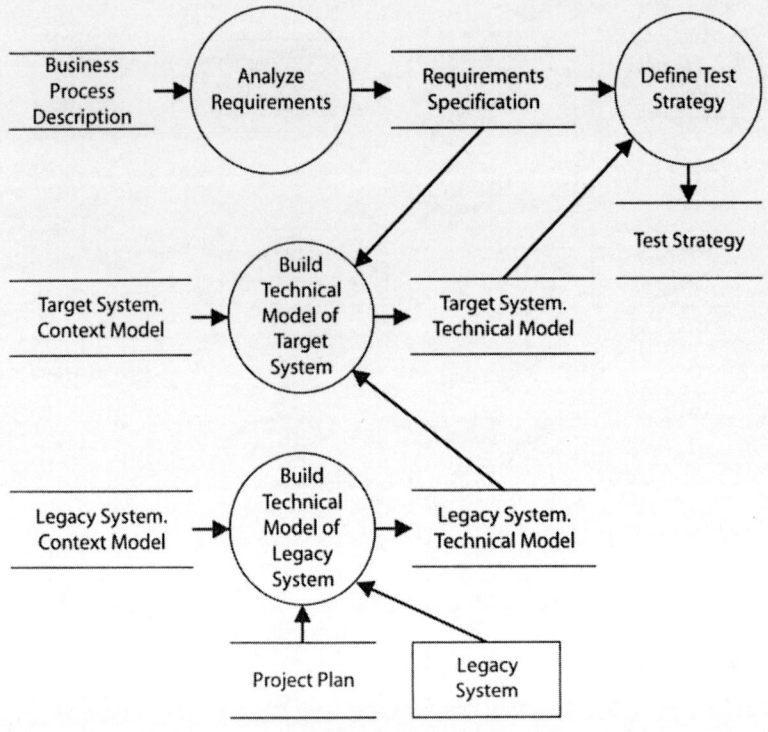

Fig. 7.4 The Design phase.

In Build Technical Model of Target System, engineers extended the legacy system's Technical Model with additional details to implement the target system's requirements. The target system's Technical Model served as a design document for the reengineered system, so our designers included sufficient information for programmers to create implementation units from it.

The last activity of phase Design was Define Test Strategy. During this activity, we documented the complete test strategy for the target system. We found that, in addition to the resources allocated to testing during earlier project planning, further resources were required. This caused us to perform another iteration of Plan Evolution Project.

Figure 7.5 shows the revised Implement phase. The objectives of this phase were to implement the target system, using the technical design model, and to test it according to the Test Strategy. We used a typical process for system testing which involved unit testing, integration testing, and system testing. We tested reusable components from the legacy system as we integrated them with the target system.

To carry out the new process, we selected individuals to meet the responsibilities shown in Table 7.2. Since we were not using Renaissance for long-term planning, system delivery or deployment, we didn't need much input from our client. In this

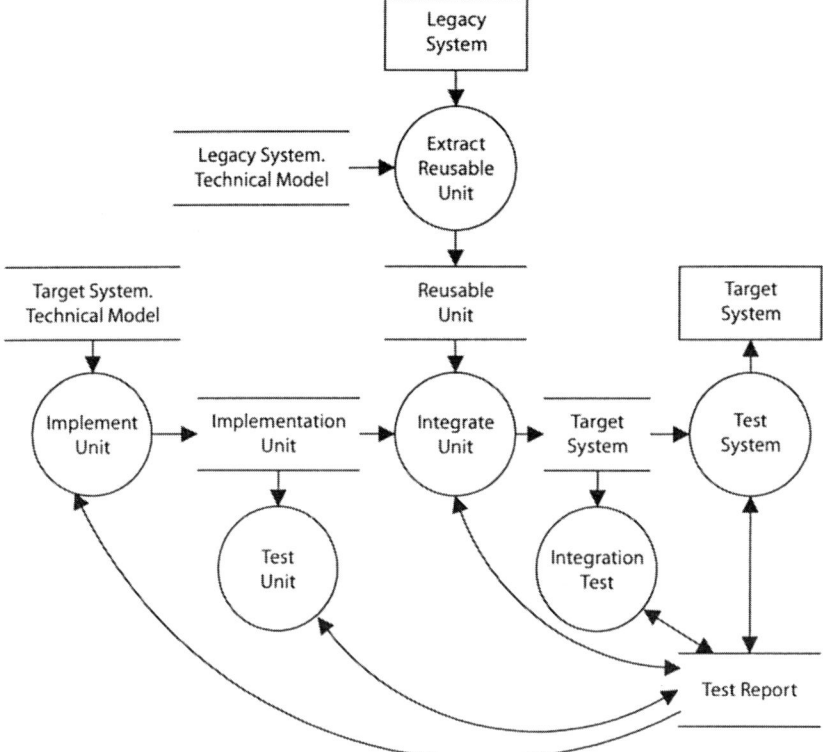

Fig. 7.5 The Implement phase.

Table 7.2 Project responsibilities

Software Project Manager
Modeller
Legacy System Developer
Software Architect
Quality Engineer
Software Engineer
Client Representative

case, we liaised with an individual from our client's organization who met the responsibilities of Client Representative.

Several of our software engineers met the remaining responsibilities. Engineers who had maintained CCS met the responsibility of Legacy System Developer. They worked with Modellers, who were competent in using the UML, to build context models of CCS. An experienced designer filled the role of Software Architect to ensure that the target system met its performance and evolvability requirements. This designer was also the Software Project Manager. For Quality Engineer, we picked an experienced software engineer who had no other involvement in the project.

7.2   Legacy System Investigation

In any evolution project, you should first gain an understanding of the legacy system. In this case, we built a context model of CCS and used it to assess the system. In Chapter 4, we explained how context models support the process of understanding legacy systems. In summary, they:

● Provide high-level documentation for the legacy system.

● Provide a basis for assessing the legacy system.

● Support the process of choosing a suitable evolution strategy.

● Help you identify reusable components.

Since documentation for CCS was out of date, we built a set of context models which covered all context viewpoints: business, functional, structural and environment.

Figure 7.6 shows, using the UML's use case notation, the business activities which CCS supports. Simple users and advanced users regularly use the services on the right of the figure. Advanced users load the system with data using the "import allocation" service. They can subsequently process that data using "allocate OAS", which generates an operational accounting sheet (OAS). A simple user with restricted access rights can query this sheet using the "evaluate OAS" service. Administrators rarely use the services to the left of the figure.

We documented the functionality viewpoint using data flow diagrams. Figure 7.7 shows a context diagram which captures the flow of data between CCS and its environment. Modellers refined this diagram with a model which shows the data flow between the system's main processing functions (Fig. 7.8).

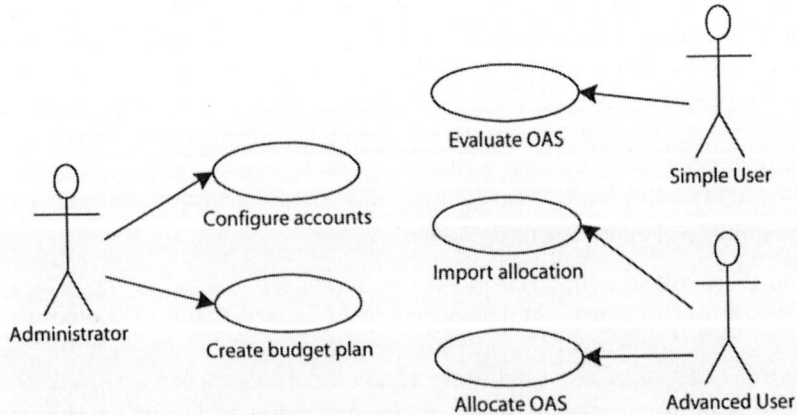

Fig. 7.6 Business activities supported by CCS.

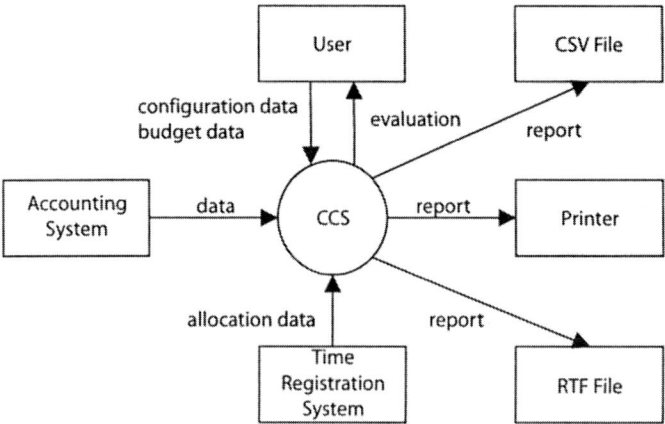

Fig. 7.7 Functional context of CCS.

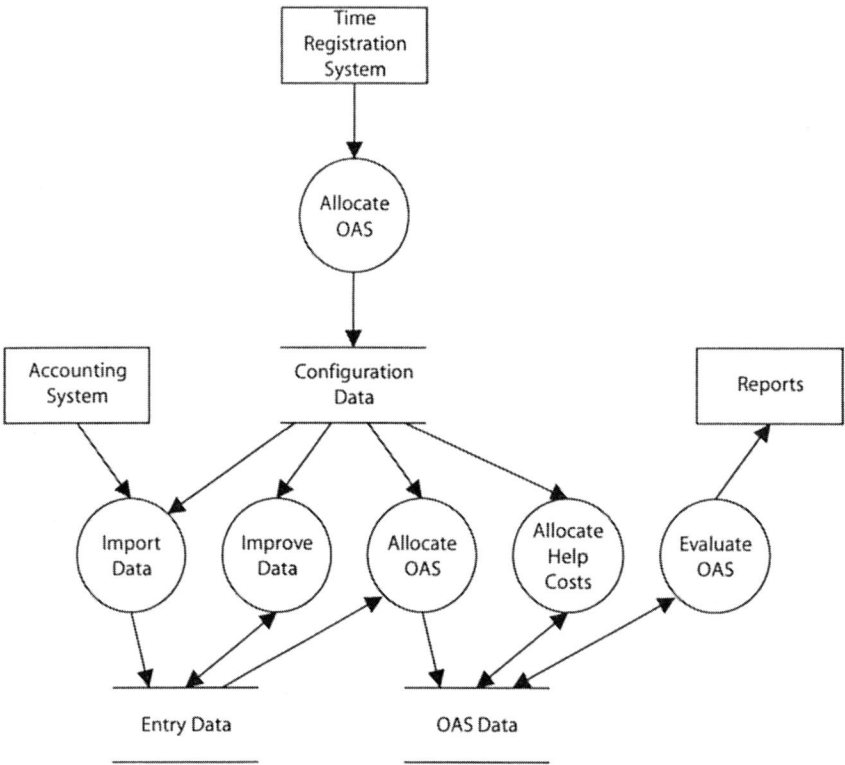

Fig. 7.8 Functional overview of CCS.

The context diagram shows that a separate system, the "accounting system", loads CCS with data. Another system, the "time registration" system, processes this data. Operators, captured in the earlier use case diagram, use the system's services to enter configuration and budget data and to receive evaluations. CCS produces a number of reports, of which the Rich Text Format (RTF) reports can be further processed by other applications.

Figure 7.8 shows CCS's internal data flow. At this abstract level we identified six functions and three data stores. CCS imports and validates the data from the accounting system using the configuration data from the time registration system. The "improve data" function optimizes the configuration data where possible. "Allocate OAS" integrates the entry data and configuration data with the OAS. The system produces the reports after it has evaluated the OAS data.

The system's functionality was implemented using a software structure which we captured with a block diagram (Fig. 7.9). CCS was built from three layers and seven logical blocks. The SQLWindows layer represents the 4GL components which implemented the application logic. BKK-Library is a collection of base classes provided by our client and Visual Toolchest is a third-party software product for SQLWindows applications.

The Component layer contains two COTS components: High Edit and Chart FX. The former is a word processor and Chart FX is a diagram generator. The Database layer comprised administration tables and CCS tables. Administration tables were implementation mechanisms and did not represent real-world entities. The CCS tables captured the application's operational data.

Figure 7.10 shows that CCS could be configured for three operational environments. The first solution involved one Windows-based PC which ran a single-user SQLBase relational database. This solution was scaled to a distributed client/server solution where clients hosted application logic and a server was responsible for data management. For larger systems, CCS could be deployed over a heterogeneous network with a Unix-based server running an Informix database.

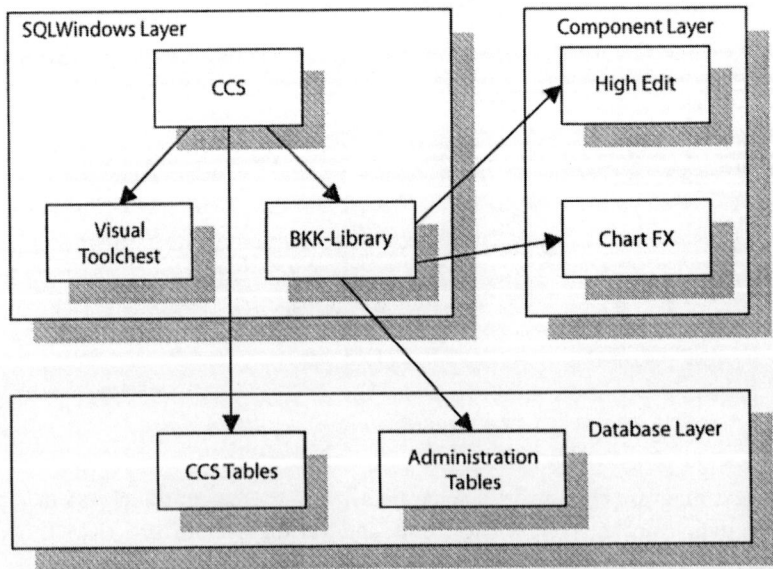

Fig. 7.9 CCS's software architecture.

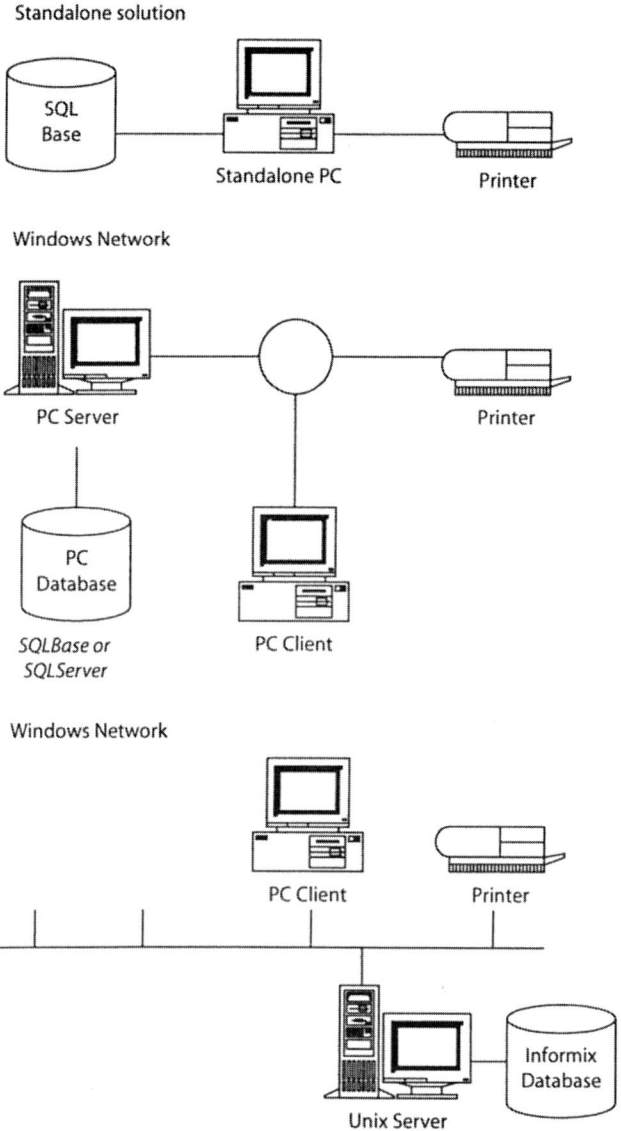

Fig. 7.10 CCS's operational environment.

Having built a set of context models, we had sufficient understanding of CCS to perform the Assess Current Situation activity. In Chapter 3, we described how you can assess a legacy system from technical, business and organizational perspectives. In this case, we did not need to assess CCS's business value, since the customer was convinced that it was sufficiently high to warrant reengineering. Table 7.3 summarizes the customer's view of CCS's business value.

Table 7.3 Business value

Attribute	Description
Supported business activities	Cost planning and monitoring
Supported functionality	Budget planning Accounting OAS evaluation
Market value	The cost explosion in national health care requires strict cost planning and monitoring. Health insurance has become a very competitive industry.
Contribution to profit	Cost control is essential to work profitably

We focused on assessing CCS's technical quality. We assessed the application at a high level and based assessment on the opinions of Legacy System Developers and Modellers. We selected system attributes from those introduced in Chapter 3 and refined them so that they were suitable for assessing a 4GL application. Rather than quantify them, we considered a brief description for each attribute to be sufficient. Table 7.4 shows how we refined attributes, such as size, and records our findings for application software.

As a consequence of implementing CCS as a pilot project for SQLWindows, CCS was more complex than necessary. During development of CCS, our engineers were learning how best to use SQLWindows and how to structure client/server systems.

Table 7.4 Technical quality of application software

Attribute	Description
Complexity	Much of the code was well structured, but we know of several components which were complex. Integrating Componentware units resulted in additional complexity.
External dependencies	Two import and three export interfaces. These interfaces provided for data input and report generation. Interface complexity was caused by support for different deployment configurations.
Test data	Some test data were available, but there were no test cases.
Age	The core components developed by us were five years old. We introduced additional components as part of our maintenance work.
Performance	CCS's performance was poor.
Failure rate	The failure rate was low and there were few bugs reported.
Size	
Forms	Fifteen forms, two of which had complex implementations.
Tables	Thirteen tables. The tables were simple and did not use any sophisticated database features.
Reports	Ten reports. All reports are easily understood.
Source files	Over one hundred files which included SQLWindows source files, report definition files, data definition files, Componentware files, and configuration files.
Documentation	
User	The client was responsible for user documentation.
Technical	The technical documentation was not very detailed and was inconsistent with CCS.

Table 7.5 Technical quality of hardware

Attribute	Description
Performance	Despite the performance problem with CCS, its hardware could meet performance requirements with an improved software architecture.
Failure rate	Unix servers rarely failed. PCs were unreliable on a small number of occasions.
Maintenance costs	Maintenance costs for PCs and Unix servers were very low.
Vendor/supplier	PCs from a variety of vendors were well supported. Similarly, there was widespread support for Unix servers.

Table 7.6 Technical quality of support software

Attribute	Description
Failure rate	The failure rate was low.
License costs	License costs for all support software products were reasonable and affordable.
Performance	There was a performance problem, but we didn't think the support software products caused this deficiency.
Frequency of fixes	Low.
Vendor/supplier	All operating system, middleware, 4GL, and database products were well supported. We expected this to continue in the future.

Based on subsequent experience, we were able to reengineer CCS using a more appropriate software architecture. Our initial experiments revealed that the "fat client" client/server model was the root cause of the system's poor performance.

Our client required a similar choice of operating environments for the target system to that provided for CCS. We assessed the technical quality of both CCS's hardware and support software to ensure that further investment in these platforms was sensible. Tables 7.5 and 7.6 show our assessment for hardware and support software.

In addition to assessing CCS's technical quality, we considered the effects of organizational factors on system evolution. In this case, our client's evolution requirements were mostly non-functional, and so any reengineering would not impact CCS's users.

From our perspective, we had several engineers who had become experienced client/server developers. They understood how to structure these systems in order to meet performance, reliability, and availability constraints. In addition, Legacy System Developers understood the IT needs of our client's industry and were available for the evolution project.

7.3 Target System Definition

Before we considered alternate target systems, we made sure we understood their requirements. From our earlier work with BPO, we identified a set of high-level requirements (Table 7.7).

Table 7.7 Evolution requirements

1	The target system will support the same functionality as CCS.
2	The target system will manage a larger volume of data than CCS.
3	The target system will be interoperable with several types of accounting systems.
4	The target system will be configurable for the same set of platforms that is provided for CCS.

To quantify the increase in the volume of data for CCS to process, our client estimated that the system would need to process over 100 000 transactions per month. At the start of the reengineering project, CCS had difficulty coping with 10 000 per month. This ten-fold increase influenced our choice of software architecture for the target system.

Since the business and functional properties of the target system were similar to those of CCS, we focused on the target system's structural and environment viewpoints. We identified two target systems:

1 An SQLWindows solution.

2 A Uniface system.

CCS conformed to the two-tier "fat client" architecture, which we introduced in Chapter 5. This model tightly couples presentation with application logic on the client and uses the server for data management. In Chapter 5, we pointed out that one of the drawbacks of this model is that the server can become a performance bottleneck.

With the SQLWindows target system, we could have resolved this problem, to some degree, by shifting part of the application logic from clients to the server. By using stored procedures or an application server, we could reduce the volume of network traffic and ultimately improve system performance. Either form of improvement would have meant changing CCS's software architecture.

In Chapter 4, we described a model for structuring evolvable 4GL applications (Fig. 7.11) which we could have used to resolve the performance shortfalls of CCS. To do this, we could have built the SQLWindows target system using either stored procedures or by hosting part of the application logic on a separate application server. In the first case, we would have implemented the stored procedures in the third layer, "database functions". For the latter, we would have deployed the "business functions" layer (layer 6) on an application server.

Figure 7.12 shows a model for structuring the application logic of the Uniface-based target system. This architecture promotes a clear structure where higher level subsystems call lower level modules. It differs from SQLWindows in that Uniface defines a data model which insulates applications from particular databases. A Uniface application is thus database-independent, which was particularly attractive in this case because of the requirement to support multiple platform configurations.

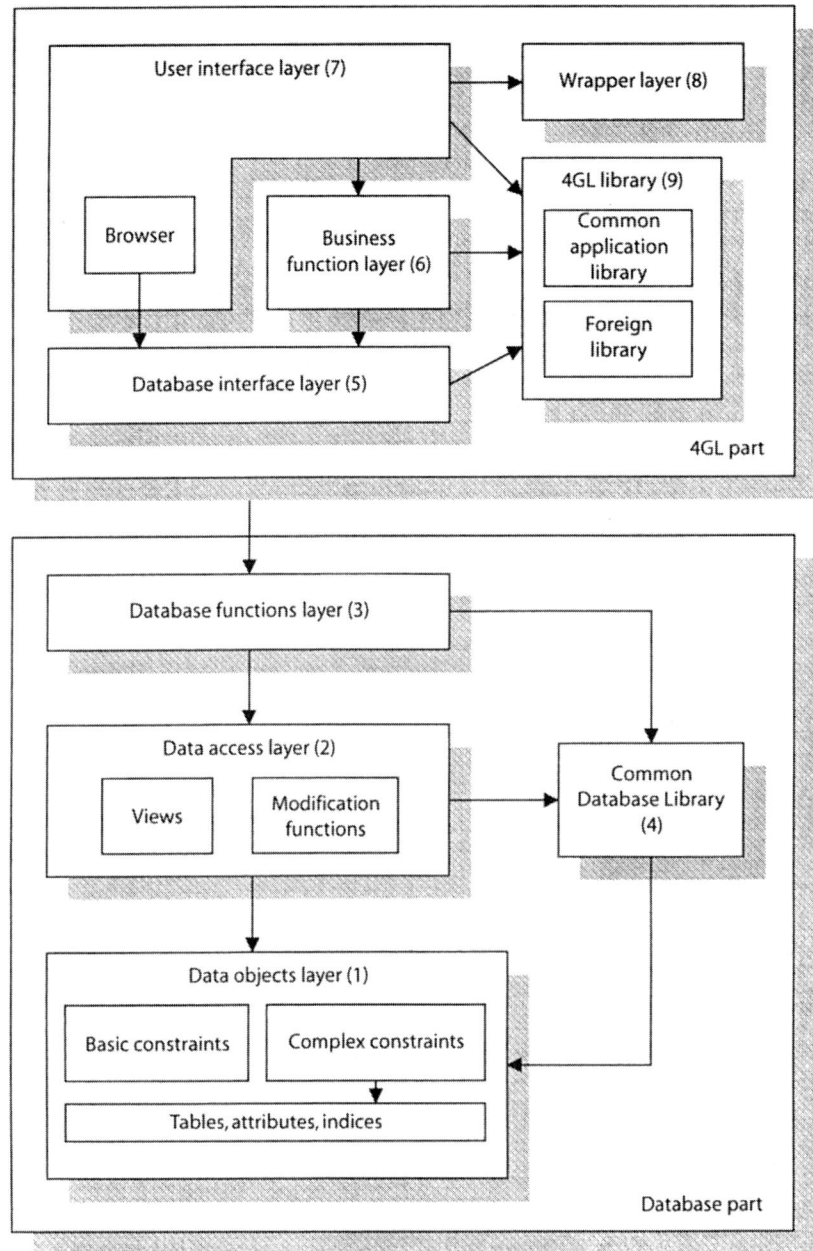

Fig. 7.11 Evolvable 4GL software architecture.

With the Uniface solution, we could have mapped server functionality onto the "business functions" layer and deployed it on an application server. Alternatively, we could have used stored procedures, but at the cost of database independence.

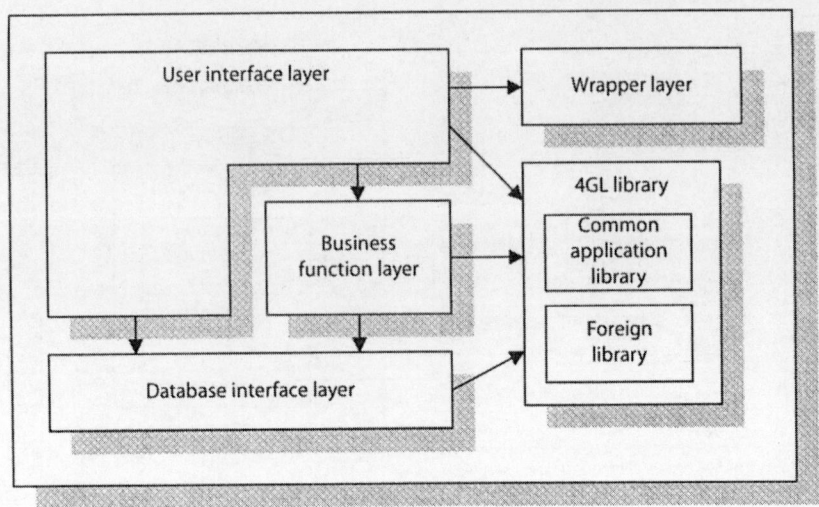

Fig. 7.12 Software architecture for the Uniface system.

Both target options had strengths and weaknesses. The SQLWindows solution offered more scope for reuse, since CCS was also implemented in SQLWindows. This meant that we could have reengineered CCS using SQLWindows relatively quickly. For the Uniface solution we could have reused the behaviour of CCS, but would have needed to reimplement it in Uniface. A Uniface solution, however, would simplify our customer's IT environment, since all systems would be implemented in Uniface. In addition, Uniface offers better support for multiple platform configurations because of its database independence.

7.4   Evolution Strategy Development

At this stage, we had a sufficient understanding of CCS and had derived a set of high-level evolution requirements. We had also identified and analyzed two possible target system architectures. We were now in a position to select one of those solutions and develop an evolution strategy for transforming CCS to that target. Table 7.8 summarizes the combinations of appropriate target systems and evolution strategies.

From the evolution strategies introduced in Chapter 3, we assessed which of them were suitable for each of the target systems. Our initial tests indicated that CCS's

Table 7.8 Target systems and evolution strategies

Target system	Evolution strategy
SQLWindows	Restructure
SQLWindows	Redesign-with-reuse
Uniface	Redesign-with-reuse

performance problems could not be solved without moving away from the "fat client" architecture. Since one of the evolution requirements involved a significant increase in data processing, which would further affect system performance, we ruled out "continued maintenance". This is a lightweight evolution strategy which precludes structural change.

We also ruled out the "revamp", "rearchitecture" and "replace" strategies. Our client was satisfied with CCS's graphical user interface, so there was no need to consider revamping CCS. Rearchitecturing was also inappropriate because CCS shared the same software and hardware technology as both target systems. All these systems conformed to client/server models and used relational database and 4GL technology. Replacing CCS was unnecessary because it was in reasonable technical condition and there was varying scope for reuse with both target solutions.

"Restructure" and "redesign-with-reuse" were more suitable strategies in this case. The former meant improving CCS's existing structure. Redesign-with-reuse suggested that we should develop a new design for the target system and reuse CCS components as part of the target system's implementation.

Restructuring, by definition, does not introduce new implementation technology. In this case, therefore, restructuring was only suitable for the SQLWindows target system. Where legacy and target systems share the same implementation technology, you can manage the restructuring incrementally. As we pointed out in Chapter 3, this often allows you to distribute the costs of evolution and reduce risks, such as building the wrong system.

If we chose redesign-with-reuse, we could transform CCS from the SQLWindows implementation to the technically superior Uniface solution. Legacy system components which we could reuse included database components and Componentware units. This evolution strategy would result in a system of better technical quality which would probably be more evolvable than the restructured SQLWindows system. Table 7.9 summarizes the benefits of each target system/evolution strategy combination.

In addition to considering the benefits of the three target system/evolution strategy combinations, we analyzed their risk factors. Table 7.10 shows the relevant risk factors which we took from Chapter 3. The first factor represented our concern that the SQLWindows solutions might have failed to conform to our client's IT strategy, which involved integrating CCS with its Uniface systems.

Table 7.9 Summary of target system benefits

SQLWindows Restructure	SQLWindows Redesign-with-reuse	Uniface Redesign-with-reuse
Much scope for reuse	Target system has a more evolvable software architecture	Evolvable software architecture
Relatively fast strategy implementation	Much scope for reuse	Common IT infrastructure for our client
		Database-independent solution

Table 7.10 Risk factors

Risk factor	Target system/evolution strategy		
	SQLWindows Restructure	SQLWindows Redesign-with-reuse	Uniface Redesign-with-reuse
1 System will not meet evolution requirements	✓	✓	
2 Experienced staff may leave	✓	✓	✓
3 Inadequate or inconsistent documentation	✓	✓	✓
4 Errors introduced		✓	✓
5 Difficulties integrating legacy system components			✓

Risk factors 2 and 3 affected all three strategies. The documentation was out of date, and we relied on a group of Legacy System Developers who had maintained the system and who had developed a good understanding of it. We controlled this risk factor by building context and technical models to document the target system. If valued engineers left, others could have used these models to understand the system.

The redesign-with-reuse strategies were more radical than restructuring. Consequently, the risk of introducing errors in the target system was relatively high for these strategies. However, our engineers had gained much experience in using client/server, relational database and 4GL technology. From a technology perspective, we did not see risk factor 4 as a threat to project success.

You can also introduce errors in a target system from a poor understanding of either the application or the evolution requirements. In our case, the evolution requirements were clear. In addition, our engineers had a good understanding of CCS and so, from these perspectives, concluded that risk factor 4 was not a critical risk factor.

The final risk factor was only applicable to the most radical evolution strategy, which involved migrating from SQLWindows to Uniface. Migrating from one implementation technology to another meant that CCS's data components and Componentware units might not integrate well with Uniface. We aimed to mitigate this risk factor by investigating what similar COTS components were recommended for Uniface. We also aimed to build time-contingency into the project plan to reimplement data components in the event that we could not integrate them with the Uniface solution.

Having assessed the benefits and risks of each evolution strategy, we moved on to consider their relative costs (Table 7.11). In this case, we derived cost items from the customized method's process, where each activity represented a cost item. In addition, we also estimated project support costs. Table 7.8 shows these cost items, which were common to both evolution strategies. To quantify them, we used a combination of two techniques: expert judgement and analogy-based methods.

We based our cost estimates on the following assumptions:

● The effort needed for project support was constant for all three target system/evolution strategy combinations.

Table 7.11 Cost items

Process costs
Analyze Requirements
Build Technical Model of Legacy System
Build Technical Model of Target System
Define Test Strategy
Implement Component
Test Component
Extract Reusable Components
Integrate Units
Do Integration Testing
Test System

Project support costs
Project Management
Quality Assurance
Delivery
Documentation

- The effort for building technical models of the legacy system and extracting reusable components from CCS increased the more we tried to exploit reuse.

- In contrast to the above assumption, the effort for the Implement Unit activity increased as reuse decreased.

Table 7.12 shows the results of our cost estimation exercise. Of particular interest was that effort was more dependent on the choice of target architecture than the evolution strategy. This was because the SQLWindows solutions offered more potential for code reuse.

Based on our analysis of the strategies' relative benefits, costs and risks, we were able to select the most appropriate target system and evolution strategy. We chose the Uniface system, which required the redesign-with-reuse evolution strategy. We anticipated that this combination would result in a system which would better fit our client's IT strategy than the SQLWindows alternatives. We traded reuse for a more evolvable system and a more manageable set of information systems for our client. The former was due to the use of an appropriate software architectural model and the latter because of a common implementation technology.

Table 7.12 Cost estimation results

SQLWindows Restructure	SQLWindows Redesign-with-reuse	Uniface Redesign-with-reuse
75 person days	85 person days	110 person days

7.5   Target System Modelling

As we pointed out in Chapter 4, software design is as important for 4GL applications as it is for 3GL systems. Although many 4GL development environments support prototyping techniques, a visual "drag-and-drop" approach does not lead to well-engineered systems. During our Design phase, we used the UML to document our design for the Uniface target system.

We used the target system's structural context model (Fig. 7.12) as a starting point for technical design. Figure 7.13 shows, using a UML package diagram, the resulting architecture. To the left of the figure is the well-established structure of user interface, business functions and application model layers. Unlike the traditional model, however, we made the application model directly accessible to the user interface. We chose this architecture because it better exploited Uniface's support for reuse and application partitioning. The wrapper layer contained classes which encapsulated the component layer's Componentware units.

We decomposed the application layer into further packages and classes. Figure 7.14 shows that we used two packages: "CCS tables" and "global definitions". The former contained the data structures for the target system, and the latter defined global resources such as template definitions and global procedures. We used the UML's stereotype construct to customize the UML to our needs, as described in Chapter 4. For example, we used classes to represent Uniface entities and stereotyped them "table". We used class attributes for entity attributes and class relationships for entity relationships.

The "global definitions" package contained a class named "global procedures", which documented the system's global subprograms. To show the relationship between entities and global resources, we used class relationships. For example, the OAS entity used global procedures and the attribute interface.

For the user interface layer, we identified several forms, services and tables. Figure 7.15 shows the user interface components. We used class dependency relationships

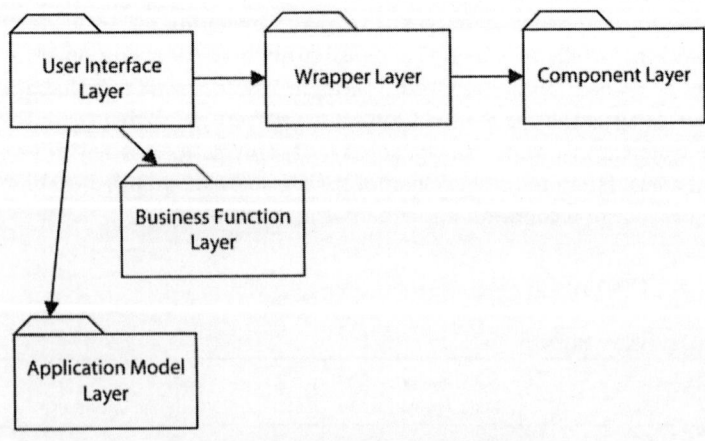

Fig. 7.13 Technical structure of the target system.

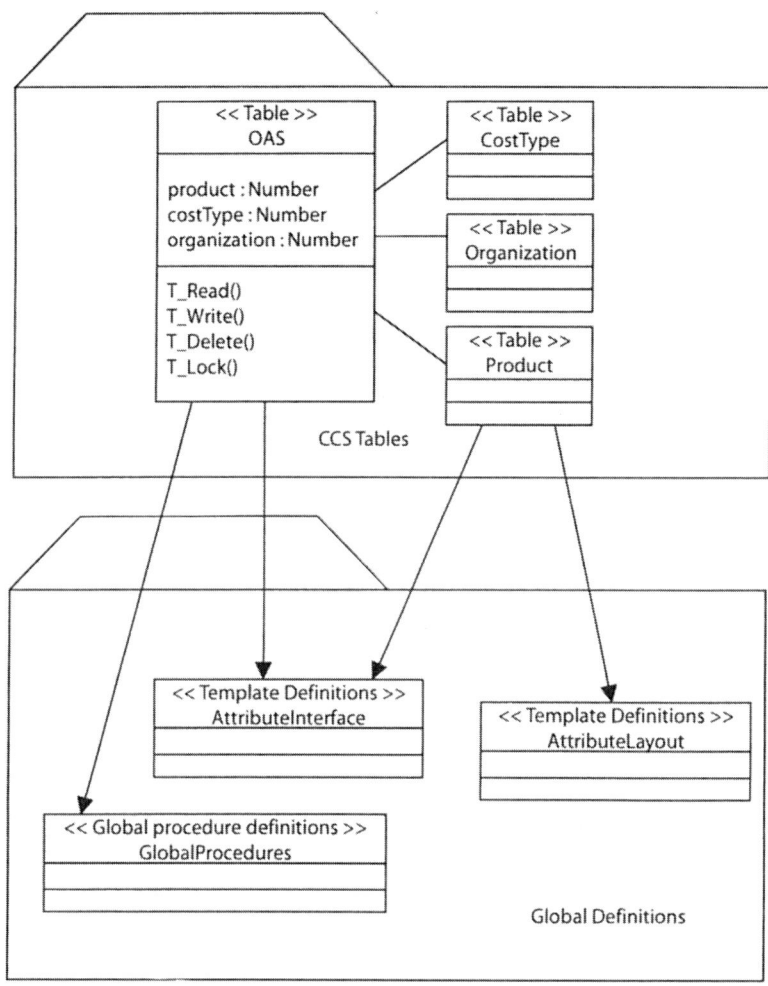

Fig. 7.14 Application model structure.

to document the "use" relationships between the components. We supplemented this structure with diagrams which showed the dynamic interaction between these components. Figure 7.16 shows a UML sequence diagram for a typical trigger and procedure activation for the target system.

Further Reading

RENAISSANCE Consortium (1998) *Renaissance Method Handbook.* http://www.comp.lancs.ac.uk/projects/renaissance/.
RENAISSANCE Consortium (1998) *Evolution Planning.* Consultancy report, http://www.comp.lancs.ac.uk/projects/renaissance/.

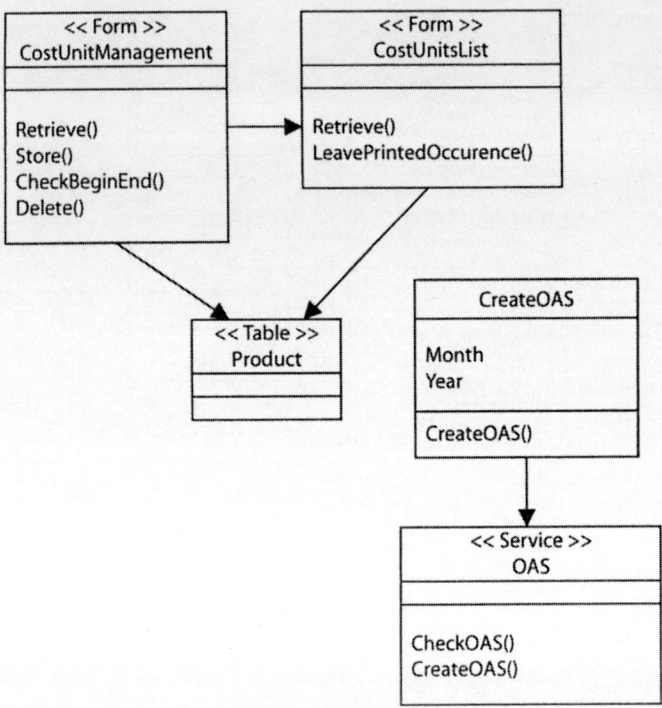

Fig. 7.15 User interface structure.

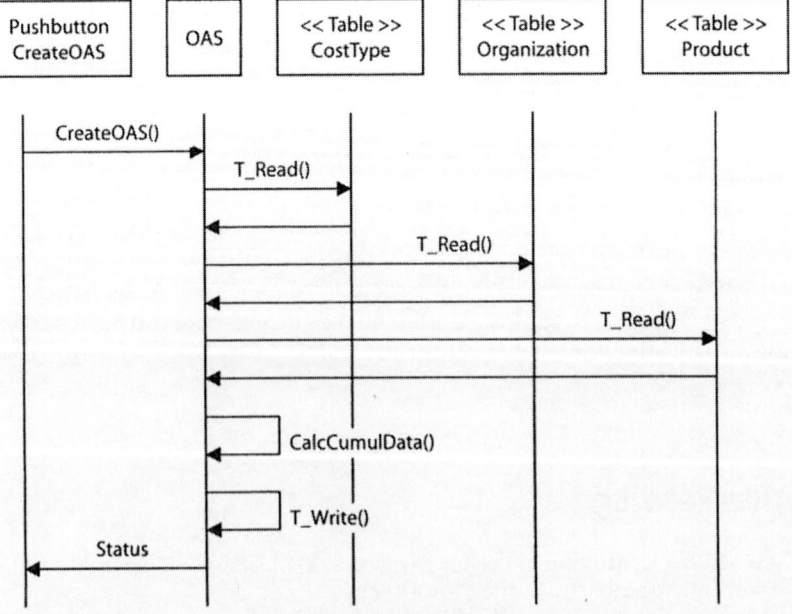

Fig. 7.16 Operation activation.

RENAISSANCE Consortium (1998) *Architectural Modelling*. Consultancy report, http://
www.comp.lancs.ac.uk/projects/renaissance/.
RENAISSANCE Consortium (1998) *Client/Server Migration*. Consultancy report, http://
www.comp.lancs.ac.uk/projects/renaissance/.

Key Points

- There is no fundamental difference between 3GL and 4GL evolution projects. You can customize Renaissance to support both types of project.

- An explicit design phase for distributed 4GL-based systems is useful to ensure that the resulting application meets both its functional and non-functional requirements.

- Context modelling helps you to understand a legacy system. This enables you to assess the system effectively.

- The UML is an appropriate notation for building technical models of 4GL applications. You can customize it to support specific features of particular 4GLs.

- For evolvability, you should structure distributed systems according to a sound architectural model.

Appendices

Appendix A   *Online Software Reengineering Resources*

The increasing popularity of the WWW has made it a valuable resource for locating information on software evolution and reengineering. While there is considerable material of interest to the software reengineering community on the WWW, finding particular information can be a difficult and time-consuming task. This appendix is designed to guide you through the online jungle of software reengineering resources. Table A.1 summarizes the WWW sites which we introduce in this appendix.

Table A.1 Software reengineering WWW sites

WWW site	URL
RENAISSANCEWeb	`http://www.comp.lancs.ac.uk/projects/renaissance/`
SEI Software Reengineering Centre	`http://www.sei.cmu.edu/reengineering/`
Software Technology Resource Centre	`http://stsc.hill.af.mil/`
Virtual Software Engineering Library	`http://rbse.jsc.nasa.gov/virt-lib/soft-eng.html`
Software Reuse Initiative	`http://sw-eng.falls-church.va.us`
SEWeb	`http://seweb.dit.csiro.au/`
IEEE Committee on Reverse Engineering and Reengineering	`http://www.tcse.org/revengr/`
Reengineering Forum	`http://www.reengineer.org/`
IEEE Reengineering Bibliography	`http://www.cc.gatech.edu/reverse/bibliography/`

A.1   The RENAISSANCEWeb

`http://www.comp.lancs.ac.uk/projects/renaissance/`

The Esprit project, RENAISSANCE, which has provided much of the material for this book, manages its own software reengineering WWW site. This site is a good place to start since it provides access to RENAISSANCE documents which complement this book and links to other sites.

171

RENAISSANCEWeb is divided into two sections. The first contains information about the RENAISSANCE project, and the second is dedicated to reengineering in general. In the first section, you can find out about the project's background and rationale, see how to contact individuals involved in the project, and access a set of documents which we produced during the course of RENAISSANCE.

RENAISSANCE documents are classified as follows:

- *Renaissance method.* In Chapter 2, we presented an overview of the Renaissance method. The "Method Handbook" provides a complete and detailed definition of the method. The "Method Framework Description" provides the background and rationale for Renaissance.

- *Consultancy reports.* These documents support Chapters 3–5 of this book. They contained detailed advice on how to perform the Renaissance method's activities. There are three consultancy reports:

  1 "Evolution Planning". This report is aimed at consultants who are assisting clients to reengineering their systems. In particular, it provides advice on assessing legacy systems for fitness for evolution, choosing an appropriate evolution strategy, managing risks in evolution projects and estimating costs for evolution projects.

  2 "Architectural Modelling for Evolution". This document explains how to model both legacy and modern systems at a range of abstraction levels.

  3 "Client/Server Migration". This report provides technical guidelines for migrating legacy systems to distributed client/server architectures. It focuses on reusing, integrating and encapsulating legacy system components within a modern architecture.

- *Technology briefing reports.* These were developed as working documents during the initial months of RENAISSANCE. They provide you with an overview of key technologies which are relevant to software reengineering. We produced briefing reports for the following technologies:

  - *System modelling.*

  - *Process support.*

  - *Middleware.*

  - *Rapid application development.*

  - *4GLs.*

  - *Internet technologies.*

  - *Database technologies.*

  - *Reverse engineering.*

  - *Evolution management.*

  - *Distributed object technology.*

A.2   Additional WWW Sites

The second part of RENAISSANCEWeb gathers a set of links to other software reengineering WWW sites. These sites fall into two broad categories: information provided on a non-profit basis and information which is provided for commercial purposes. Sites that deal with the former are typically run by research organizations and are generally funded, either directly or indirectly, by government grants. The growing body of commercial information relates to services or products offered by their providers.

To review all online information would be a futile activity because of the dynamic nature and growth of the Internet. Our approach is to provide you with pointers to interesting WWW sites.

- *Software Reengineering Centre.* The Software Engineering Institute (SEI) is a research and development centre which is part of Carnegie Mellon University, and is funded by the US Department of Defense (DoD). The centre aims to provide leadership in advancing the state of practice in software engineering. It has its own software reengineering group, which is well documented at its WWW site.

- *Software Technology Resource Centre.* This site is managed by the US Air Force and focuses on DoD requirements. This site describes the services and products which the centre provides. In addition it provides general software reengineering information. The site also hosts *CrossTalk*, the journal of defense software engineering.

- *Virtual Software Engineering Library.* This is the WWW's oldest catalogue, created by Tim Berners-Lee, who is credited with the creation of the WWW. The catalogue is run on a non-profit basis by a distributed group of people who are experts in the field. The Virtual Library includes software reengineering and has become a *de facto* standard catalogue for many academic disciplines.

- *Software Reuse Initiative.* This site offers extensive information and resources for software reuse. It includes an executive primer on reuse with case studies, lessons learnt, training material and source code. This site also contains links to other reuse-oriented sites.

- *SEWeb.* The Australian Software Reengineering Online Extension Service is an online resource centre for software reengineering. A consortium of industrial and academic organizations in Australia created it. The site includes information on databases, client/server solutions, metrics, process modelling and risk management.

- *IEEE Committee on Reverse Engineering and Reengineering.* This committee promotes technologies for examining existing systems and approaches for reengineering them. The site covers a wide range of topics, which include program understanding, restructuring, language translation, data reengineering, system migration and business process reengineering.

- *Reengineering Forum.* The Reengineering Forum is an industry association that seeks to encourage a combined industry/research review of state of the art practice in reengineering software systems and business processes. This site disseminates reengineering news and publicizes current events.

● *IEEE Reengineering Bibliography*. This is an annotated bibliography of software reengineering which has been compiled by the IEEE. The site enables users to add their own opinions to the bibliographic database. You can search the database online or download it as a BibTeX database.

Appendix B   *Tool Vendors*

In this appendix, we provide a list of vendors which offer CASE tools for software reengineering. The growing market for CASE tools is well represented on the WWW. While some vendors use their WWW sites to provide extensive product information, others use their sites only to publicize the existence of their tools. Table B.1 provides URLs for some tool vendors. The table is not exhaustive, and since we have had no experience with the tools we do not endorse the companies or their products. We include the table, however, as a starting point for your own investigation.

Table B.1 Tool vendors

Vendor	URL
Aonix	http://www.ide.com
Blue Ice	http://www.blueice.com
Bozeman Legg	http://www.bozemanlegg.com
Cayenne Software	http://www.cayennesoft.com
Class Solutions	http://www.class-solutions.com
Cognizant	http://www.dbss.com
Cyrano	http://www.cyrano.com
Fieldex	http://www.fieldex.com
HAL	http://www.halinfo.it
Imagix	http://www.imagix.com
Innovative Software	http://www.isg.de
Interfacing Technologies	http://www.interfacing.com
International Software Automation	http://www.softwareautomation.com
Leverage Technologists	http://stout.levtech.com
Lockheed Martin	http://www.imco.com
Mark V Systems	http://www.markv.com
McCabe	http://www.mccabe.com
META Software	http://www.metasoftware.com
Objective Software Technology	http://www.objectivesoft.com
One UP	http://www.1up.com
Rational Software	http://www.rational.com
Reasoning Systems	http://www.reasoning.com
Science Applications International	http://www.saic.com
Sector 7	http://www.sector7.com
Select Software Tools	http://www.select.com
SEMA Group	http://dis.sema.es

Table B.1 Tool vendors *(continued)*

Vendor	URL
SiC.com	`http://www.s-i-c.com`
Software Emancipation	`http://www.setech.com`
Software Validation	`http://www.software-validation.com`
TakeFive Software	`http://www.takefive.com`
Transition Software	`http://www.transition-software.com`
Verilog	`http://www.verilogusa.com`
Viasoft	`http://www.viasoft.com`
Visible Systems	`http://www.ozemail.com`
Whitfield Software Services	`http://www.wssnet.com`
Xinotech	`http://www.xiotech.com`

Appendix C *Implementation Technology Vendors*

This appendix supports Chapter 5 (Migration to Distributed Architectures). Table C.1 lists vendors which support products such as 4GLs, distributed object technology, database management systems and general middleware. You can use many of these products to integrate legacy components within a modern distributed architecture. Similarly to Appendix B, the table is not exhaustive, but it provides a starting point for locating vendors of distributed and client/server products.

Table C.1 Product vendors

Vendor	URL
Borland	http://www.inprise.com
Centura	http://www.centurasoft.com
Componentware	http://www.componentware.com
Compuware	http://www.compuware.com
DEC	http://www.dec.com
Expersoft Corporation	http://www.expersoft.com
IBM	http://www.ibm.com
Information Builders	http://www.informationbuilders.com
JavaSoft	http://www.javasoft.com
Microsoft	http://www.microsoft.com
Momentum Software Corporation	http://www.momentumsoftware.com
Netscape	http://home.netscape.com
NetWeave Corporation	http://www.netweave.com
Novell	http://www.novell.com
OLE Broker	http://www.olebroker.com
Oracle	http://www.oracle.com
Orbix	http://www.orbix.com
PeerLogic	http://www.peerlogic.com
Seer	http://www.seer.com
Sun Microsystems	http://www.sun.com
SAP	http://www.sap.com
Sybase	http://www.sybase.com
Transarc Corporation	http://www.transarc.com

Index